Date Due			
NOV 9			
DEC 3 0			
OCT 16			
NOV 6			
DEC 4			
NOV 1 0			
MAR 2 2			
MAY 0 8 2009			

The Murderers

THE STORY OF THE NARCOTIC GANGS

By HARRY J. ANSLINGER

U. S. Commissioner of Narcotics

and WILL OURSLER

FARRAR, STRAUS AND CUDAHY, NEW YORK

NOTE

In a few cases in this book—either to protect the innocent, or because there appeared no need in a specific case to rake up old coals of guilt—a fictitious name is used. The following names fall into this category: Joe Sing (Chapter 2), Sol the Oil (Chapter 10), Dr. Howard (Chapter 14), Mr. Phoenix, Hugo and Elmer (Chapter 17), John Osgood (Chapter 18), Dr. Fritz (Chapter 25).

Contents

Preface   ix

PART ONE EMBRYO

    1. Roots   3
    2. Slavery, Inc.   25
    3. Hemp Around Their Necks   35
    4. Lepke   43
    5. Baron   56

PART TWO INSIDE MAFIA

Portrait Parlé   77

    6. From the Mafia Files . . .   79
    7. Il Capo   100
    8. Aliens Bearing Gifts   110

PART THREE AGENTS AND INFORMERS

Personnel   123

    9. A Man Named X   125
   10. Oozy: Informer Extraordinary   135
   11. An Agent Named Kip   146
   12. A Game at Monte Carlo   153

PART FOUR SCOPE OF EVIL

Survey   165

   13. Locale: Anywhere   166
   14. Tentacles   171

15. A Girl Who Died   183
16. Stardust   194
17. Western Story   201
18. The Vice President Requests . . .   207

PART FIVE   EXTRA-CURRICULAR

Specialties   217

19. Incident at the UN   218
20. Chinese Red Lullaby   226
21. Dr. Addison and Others   231
22. H Is for Horse   244

PART SIX   PORTFOLIO

Characters in a Book   257

23. "The White House Calling . . ."   258
24. Literary Lion   263
25. Pirates, Derelicts and Con Men   273

PART SEVEN   PERSONAL TO AMERICA

Meanings   287

26. For the Defense   288
27. Final Report   294

Appendices   297

PREFACE

This is the record of a world-wide apparatus of criminal conspiracy, civic corruption and murder by appointment. It is the story of the crime syndicate's national and international dealings in commercialized drug addiction.

It is a report to the public on an enemy who seeks to destroy whole segments of our communities in his quest for vast profits from the illegal sales of narcotic drugs. It is a report on action and counter-action, deception and counter-deception, a record of men who have fought—and in some cases died—in this little-known and little-understood struggle.

I do not explore deeply here the chemistry or technical aspects of the drugs themselves. This complex field has been covered in many books and scientific papers. The pharmaceutical aspects of narcotic drugs fill volumes. For the general reader's reference, the appendix includes a list of the most important drugs and narcotics and the synthetics, with a brief comment on the makeup and the effects of each.

I want to show here the nature of the men and women behind the traffic, who and what they are, their purposes and methods, both in America and abroad, and the extent of their infiltration of legitimate business. I also intend to reveal our countermeasures against these enemies.

Falsehood and confusion are spread by the paid publicity men of the underworld. Many people, wittingly and unwittingly, try to tear down our work without realizing the danger in which they put themselves and their own families and homes. A dangerous uncertainty has been planted in the public's mind

by misinformed, misdirected, or deliberately dishonest advocates of all sorts of wild schemes for lifting controls, for
government-sponsored narcotic "feeding stations," for opening
wide the doors to addictive drugs. Such deliberately cultivated
confusion must be dispelled, for the safety of our country and
its future.

As a veteran front-liner in the battle against organized crime,
I believe I qualify as an expert. I believe also that the public
has a right to the facts.

HARRY J. ANSLINGER

PART ONE

EMBRYO

1. Roots

For more than thirty years I have been engaged in the war against the murderers. These are the men who control and direct the international traffic in narcotics. They represent many types of individuals, ranging from diplomats and ladies of society to silk-shirted racketeers, killers, and the sidewalk vermin who serve as couriers and front-line vendors of dope.

I have waged this protracted campaign in the criminal jungles since 1930, when I gave up other government service to become United States Commissioner of Narcotics and chief of the Federal Narcotics Bureau, charged with enforcing the provisions of the Harrison Act and related narcotic control legislation. Ours is a war fought on unsuspected battlefields, unseen and unrecognized in the midst of average, everyday communities. It may be the salon of our latest trans-Atlantic jet, the office of a governor—or the upstairs linen closet of a Westchester housewife.

Many of the big dealers in the business of narcotic agony move in the most elite circles in both Europe and America. One notorious international trafficker, responsible for the addiction of millions in Africa, Asia, Europe, and America, was virtually lionized by New York society when he dropped into the United States as a refugee at the end of World War II. The sophistication of this bald-headed Parisian, with his edge of accent and his impeccable grooming, melted easily into the Park Avenue cocktail hour. Any crass mention of court trials, acquittals on technicalities, or deportation proceedings, was shrugged off. The Parisian was not only a gentleman; he was attractive and amusing.

The world of dope is a misshapen, hallucinatory cosmos that thrives on its own secrecy, its shifting argot and coded terminology, its unseen "passes"—from one hand to another in the shadows. Which is the criminal and which the victim in this secret world within a world is not as easy to define as some social caseworkers insist. Is it the Washington politician who stays on the fringes of the crime syndicate but consorts with penthouse prostitutes who provide boudoir marijuana and cocaine as a special service to the customers? Is it the habitual criminal—the car thief or stickup artist who picked up his drug habit in prison? Is it the unseen "investor" who puts up the cash needed for the raw merchandise, but takes no part in the actual purchase or transportation, the preparation in tenement laboratories, the delivery to addict customers in New York, Chicago or Los Angeles?

Or is it a flaxen-haired eighteen-year-old girl sprawled nude and unconscious on a Harlem tenement floor after selling herself to a collection of customers throughout the afternoon, in exchange for a heroin shot in her arm?

From the start I have thrown the full efforts of the Bureau not against minor characters trapped in their weakness and despair but against the sources—major violators, the big hoods, the top-drawer importers and wholesalers in the international traffic and on the national syndicated crime scene. Some of the members of this clandestine cosmos have controlled whole communities and cities, police departments and mayors, judges and district attorneys and juries.

Getting evidence to convict hoodlums who thrive in this heavily protected level remains one of the most challenging assignments in law enforcement. The victims—the addicts—their husbands or wives, parents or children all live in constant fear. Those on the inside of this furtive world must abide by the code. The penalty for anyone who talks is death.

Yet there are those in this underworld who do talk. They

talk for their private reasons—for profit, for special consideration in their own cases, help for a wife or mother who may be ill or dying, for revenge, or merely to salve their conscience. Secretly they work for us, while remaining members of the mob. Such "special employees" of the Bureau come from every stratum of the underworld. They provide us with an entry into the most sensitive circles of the hoodlum hierarchy.

Somewhere in the background of almost every major case there is a special employee who fingered the deal in its preliminary stages. We protect these men to the fullest measure. Their names are never mentioned in reports, they are brought into court only if it is their desire to speak out regardless of the personal risk.

Some of these who did speak are dead because they would not heed my warning to move out of the reach of syndicate vengeance. In some cases we have paid for transportation to other continents where they can start a new life. But they can never come back. This is the price they pay to live.

Vital as is the contribution of the special employee, the job of actually bringing in the violators and securing the evidence we can take into court is carried on by Bureau agents using undercover techniques developed to meet the unique problems of narcotic investigations and courtroom prosecution.

The Bureau agent merges with his assignments; he plays his part as if it were reality itself. For weeks or months, even years, he may live with the narcotic gangsters whom he will one day bring before a jury. He becomes a part of the gangster's intimate life and family. Whatever his cover story, he clings to it until the final moment when the arrests are made. If asked to guard a shipment of heroin—as happened in one California case—the agent guards it as a sacred trust.

The world in which he lives on assignment is one of violence. One slip—one false word—could cost his life. Yet there is twisted logic in the underworld code; where an informer would be shot or stabbed to death, the Bureau agent, who makes his case and brings the violators into court, is in no danger of reprisal; the hoods accept him as a part of the routine business risk.

One violator told our man in a Federal courthouse corridor, "Johnny, I gotta hand it to you. I didn't know you agent. I thought you goddamned informer and I would kill you. Now I no have to."

It is their delicate differentiation between one of us and one of their own.

The syndicate which the agent infiltrates to make his case is a modern phenomenon. In 1914, when the Harrison Act was passed, narcotic trafficking in America was largely in the hands of the Chinese. Opium, produced from the opium poppy, was the most popular addictive drug in use. Only later did the so-called "white drugs"—morphine and heroin, both made from opium, and cocaine, made from the coca leaf—replace opium in popularity. The "white drugs" are quicker in effect, more dangerous, more addictive—and more profitable.

With the Harrison laws, addiction in America was curtailed drastically—from one addict in every four hundred persons to one in every four thousand. But as the figure dropped, the underworld traffickers got bolder. The hoodlums were willing to take chances because the profits were immense. They killed when they had to. They cut each other's throats for extra profits. They sold each other narcotic merchandise and then reported shipments in transit to the authorities to collect full legal rewards offered for tips leading to seizures of contraband.

Marijuana was not considered a narcotic drug nor was it under any form of Federal control as late as 1930, when the Bureau of Narcotics was started. The underworld leaped through this gap in the law. Use of marijuana spread across America like a roadside fever from state to state. The dealers employed marijuana cigarettes—"reefers"—as an introductory drug that could bring in new customers, primarily high school age youngsters, for the trade in heroin.

The syndicated narcotic underworld that came into being in the 1920's and 1930's was a part of the larger organized rackets, yet it had its separate identity. Although amorphous and made up of seemingly isolated individuals and groups, it nevertheless had an identifiable unity of its own, a loosely formed yet interlocking world-wide fraternity. In the late twenties and the thirties, a handful of men—thousands of miles apart—shaped the dope syndicate. Each step in this story was a struggle for power between the groups within this special department of international crime.

Spread out from New York to Paris, from Istanbul to Shanghai, from Rome to Roanoke, the mobs and their leaders trusted no one. They informed on each other, double-crossed each other, plundered each other's shipments, betrayed and killed for revenge or a fast payoff. One group rose to power over the corpses of another.

As the smaller mobs destroyed each other, the shadow of one grew larger with each new "execution." This was the Grand Council of the Mafia, with its plan of an international cartel controlling every phase of criminal activity.

When we in the Bureau first warned the public about the neo-Mafia menace, many criminal authorities jeered at our warnings. Mafia was a myth, they said. If it had ever existed at all, it was long dead. Mafia's press agents in America joined the chorus.

Meanwhile, in a New York State prison a graying, bespectacled inmate paced nervously in his cell staring up fretfully at a chunk of blue sky beyond the bars of the window. Notorious Lucky Luciano only waited for the commutation of sentence and deportation to put together a super-syndicate that would dominate international crime, particularly the traffic in dope.

When I was born—May 20, 1892, in Altoona, Pennsylvania—opium was the base of familiar household tonics and elixirs, obtainable without prescription at any pharmacy. Opium for smoking was sold openly throughout the civilized world; in

China alone, an estimated thirty to forty million human beings were opium addicts.

Several miles from Altoona was a rural township of some six hundred people in my boyhood. Of that number, approximately sixty—one in every ten inhabitants—were addicts. Two of the pharmacists in our town died of narcotic addiction.

As a youngster of twelve, visiting in the house of a neighboring farmer, I heard the screaming of a woman on the second floor. I had never heard such cries of pain before. The woman, I learned later, was addicted, like many other women of that period, to morphine, a drug whose dangers most medical authorities did not yet recognize. All I remember was that I heard a woman in pain, whose cries seemed to fill my whole twelve-year-old being. Then her husband came running down the stairs, telling me I had to get into the cart and drive to town. I was to pick up a package at the drug store and bring it back for the woman.

I recall driving those horses, lashing at them, convinced that the woman would die if I did not get back in time. When I returned with the package—it was morphine—the man hurried upstairs to give the woman the dosage. In a little while her screams stopped and a hush came over the house.

I never forgot those screams. Nor did I forget that the morphine she had required was sold to a twelve-year-old boy, no questions asked.

As I grew up, I saw other glimpses of drug addiction and its effects in this community, this small-town symbol of Main Street America of that era, with its mixture of old families and new immigrants, rolling farmlands and new factories, miners and roadworkers, foremen and factory heads. I remember a young pool player, the best in Altoona, a bright-eyed, grinning youth who wanted to be a world's champion. He could shoot billiards with anybody on earth and once almost beat Willie Hoppe.

He was also in the choir—a pool player who sang tenor like an angel. His voice was so good that some people in New York began negotiations to have him come to New York to sing regularly in the choir of the Little Church Around the Corner.

But he did not make it, either as billiard champion or choir tenor. Opium won the contract, smoking opium, to which he became addicted. Within two years he was dead.

I knew the importance of the opiates and other drugs as a pain killer in medicine, as a tool in medical and scientific research. I had learned something of this phase in my studies in high school and later at Pennsylvania State University.

But I had also seen the other side—at first hand.

For most of us, the future has its roots in the past.

It was soon after my graduation from the University, long before I had any idea of going into law enforcement, that I had my first brush with Mafia violence in America.

I went to work as a supervisor of landscape construction gangs employed in connection with the railroad. The gangs were made up almost entirely of Sicilian Italians, most of them recent immigrants. Giovanni was one of them. He had a big family and a rugged disposition and didn't like to be pushed around. Giovanni would talk over his lunch box about his big dreams, his big chance in America.

One day I found him unconscious in a ditch. Someone had put twenty-five bullets into his body, and dumped his blood-drenched form at the side of the road.

This was the work of Mafia. *Mano Nera* they called it in Italy—the Black Hand. Giovanni thought he had left all that behind him; in America he was the equal of all other men. Why should he pay tribute out of his small earnings to some man the others called Big Mouth Sam? The others had agreed to pay Big Mouth his "cut" but Giovanni had held out.

We found him in time and got him to a hospital, gushing blood from every part of his body. While he battled for life, I personally sought out Big Mouth Sam.

Squat, black-haired, ox-shouldered Big Mouth lived off fellow immigrants by his simple "terror-tax" formula. Whoever balked was beaten, stabbed or shot. The little eyes glinted at me. He was startled, I gathered from his look, at my size. I stand six feet and weighed at that time about two hundred pounds.

I said, "I'm Giovanni's boss and friend."

"What about Giovanni?" he protested, excitedly waving his hands. "What I got to do with Giovanni? I don't know no Giovanni."

I told him I knew he was the one who pumped all that lead into Giovanni's body and dumped him in the ditch. "If Giovanni dies," I warned him, "I'm going to see to it that you hang. Do you understand that?"

Big Mouth started to object again but I cut him short.

"And if he lives and you ever bother him again, or any of my men, or try to shake any of them down any more, I'll kill you with my own hands."

He was convinced I would keep my word. The abject cowardice of his kind is sickening to see close up. He began shaking his head and muttering as he moved away, "You got it wrong, you got me wrong."

Giovanni survived. Patched up and strong again, he went back to work. Big Mouth and his crowd did not bother him or any of my construction workers after that. But this extortionist and his kind continued to plague other Italian workers throughout the state.

Such was my first direct encounter with this transplanted brotherhood of plunder, extortion, thievery and murder.

My early experiences in undercover activities started a few years later, just after the outbreak of the First World War, when I joined the diplomatic corps of the United States. I served in Holland during America's involvement in the war. My work was of a consular nature but also called for behind-the-scene intelligence reports and investigations. I spoke German and Dutch fluently and had a smattering of French. After our entry into the war, I was stationed in The Hague.

It was a time of tensions. Every government—including our own—was eager to obtain every scrap of information possible, especially as the war drew to its close. Social affairs, dinners and teas and garden parties, mingling with the nobility and near-nobility of that day, leaders of governments, and the unknown lesser lights who had most of the information anyway—this was all part of the assignment.

The most important undercover case in which I took part—one that had its role in the shaping of history—has never before been revealed.

On the day Kaiser Wilhelm the Second gave up his imperial throne, I was called in by my harassed superior officer, the American minister at The Hague. "The Kaiser will abdicate today and the Netherlands will grant him asylum," the minister announced tersely. "He will stay at Count Bentinck's castle at Amerongen. That's where Charles the Second stayed when he got out of England just ahead of the axe. You know the place?"

"I've been there. I've met the Count too—at some garden party for the Queen."

"Go down there and see what you can find out," he ordered. "We need every scrap of information we can get for the President." He paused, then added: "There's one other point. The American government does not want the Kaiser to abdicate. It's vital that this be relayed to the right people. . . ."

I reached Amerongen before the arrival of the "Abdication Special" bringing the Kaiser. An air of uncertainty and suspicion gripped the quiet Dutch town. The streets were crowded with an odd mixture of people, some of them obviously Secret Service. While I waited for the arrival of the Kaiser, a towering Dutchman tapped a pudgy finger on my shoulder. He seemed nervous, unsure of himself. He told me he was a member of the Dutch Secret Service and that no strangers were allowed in town. He asked to see my identification.

My whole mission would have been wrecked if this Dutch

official discovered my real identity. I would have been ordered out summarily and possibly thrown into jail. So, instead of obeying his order to see my papers, I countered with one of my own, speaking not in Dutch but in a harsh German, in tones of imperious outrage. "Show me *your* credentials," I commanded him.

The ponderous Dutchman was startled. I was obviously a German official, sent on ahead of the Kaiser. In the uncertain situation of that day, he had no wish to be involved in trouble. He obliged by showing me half a dozen cards and letters. I studied them carefully, noting in particular the most important —Count Bentinck's card, stamped by the town burgomaster. "These are in order," I said stiffly, handing them back. "I shall mention your efficiency to the Minister of Justice."

My Dutch friend was impressed. He bowed, beamed, and went on his way.

I strolled over to the office of the burgomaster a few minutes later, presented myself as a German official traveling ahead of His Majesty and requested my credentials. Again, because of the turmoil of the times, plus a number of realistic details I let drop about the Kaiser and his requirements, the burgomaster had no doubt that I was what I claimed to be, and handed me the necessary credentials. These enabled me to go wherever the Kaiser's party went without any interference from Dutch authorities.

I dropped over to the inn reserved for the Kaiser's staff. There I had a few drinks with the proprietor and we developed an immediate warm friendship. When the Kaiser arrived with his entourage, he and the servants went on to the castle. The staff arrived at the inn. I mingled with them, accepted as some young official brought in from somewhere in this hour of crisis. No one questioned me or my reason for being there.

During dinner most of the German staff officers, wallowing in the dejection of defeat, tried to drown German sorrow in Dutch gin. One of them got up and walked unsteadily into the lobby of the inn. I followed, putting on an act of equal dejection, and struck up a casual conversation with the man.

He introduced himself as Knauff, court councilor to the Kaiser. I told him I was a Dutch citizen working for Dutch Intelligence. He had difficulty understanding my Dutch interspersed with German, so we switched to English which I pretended to speak with a heavy Dutch accent.

"I have information of importance," I said, "that I must have relayed in complete confidence to His Imperial Highness."

Knauff was quizzical. "You wish me to carry this information?"

"Abdication was entirely useless and unnecessary," I told him. "The Social Democrats will bring on revolution, strikes and chaos. If you play your cards carefully, His Majesty will return in triumph."

I was feeding him, in effect, ideas that the State Department hoped would prevail. My purpose was to draw him out, to determine what course the Germans themselves would follow and why.

"I advised His Majesty to remain," Knauff confided, "but it has worked out otherwise because of what others said Wilson wants."

I said: "I happen to know that one of your intermediaries, a journalist, is a fool who got his information from the wrong person."

"Yes—you may be correct," Knauff admitted. He then explained that Scheideman, the German Socialist leader, had informed the Kaiser that the government must have the views of President Wilson. The German ambassador at The Hague called in the journalist and asked him to get this information for the Kaiser and Germany. The journalist reported that he talked at The Hague with an American of great importance who was close to Wilson, and who agreed to find out the President's view.

"This was followed by another meeting," Knauff said, "at which our journalist intermediary learned through his important contact that the President desired immediate abdication."

"But the President wants nothing of the kind," I protested.

"We do not know that. Our ambassador at The Hague believes the journalist, and the Kaiser believes the ambassador. Perhaps there was more alcohol than truth in that meeting. Perhaps this important man was a liar who never even talked with Wilson. We do not know, you see."

The following day, authorities began double-checking the identities of everybody at the inn, and I slipped out of town on the last train departing for The Hague.

Our minister was greatly disturbed at my report. Cables flew back and forth. The President, who had believed that German stabilization under the reigning monarch was essential for the kind of peace the world needed, was furious at the role one of his chief advisors appeared to have played. Scheideman was informed of President Wilson's actual views but by then was too well intrenched to give up the Socialist victory. For a brief period General Krupp and his Balkan troops occupied Berlin with a plan to restore the monarchy. But the Socialists called a general strike and Krupp and his troops left Berlin, firing machine guns as they left.

I was at the Adlon Hotel when they fired a burst into the lobby, injuring several persons who were crouched in terror. Blood spattered my hands.

I learned later that the man who had informed the Kaiser's intermediary so erroneously about Wilson's views had not even talked to Wilson, or cabled for information of any kind. A few drinks had given him sufficient self-confidence to put his own interpretation on the Fourteen Points, the aims of Wilson, and the needs of the world.

Had he not done so, the Kaiser might well have stayed on the throne, as the Emperor did in Japan after World War II. A decent peace might have been written, forestalling any change for a future Hitler gaining power, or a Second World War erupting.

One learns in government service to accept both unsung
victory and unrecognized defeat.

In December, 1918, Colonel Luke Lea of the U.S. Army
took twenty American soldiers from Brussels to Amerongen in
an attempt to kidnap the Kaiser and bring him to Paris as a
Christmas present for General Pershing. The raiding party got
as far as the closed gates of the castle. Count Bentinck appeared
and talked the colonel out of any rash assault. Lea and his
caravan turned back to Brussels, where Dutch police picked
up their arms and records. As a result of this childish episode,
Lea became a hero and was elected governor of Tennessee.

The State Department instructed me to investigate. Having
been to Amerongen on my earlier undercover visit only a
month before, I hoped that the chaos and confusion which had
prevailed at that time would keep anyone from recognizing
me now.

At the castle I talked with Count Bentinck about restrictive
measures and visa controls to prevent any reoccurrence of a
kidnap attempt. Count Bentinck told me, "Not only did they
try to kidnap the Kaiser but when we had our parley somebody stole my silver ashtray with my coat of arms."

The count had been active in setting up arrangements at the
inn when the Kaiser first arrived. I knew he had seen me
there. As I was leaving now, he said, "Haven't I seen you
somewhere before?"

I mentioned a social function we had both attended, given
by Holland's Queen at her summer palace. I recalled how we
had met as we walked through the gardens with the Queen's
Consort, the Duke of Mecklenberg.

"Oh, to be sure," the count replied.

I cannot here go into the details of many other assignments
during that period. I can disclose, however, that I was allowed,
as an unpublished reward of the American government, to keep
as my own the field utility kit and certain other minor personal
possessions of His Imperial Highness, Kaiser Wilhelm II.

For any who may be interested, these possessions are on display at the Smithsonian Institute in Washington, D.C., to which I donated them in 1957. How I obtained them must remain a state secret.

Immediately after the Treaty of Brest-Litovsk and the take over of Russia by the Communists, the British had tried to get intelligence people inside Russia, but most of them were soon discovered and executed. The Russians caught all but one who is, in fact, still inside Russia, although no longer an employee in intelligence activities or associated any longer with the British government.

I was at that time American Vice-Consul in Hamburg, Germany. In this post I helped repatriate many American seamen. Young Americans, most of them, young fellows whose faces bore the stamp of the opium smoker, the user of morphine or the new "kick" called heroin. I saw it also on the skeleton faces of men of other countries, seeking visas or other help from us.

You always knew—and always with a stab of pity. The loathing that had begun in me as a boy in Pennsylvania increased as this blight was revealed in so many faces.

Our offices were a center of information and rumor. The grimmest stories—then as now—came from the refugees who managed to get out of the iron shadows of the new paradise-on-earth, Russia. Stories of what was going on were all cut from the same cloth of cruelty—daily liquidations, murder, pillage and unspeakable brutality. I was sending back reports on all this. One of my informers, a Dutch citizen, told me that he had heard there would be a meeting of the Third International in Amsterdam. There had not been a meeting of these conspirators for years and this was important news. Furthermore, he said, the International was going to dispatch agents to spread disorders and dissension, labor disputes and strikes, riots and revolutions, to every possible country. I cabled this information in code to Washington. They told me to keep in touch if I got any further information.

Through my Dutch informant I obtained a number of documents concerning this Third International meeting and—among other information—the names of two Russian youths who had been designated to go to the United States and aid in the formation and expansion of the Communist Party of America.

I asked my informant, "Have you any guess how these men are planning to get into the States?"

"I know how they will get in."

He stopped, flustered. "It is through one of your own men," he finally said.

I asked, "Who is it?"

He told me the name. "He's one of your American officials in Rotterdam," the informant reminded me. "He's slipping a lot of fellows—Communists and others—into America. He puts them as workaways at one cent a month on ships going to the States."

"How much does he get out of it?"

"A hundred dollars a man."

I wanted urgently to locate these two Russian agents who were going to America. I assigned this informant to go to Rotterdam, pay his hundred dollars and get to America. This he did with ease, as he was officially a member of the Dutch Communist Party and had no trouble convincing the Rotterdam official that he also should be "slipped through" to America.

Unfortunately we were not able to catch up with the two agents in America. They jumped ship and vanished into the labyrinth of America in the early twenties. There was not, at that time, any fully organized FBI as there is today and the immigration people had no large staff of investigators to run down every sailor who jumped ship at some American port.

I reported all the facts of the case to my superiors in the State Department. The man in Rotterdam was quietly removed. I was informed that an open scandal would have done harm to the nation at that moment.

I was still after information on the two Communists. Unwilling to quit, I went to Rotterdam myself. I had obtained an address where the two men had stayed, an obscure back-street tavern. I asked the woman behind the counter if either man was there.

"Oh, they have both shipped out," the woman said.

I said I was going to America too and had promised to pick up their mail and bring it to them; I was their close friend. She seemed to understand that this meant I was a comrade. We shared a secret bond. She handed over the mail to me without any question, and thanked me for taking it to them.

Although we did not locate either man I found among the letters a pathetic note from the mother of one of them. The letter when translated left no doubt as to their assignment—to spread in America the Red doctrine of revolution which has always been their fundamental tactic throughout the world.

Give up these wild ideas, the letter pleaded with the boy. This mission to America was too dangerous; he could be hurt or thrown into jail or killed. Give it up. Come on home. Unfortunately we had no forwarding address for her son. I decided to make further investigations on my own for eventual report to the State Department, and discovered that the Reds were making it a business to get *real* passports—chiefly Polish—by posing as refugees from Russia. To these they would then affix *fake* American visas. I had the Warsaw Consul General send me a genuine visa with his own stamp. With this to go on, the new Rotterdam Vice-Consul, Russell Brooks, and I, took our places at the gangplank on the day of the departure of the ocean liner *Rotterdam*, bound for New York. I stood behind Brooks to confirm his findings. As each passenger began the ascent up the gangway, Brooks would halt him and ask to see his passport and visa. Long before sailing time, we had lifted the passports of more than one hundred would-be passengers, turned back because their visas were forged. This "bag" on a single ship and a single voyage indicated the extent of Communist effort to get a honeycomb of agents into the United States.

I cabled the State Department regarding this development
with its dangerous implications for our country, and urged
that they send instructions immediately to all ports of de-
barkation in the States, and to all immigration officials, giving
them samples of genuine visas issued by our consuls throughout the world, as the one way to clamp down this traffic in
Communist agents. I asked the State Department also to forward this information to all friendly governments. Washington, however, remained unconcerned.

The Communists, my superiors told me, would collapse
within eight years. I was told to go about my career without
worrying any more over this problem, because the American
people were in no mood to worry about such trifles.

Decades later, in the world of narcotics, I met this same
Red enemy—with the same ultimate goals. And in some measure, I also met the same puzzling unconcern.

My diplomatic training carried me beyond the routine of
the average legation or embassy. It was a world-wide education in what went on behind the scenes. After my service in
Holland and Germany, I was consul at LaGuaira, Venezuela,
and after that at Nassau in the Bahamas. Problems of legal
and illegal immigration, and problems relating to smuggling of
all kinds, occupied my attention. Efficient smuggling controls
were essential for America's safety. Later I was to tangle with
those smuggling alcohol into the States and I saw in that
activity the start of the syndicated criminal effort in America.

In 1926 I was made chief of the division of foreign control
in the Treasury Department. In 1926 and 1927, I was the
United States delegate to international conferences on the
suppression of smuggling, held in London and Paris. These
conferences dealt with control of smuggling through application of international treaties and exchange of information. In
1928, I was American delegate to the international conference
in Antwerp, Belgium, on the suppression of alcoholism.

In 1929, I became assistant commissioner of Prohibition. So
long as I held this post, I labored to my fullest strength to en-

force and make effective the anti-alcohol laws of the United
States. But it was becoming obvious that this was a thankless
and impossible assignment. The people of the nation had rejected Prohibition. Criminal gangs were feeding this appetite.
Liquor poured across the borders not in a trickle but in a flood.

Another danger was growing almost unnoticed. The big
organized bootleg gangs were looking to the future when
Prohibition would be out. They would have to find other outlets. One lucrative outlet, even then occupying much of the
international underworld of that time, was that of narcotics.
Big chemical plants of Europe and Asia already were producing vast quantities of drugs which came into this country by
various routes and smuggling techniques.

In 1930, President Hoover asked me to take on a new responsibility—that of United States Commissioner of Narcotics
in charge of the newly formed Federal Bureau of Narcotics
under the over-all control of the Secretary of the Treasury.*
I had been in office only a few weeks when I found myself and
the new Bureau the object of a blistering assault from the floor
of the Senate.

Senator Cole Blease of South Carolina had purchased opium
through an undercover private detective he had hired, to prove
how easy it was to buy dope in the capital of the United
States. The Senator now rose from his seat, waving in his
hand the tin of opium. "This was purchased," he shouted,
"only one block from where we are now deliberating."

I knew that what he said was true. I had been working on
the case since my first day in office. With this blunt charge
from the floor of the Senate, however, time was running out—
if the newly formed Federal Narcotics Bureau was to win and
hold the respect and support of Congress and the public, it
would have to act fast.

In 1930 the Chinese still had a virtual monopoly on the

* For Bureau organization, as well as information on international control
development, see appendices.

pium trade in America; opium dens could be found in almost
ny American city. The Chinese underworld of dope—com-
ined with gambling and prostitution—had its own special
)riental ruthlessness which fitted the aura of violence and
rutality and killing that has always been the hallmark of the
arcotics underworld.

Among the criminal elements, life was the cheapest of all
ommodities. The tongs—the On Leongs and the Hip Sings
articularly—had professional "hatchet men" who carried out
illings on order; the more important the individual or tong
fficial, the higher the fee for the execution. The tongs had
mething of the overtones of an Oriental Mafia, except that
ney existed openly, and only in the United States, following
ne heavy Chinese immigration of the last half of the nine-
enth century. China itself has never had any tongs. They
vere American-spawned fraternal organizations, brotherhoods
f mutual protection. The Hip Sings and the On Leongs were
ne two most powerful. Both had extremist elements.

Chinese brothel keepers were equally brutal. Murder was
ommonplace. Prostitutes were brought in on stinking smug-
ling boats; if immigration or customs spotted the craft, the
Chinese "importers" thought nothing of drowning half a dozen
f these slaves to get rid of incriminating evidence.

I was convinced that the tongs, particularly the Hip Sings,
vere the distributing agents for opium on a national scale. But
t that time we were a newborn bureau. We had only begun
o train our undercover agents. Because of the Chinese in the
merican narcotic picture, several of the agents we had
rought in were of Chinese origins.

Our preliminary investigations had revealed that the tongs
nd other Chinese individuals were operating opium dens,
long with gambling and brothels, on both sides of Pennsyl-
ania Avenue, from Washington's Chinatown on Seventh
treet all the way to the Capitol. Working closely with the
Vashington metropolitan police, I ordered all available agents

thrown into this investigation. Within a few days, we h.
our first taste of tong violence.

One of the On Leong Tong members had come over to o
side and was working as a "special employee" of the Burea
Someone within his tong learned the truth, and only tv
blocks from the Capitol dome, our man was shot dead on t'
street as he collected data on dens we intended to close. T'
killing was skillfully carried out. No witnesses were availabl
No one was ever brought to trial.

Despite this, our agents made a number of "buys" of opiu
at Chinese establishments. The purchases, paid for with sp
cially allocated government funds, had to be witnessed by
second agent, in order to be acceptable as substantiated ev
dence in a court of law. Following the purchases we obtain
secret warrants for raids on thirty opium dens in Washingto
all located on or close to Pennsylvania Avenue, some of the
underground and actually extending directly under the aven
traversed by presidents and diplomats and world leaders.

I had no desire to risk another life, so I decided to raid the
dens all on the same night, and close all the places for goo
I picked a special occasion, a night when the Chinese we
holding an annual convention in Washington and family re
resentatives and tong leaders from cities all over Ameri
would be on hand. Washington metropolitan police patrolm
agreed to join with us. They "lent" us about four hundre
patrolmen. In addition, I had almost two dozen top unde
cover agents heading up approximately ten raiding parties.
was one of the largest and most carefully coordinated actio
of metropolitan and federal authorities, pooling their effor
in a single police operation.

We began in the early evening, sending out raiding parti
in cars, followed by patrol wagons. We would swoop down o
a center, break in, drag out the participants, the operators, th
opium-smoking paraphernalia and tote the whole business o
to the police station. While we took them off, another raidir

party would launch the next wave. This went on throughout the night.

Chinese operators simply could not believe that this was a series of "saturation raids" and they would be next on the list. As the raids continued, hour after hour, operators of places not yet raided must have heard what was happening. Yet the next place we hit would be going strong.

I went on more than a dozen of these raids personally. To get a closer look at the setup in these establishments, I stayed behind in one of the last places we raided to make my own survey of the upper floors, after the occupants had been removed to the police station.

These upper areas were dimly lit. The raid was over and there were only a couple of detectives on duty outside. There was an almost oppressive silence as I started up the stairs. When I reached the next landing I thought I heard a sound. I turned on my flashlight, crouching down to see where the sound came from. I was aware that someone was standing behind me.

For a moment I did not move. Then I turned as casually as I could and looked up. In the half light I saw a man looking down at me. He wore a gray business suit. He carried no weapon and looked almost friendly. "Why didn't they cart you off with the others?" I demanded.

In flawless English he replied, "The police captain downstairs told me he thought you were up here, Commissioner. I'm the mayor of Chinatown."

The mayor protested against the raids but I cut him short. "Let me tell you something, Mr. Mayor," I said. "You get these dens out of here. I don't care where you take them but get them out of here. If you or the tongs try to open up these joints," I added, "I'll raid them night after night. We'll smash them into a teakwood pulp."

The raids plus the chat with Chinatown's chief executive paid off in this first major case of the Bureau. The dens were either closed up permanently or moved to other cities where we would take care of them at a later date. It was an auspicious beginning, this first victory at close quarters with the narcotic underworld. The main street of the nation's capital, at least, was no longer polluted.

2. Slavery, Inc.

Chinese seduction of teen-aged girls into addiction and prostitution presented serious problems to our Bureau in the years immediately after 1930. The Chinese not only dealt with prostitutes imported from Asia; many of their customers had developed a liking for the charms of Caucasian girls. The result, I learned, was a primitive Chinese-American call-girl organization loosely interlaced through Chinese family associations and the tongs.

Little of this incense-flavored depravity was published in the American press. The girls were from good families. The clientele put a high premium on white girls with cultured backgrounds. Even where Chinese operators were arrested and convicted, details were suppressed when necessary to protect underage girls and their families.

Narcotics and prostitution, I had long realized, were hand-maidens in the underworld. This was even more apparent later, when the call-girl and dope tie-in became an important part of syndicate operations. It offered the promise of big profits. The girls produced a safe and predictable market for narcotics; and the drugs dulled their senses and the measure they had to give of themselves. The pattern also gave the syndicate a hint-and-wait wedge of blackmail—a pressure point against public officials gulled into their power. Heroin and morphine were the principal drugs the syndicate later promoted for their prostitution trade. But in those earlier days it was opium.

In the mid-1930's I began to receive reports involving what we called the "dream girls." One of the dreamers, found alone and dazed on the streets of a West Coast city at four in the morning, was arrested by police and taken in for questioning. She was nicely dressed, a raven-haired, round-faced, pink-cheeked seventeen-year-old, seemingly from an upper-class background. She gave them her name and address, and admitted that she was an opium user. She would not tell police where she had been, or who had given her drugs. She had no narcotics in her possession. Police called her parents to come and take her home.

I received reports of other girls picked up by the authorities in West Coast cities over a period of weeks. They were all white girls from good families. All appeared in a bewildered, semi-comatose condition. All apparently had been smoking opium. The rise in the number of these cases was startling. Complaints began to come in to local authorities and to West Coast offices of the Bureau from parents who were alarmed and suspicious over the late hours, the aura of secrecy, the list-less, blurred lethargy of the girls. When picked up the girls would say little. One or two hinted that they were working with a Chinese "businessman."

Gradually we began to find a few scattered leads. Some of the parents began to talk more freely. Our investigations throughout the West Coast area revealed that the number of female addicts had gone up but we found no reported increase in the number of male addicts. At the same time, we had reports of sex orgies in several parts of the city, in which these girls participated, at what were reported as "fantastic prices."

Over the long distance phone I conferred with my supervisors and agents in California. All their leads had dried up. I told them to start looking back over the criminal files for the past year or two. "Check every case that had anything to do with sex, perversion, prostitution, opium, or violence, and raids involving young girls." Some place along the road, I figured, the Chinese "businessman"—if one were involved—must have made at least one misstep.

For days it appeared he hadn't. Then one of our men came upon a six-months old item that held a hint of possibility. It was listed in routine terminology as "an unusual death" of a white girl whose nude body had been found in the apartment of a Chinese named Joe Sing. She had apparently died of natural causes but police had questioned Joe at length.

Sing's story had been that the girl knocked at his door and told him she had been on a party nearby and felt sick. She wanted to rest. He led her to the bedroom, he said, where the girl said she wanted to disrobe and lie down. Would he get her a glass of water? When he returned with the water, according to his story, she was lying naked on the bed and when she did not move he went over to the bed and realized that she was dead.

Frightened, he said, he called a neighbor and the two attempted to dress the girl and take her out of the building. Then they gave this idea up and called the police, telling them the entire story. After the grilling by authorities, Joe Sing was released for lack of evidence. The medical report, based on a routine cursory examination, called it death from "natural causes." A few days after this report, Joe Sing disappeared.

We wanted to talk to Joe Sing. I assigned one of our most extraordinary agents to find him—a lean, full-blooded Cherokee Indian who sometimes passed as a Chinese, sometimes as an Indian, Mexican, Negro or Eurasian. Whether he played the part of peddler, addict or underworld bookkeeper, his performance was invariably brilliant. I do not recall that he was ever "made"—that is, spotted—by suspects against whom he was trying to get evidence.

We gave him a full set of papers identifying him as a Chinese immigrant who had been living in Chicago. For days he toured Chinese restaurants, regaled himself with the best Chinese food, chatted with Chinese customers but did nothing and asked nothing that would make anyone suspicious. In the course of this he happened to overhear two Chinese waiters talking about girl friends. Several times he heard them mention "white girl" and "apartment 10A." The agent said he believed —from the tone of the waiters—that the term 10A was more than an apartment number. It was used like a name. Perhaps it was Joe Sing.

So we had to find an apartment 10A, address unknown. The area in which we figured Joe Sing might operate covered about two square miles. There were perhaps five hundred apartment buildings of various sizes.

Our Cherokee "Chinese" began an arduous door-to-door canvass, from one apartment house to the next, presenting himself as a vacuum cleaner salesman, complete with samples. After two plodding days he came to an apartment house tucked away on a quiet side street. It had a pleasant courtyard and a cool, shadowed lobby, and an air of tidy window-box respectability. But on one of the mailboxes the agent saw a card with a scrawled figure: 10A.

He found the apartment on the second floor—with the same identification on the door. He knocked and waited. There were noises inside, but no one answered. He next located the apartment house owner and identified himself as a U.S. government agent. The owner, obviously nervous, but apparently eager to cooperate, declared that apartment 10A was occupied by a Chinese male who occasionally rented the place out for "private parties." Exactly what kind of parties he did not know. The agent took out a picture of Joe. The building owner said, "Well, it could be him. He's husky enough. And ugly enough."

We staked out the building so that our agents could observe everybody going in and coming out of this apartment house. Among possible suspects they observed a woman whom they recognized as a known heroin pusher. Our agent made several purchases of heroin from the woman, who went by the name of Marie. He established that she was obtaining the heroin directly from Joe Sing in the apartment. He also learned from her that she tapped out a secret code word on the door before they would admit her.

The following day we seized Marie just after she walked out of Joe Sing's apartment, carrying heroin. Our agents then knocked at the door, using the signal Marie had disclosed. The door opened a few inches. A Chinese peered out. The agents barged uninvited into the apartment.

Four nude girls—all about eighteen years old—were surprised in a scene of unspeakable sexual depravity. Leaping up and crying out in high-pitched alarm, they ran for their clothes, while a naked Chinese cowered against the wall.

The agents identified themselves. The man who opened the door admitted he was Joe Sing. "You won't find any evidence against us," he told the agents. "We had a tip some detective moved in next door and we threw out all the apparatus. You'll find nothing to use in court."

He was almost right. All we found were some empty "toys" of opium. (A toy is a small tin container; the opium is dipped out of the "toy" onto the needle for "cooking" preparations before it is smoked.) In the dimly lit bedroom, agents found a woman's purse with 62 capsules of heroin. Sing accepted the inevitable with Oriental calm. He even reached under the sofa and brought out another box. "Here's some more," he said smiling.

All the girls were questioned. They gave us their names and addresses as well as the names and addresses of other patrons, including both men and women. Their naïvely related accounts of sexual acts were pathetic, and shocking. One half-hysterical girl told us of how Joe had taken her and other girls through the apartment, shown them his bedroom with nude photographs all over the walls, shown her an opium pipe and explained its uses "in my country," as he put it. Then, a little later, he induced them to try just a little opium smoking themselves.

This girl's story, like the others, depicted a deliberate and carefully organized business. She said that all the girls were young and from good families; all the men were Chinese, either merchants or youths out for adventure. She told us that people came and went during the evening. Couples danced together to a record player.

The opium she had smoked that first evening did not make her sleepy but seemed to quicken all her sensibilities. "I felt simply wonderful," she told us. "I thought it was great. We ate little bits of Chinese candy. I was dancing with a Chinese boy. We danced a lot."

She saw another girl, apparently a professional dancer, take off her dress. Underneath this she had on an abbreviated costume and she did a solo dance. Other couples were lounging around the room, watching her dance, or indulging openly in love making. "It was terribly hot in the apartment," she said. "He keeps it hot like that. Some girls took off their dresses and slips—they always do that at Joe's—and one was in nothing but panties. I pulled off my dress too because it didn't seem to me to make any difference and I was in a sort of dream state. . . ."

She said the boy she was dancing with began kissing her and trying to make love to her but nothing she was doing seemed real to her. This unusual effect she described had a definite cause. In addition to the opium symptoms, she was fed candy. We tested the candy when we raided the apartment. It contained cantharides, a powerful stimulant used as an aphrodisiac.

In the midst of her love making the girl had collapsed. When she came to it was daylight. The girl who had brought her to the apartment was lying on the floor near her, in a deep opiate sleep. The love-making youth was gone. Joe Sing, however, was there. He insisted he wanted to help her. He gave her some capsules that he said would "fix her up." The girl took the capsules and—still in a half-dazed condition—left the apartment. Sing made no effort to stop her.

She did not tell her parents anything of what had occurred. She said merely that she wasn't feeling well and wanted to sleep. In the next few days she found that using the capsules he had given her helped to soothe her nerves and ease the pain she felt in her abdomen.

The capsules contained not medicine but heroin, and when the effects of the capsule wore off, the girl was in pain again even worse than before. She went back to Joe Sing—and he gave her more capsules. Eventually he told her he couldn't give them away any more but he would let her have some if she went on a party for him with another girl. The men involved on these "dates" were always Chinese.

Girl after girl in a pitiful repetition related essentially the same story and sequence of events. We talked with the parents who in most cases had no real idea of what their daughters were involved in. The facts, times and other details and the stories checked out. Sing seemed to have thought of every angle. If the girls didn't go for the opium at first, the "loaded" candy helped to suck them in. If they got a little reckless and danced naked or half-nude, he would get photos of them in various stages of disrobing or love making. One of the girls told us that Joe Sing offered her free heroin supplies for every girl she introduced into his network. All the girls had to be white. The more beautiful and youthful, the higher the fee in heroin.

These girls now went back to their homes, their families— and a new chance.

Marie, the female heroin pusher, pleaded guilty—there was little else she could do with the case we had against her—and got eight months. Joe drew ten years. He was released after serving part of it, and immediately went back to selling dope to white girls. We made a second case against him, and again sent him away.

The technique developed by Joe Sing parallels in many respects that employed later by Lucky Luciano and made standard operational procedure for recruiting fresh batches of prostitutes out of high school and teen-age ranks. We have dealt with hundreds of these cases since those first Chinese-

American call-girl operations. The pattern is sickeningly similar. She begins with the smoking of "tea"—marijuana—and from there moves to the "white drugs"—heroin usually. She starts by sniffing or smelling heroin—a grain or two on the corner of a handkerchief. From there she moves to injecting the drug subcutaneously into the muscle or intravenously—"main lining," this is called. Then she turns to the only avenue that will provide the quick and ready cash she needs to support this habit.

In the hands of the emerging syndicate, the pattern was refined, as the hoodlums put addiction and call-girl routines on what they called a "pay-as-you-sleep" basis. In their new business-like techniques, the girl-and-dope operations dovetailed into other equally and even more important syndicate by-products.

Peggy W. is a svelte, sophisticated sample of the latter-day operation. Peggy is only one of the names she goes by. She dresses like Park Avenue, has the *hauteur* of a Newport matron and the moral horizons of a Times Square tramp. She moves in rarefied circles, normally unassociated with madames or female dealers in dope. This "first lady" of the underworld came herself from a family of pimps and prostitutes, but she has carried the family tradition to a level of elegance in vice rarely achieved. Her customers represent the finest people in the nation, and on the international scene as well. She deals with the highest level in business, politics, industry, and the professional arts.

Evidence indicates that she is the chief supplier of prostitutes used by the group known as "café society" in New York City. These girls operate out of apartments, primarily, but also through a number of elegant barrooms where they gather informally. Our files on her state:

She was the former mistress of _____ _____ [one of America's richest young men], and is also the associate of important criminals and hoodlums, as well as of many influential persons in manufacturing and professional circles who obtain the services of prostitutes through her for use personally or in their business.

In June, 1953, she was arrested under a New York State law charged with possession of narcotics with intent to sell. She was at that time in possession of opium, opium smoking paraphernalia, marijuana and amidone, a highly dangerous and addictive synthetic narcotic. A year later she was convicted on these charges and sentenced from one to three years in state prison. Because of her powerful political influence in New York, Washington, and Albany, this sentence was suspended.

She returned at once to her big operations. One month after her release, she was arrested again at her elaborate mid-town apartment and charged with possession of heroin and marijuana. At this time, in association with a number of well-known syndicate hoodlums, she was selling through the pushers to teen agers, taking her profit from these sales—and building a reserve of candidates for her call-girl ring.

Peggy was charged with violation of federal laws by our agents. Her New York State probation was revoked and she was resentenced in July 1954 to three years in a New York City prison—much to be preferred to a federal prison. The federal charges against her resulted in two three-year terms in addition, but these were suspended and she was given three years probation on each, the probations to run concurrently after she served her New York prison term. This was a fantastic sentence for such a woman. Her time in prison was no more than the first sentence, in spite of her persistent activities in dope and prostitution.

The chilling fact we must recognize is the influence of Peggy's clientele; the people of importance who dared not cross her because of what she could reveal. This is not guesswork or imagination. We know who some of her customers and clientele were. We found the little black book which listed her $100 to $500 a night customers. Blackmail is an ugly word but there is no other. This is what happens when leaders of a community—state and national leaders—put themselves in the power of such people.

3. Hemp Around Their Necks

In 1930 there was no federal law against smoking marijuana, and the average American citizen in an average community had probably never heard of "reefers" or "tea" or other words in the argot of marijuana users. But by the middle thirties we began to see the serious effects of marijuana on our youth. An alarming increase in the smoking of marijuana reefers in 1936 continued to spread at an accelerated pace in 1937. Before this, use of reefers had been relatively slight and confined to the states of the Southwest, particularly along the Mexican border. Seizures by state officers in these two years, however, had increased a hundred percent and by hundreds of pounds. Reports I received from thirty states showed an "invasion" by this drug, either by cultivation or underworld importation. Marijuana was something new and adventuresome. The angle-wise mobsters were aiming their pitch straight at the most impressionable age group—America's fresh, post-depression crop of teen agers.

One adolescent gave a picture to an agent of a typical "smoker" in an apartment or "pad":

"The room was crowded. There were fifty people but it seemed like five hundred. It was like crazy, couples lying all over the place, a woman was screaming out in the hall, two fellows were trying to make love to the same girl and this girl was screaming and crying and not making any sense. Her clothes were mostly pulled off and she was snickering and blubbering and trying to push these two guys away. . . . The place was nothing but smoke and stink and these funny little noises I could hear but they were way out, that far I could hardly hear them and they were right there in the room, that laughing and crying and the music and all that stuff. It was crazy wild. But I didn't want to do anything, I didn't want to sleep with those women or like that. I just wanted to lie down because the room seemed big and like a great tremendous crowd like at a ball game or something. . . ."

Made from the hemp plant known as *Cannabis sativa americana*, marijuana is almost a twin brother to *Cannabis sativa indica*, otherwise called hashish. There are said to be almost three hundred names for the varieties of the hemp weed. In some parts of Asia it is called *bhang;* in South Africa it is called *dagga*. It is also challed *chira* and *ganja*. And many other names.

The hemp weed grows best in warm climates but has also been found along roadsides north of Boston. It grows to heights of from five and a half to fifteen or sixteen feet. Its leaves, seeds and flowers contain a substance which when chewed or smoked produces hallucinatory effects.

Elaborate technical processes have been developed for the manufacture of Cannabis cigarettes from the resin in the plants. Although pharmacists have never been able to isolate completely the nature of the Cannabis "principal" that produces the narcotic effect, it is known to exist in the little fringes or hairs on the leaves and in the flowers, and in the thick resin that flows through the stalk and other parts of the plant.

Cannabis grows wild in many parts of the world, and is cultivated in India, and illegally in certain areas of Africa, Mexico, Brazil and the United States. It also grows wild in parts of the United States, although we have been able to root the wild Cannabis out of most communities.

Origins of hemp weed are ancient. Rites that go back thousands of years, in temples long vanished, may well have evolved around the effects of some variant of the hemp weed. Worshipers of the Hindu god Siva were said to use Cannabis indica. In the eleventh century A.D., the Mohammedan sect called the Assassins, used hashish in so-called religious observances. They made homicide a high ritualistic art. Their name itself is today a synonym for murder.

Marijuana effects on the average user are described in a brochure we published in the Bureau for the information of lay groups. "The toxic effect produced by the active narcotic principle of Cannabis sativa, hemp, or marijuana," the report states, "appear to be exclusively to the higher nerve centers. The drug produces first an exhaltation with a feeling of well being, a happy, jovial mood, usually; an increased feeling of physical strength and power, and a general euphoria is experienced. Accompanying this exaltation is a stimulation of the imagination followed by a more or less delirious state characterized by vivid kaleidoscopic visions, sometimes of a pleasing sensual kind, but occasionally of a gruesome nature. Accompanying this delirious state is a remarkable loss in spatial and time relations; persons and things in the environment look small; time is indeterminable; seconds seem like minutes and hours like days.

"Those who are accustomed to habitual use of the drug are said eventually to develop a delirious rage after its administration during which they are temporarily, at least, irresponsible and prone to commit violent crimes. The prolonged use of this narcotic is said to produce mental deterioration."

One of the great difficulties with Cannabis is its unpredictability. Physicians who have made hundreds of tests with Cannabis report that there is no way to predict what effect it can have on the individual, both under controlled and non-controlled conditions. One man has no reaction at all; the next may go berserk and try to stab somebody or harm himself. The medical profession after many such experiments was forced to drop the narcotic as a possible analgesic because of this unpredictable quality.

Much of the most irrational juvenile violence and killing that has written a new chapter of shame and tragedy is traceable directly to this hemp intoxication. A gang of boys tear the clothes from two school girls and rape the screaming girls, one boy after the other. A sixteen-year-old kills his entire family of five in Florida, a man in Minnesota puts a bullet through the head of a stranger on the road; in Colorado a husband tries to shoot his wife, kills her grandmother instead and then kills himself. Every one of these crimes had been proceeded by the smoking of one or more marijuana "reefers."

As the marijuana situation grew worse, I knew action had to be taken to get proper control legislation passed. By 1937, under my direction, the Bureau launched two important steps: First, a legislative plan to seek from Congress a new law that would place marijuana and its distribution directly under federal control. Second, on radio and at major forums, such as that presented annually by the New York *Herald Tribune*, I told the story of this evil weed of the fields and river beds and roadsides. I wrote articles for magazines; our agents gave hundreds of lectures to parents, educators, social and civic leaders. In network broadcasts I reported on the growing list of crimes, including murder and rape. I described the nature of marijuana and its close kinship to hashish. I continued to hammer at the facts.

I believe we did a thorough job, for the public was alerted, and the laws to protect them were passed, both nationally and at the state level. We also brought under control the wild-growing marijuana in this country. Working with local authorities, we cleaned up hundreds of acres of marijuana weed and uprooted plants sprouting along the roadsides.

The 1937 law does not prohibit the sale of marijuana but puts a tax of $100.00 an ounce on any sale or transfer of the drug, and makes such sale or transfer illegal without proper registration and approval from the Bureau. Possession without proper authorization can bring a prison term.

The Marijuana Tax Act is patterned in general after the Harrison Act, but with some major technical variations, principally based on the fact that while marijuana is used in laboratory tests it is not used for medical purposes.

There were still some WPA gangs working in those days and we put them to good use. Just outside the nation's capital, for some sixty miles along the Potomac River, on both banks, marijuana was growing in profusion; it had been planted there originally by early settlers who made their own hemp and cloth. The workers cleaned out tremendous river bank crops, destroying plants, seeds and roots. All through the Midwest also, WPA workers were used for this clean-up job. The wild hemp was rooted out of America.

During the Second World War, after Axis powers in the Far East and Europe cut off our access to countries where hemp was grown for the making of cord and cloth, we developed, under strict controls, our own hemp growing program on the rich farmlands of Minnesota. Less than one thousandth of one percent was ever diverted into illegal channels. After the war this production stopped and the fields went back to corn and wheat. With the war's end, however, the narcotic branch of the underworld was given a new lift by the publication of an extraordinary document which has come to be known as the La Guardia Report.

The title was a misnomer; it was actually a report of a committee on marijuana which had been appointed by the "Little Flower" of New York to give an objective picture of marijuana from a scientific point of view. La Guardia was always not only an honest official who warred against the syndicate "tin horns," as he called them, but was also a good friend of the Bureau of Narcotics. In Congress he fought consistently for increases for our Bureau to help us to achieve the manpower needed to do our job.

The men who issued this document were men of science, doctors, technicians, authorities. Published as a book by the Jacques Cattell Press in 1945, the report bore the title: *The Marijuana Problem in the City of New York: Sociological, Medical, Psychological and Pharmacological Studies*, by the Mayor's Committee on Marijuana.

This report declared, in effect, that those who had been denouncing marijuana as dangerous, including myself and experts in the Bureau, were not only in error, but were spreading baseless fears about the effects of smoking Cannabis. I say the report was a government printed invitation to youth and adults—above all to teen agers—to go ahead and smoke all the reefers they felt like.

Relying solely on a series of experiments with a group of 77 prisoners who volunteered to make the tests, the Mayor's experts asserted that they found no major menace in the use of this narcotic, which they termed "a mild drug smoked by bored people for the sake of conviviality."

The report further claimed that there was "no apparent" connection between "the weed" and crimes of violence, that smoking it did not produce aggressiveness or belligerence as a rule, that it could be used for a number of years without causing serious mental or physical harm and that while it might be habit forming it could be given up abruptly without causing distress; in other words, it did not produce the bodily dependence found in heroin, cocaine, morphine and other drugs.

Finally, the report suggested that the drug is so mild that it might well be used successfully as a substitute in the process of curing addiction to other drugs, or even in the treatment of chronic alcoholism.

Doctors and other authorities who studied the effects of this drug, however, tore the report apart for its inaccuracies and misleading conclusions. The *Journal* of the American Medical

Association joined the Bureau in condemning it as unscientific.

"For many years medical scientists have considered Cannabis a dangerous drug," the *Journal*'s editorial of April 26, 1945 stated. "Nevertheless, . . . the Mayor's Committee on Marijuana submits an analysis by seventeen doctors of tests on 77 prisoners and, on this narrow and thoroughly unscientific foundation, draws sweeping and inadequate conclusions which minimize the harmlessness of marijuana. Already the book has done harm. One investigator has described some tearful parents who brought their 16-year-old boy to a physician after he had been detected in the act of smoking marijuana. . . . The boy said he had read an account of the La Guardia committee report and this was his justification for using marijuana. . . . A criminal lawyer for marijuana drug peddlers has already used the La Guardia report as a basis to have defendants set free by the Court.

"The value of the conclusions," continued the editorial, "is destroyed by the fact that the experiments were conducted on 77 confined criminals. Prisoners were obliged to be content with the quantities of drug administered. Antisocial behavior could not have been noticed, as they were prisoners. At liberty some of them would have given free rein to their inclinations and would probably not have stopped at the dose producing 'the pleasurable principle. . . .' Public officials will do well to disregard this unscientific, uncritical study, and continue to regard marijuana as a menace where it is purveyed," the *Journal* concluded.

There can be no doubt of the damage done by the report. Syndicate lawyers and spokesmen leaped upon its giddy sociology and medical mumbo-jumbo, cited it in court cases, tried to spread the idea that the report had brought marijuana back into the folds of good society with a full pardon and a slap on the back from the medical profession.

The lies continued to spread. They cropped up on panel discussions, in public addresses by seemingly informed individuals. They helped once again, in a new and profitable direction, to bewilder the public and make it unsure of its own judgments. This carefully nurtured public doubt was to pay off with extra millions in the pockets of the hoods.

One killer who helped to nourish that doubt—a hoodlum called Lepke—took a multi-million-dollar cut in exchange for the terror inspired by the mere mention of his name.

4. Lepke

The narcotics role of slovenly Louis (Lepke) Buchalter, boss of Murder, Inc., was unique. This mass murderer headed a world-wide dope ring from which he took a better than fifty percent cut from every incoming dollar. The profits ran into many millions, but for Lepke it was only a side line.

The full truth behind Lepke's role in crime has been kept from the public, for his power reached to the highest pedestals of authority and held some of our most honored citizens in servitude.

My personal role in the Lepke story began on June 14, 1937, as I was coming down the gangplank of the S.S. *Washington* on her arrival in New York from Europe. I was returning from a meeting of the Opium Advisory Committee of the League of Nations in Geneva. A blonde pushed through the crowd at the foot of the gangway, handed me a note and lost herself in the throng on the pier. I opened the envelope the woman had handed me and read the following typewritten message:

"Mr. Harry J. Anslinger

"Dear Sir:

"I read in the paper that you were arriving on this ship and I am sure I can recognize you from your picture.

"I can furnish you with valuable information about the smuggling of large quantities of heroin by a certain gang.

"I must deal directly with you, otherwise a leak might upset everything.

"Please answer in the New York Times personal column, saying, 'X-2—telephone me.'

"Hoping you give this letter your immediate attention.

Sincerely yours,
X-2"

No one in law enforcement could afford to ignore this kind of tip. It could be a madwoman reveling in her hallucinations; or it could be someone willing to disclose information for vengeance. I inserted the advertisement as X-2 requested. The following morning I received a phone call. The caller was a woman; the voice sounded rational and intelligent. "I have something of importance to tell you," she said. "I do not want money. I want only to see that our laws are kept inviolate."

I did not believe her motive was so simple but I wanted to know the whole story. She agreed to come to Washington and meet me at the Mayflower Hotel.

Madame X-2 now seemed relaxed and sure of herself. I cannot reveal any more of her identity, even now. She talked freely with me for several hours. "My story," she told me, "concerns a gang of murderers operating in New York City. I have known some of this crowd in other ways."

The blonde informant hesitated. I said, "All right. Go ahead."

"Someone double-crossed me. I don't give a damn about any of them. I hope they go to hell."

She waited, her fingers twisting nervously. It sounded to me like a familiar pattern—the lady pushed aside by some ambitious gangster boy friend. "If you're talking about murder *per se*," I told her, "you've come to the wrong place. We deal in narcotic violations—and violators."

She leaned toward me. "This is the biggest name in the hoods right now. He's the head boy. He's got them all scared to hell. The mobs cut him in on anything he wants. And he's taking big in dope. They need his bankroll."

The name she gave me was Lepke.

The name was not widely known to the public in those days. But some of the early background of the man was already known in detail by the FBI and other agencies, local, state, and federal. Born just before the turn of the century, a native New Yorker, he had grown up in the city sidewalk gangs at a time when juvenile violence and lawlessness closely paralleled that of the post-World War II era half a century later. It was in New York City in 1910, as a reaction to the juvenile gang violence of that day, that the first plans for launching the Boy Scouts of America were put together. Lepke was not one of those they reached.

By the 1920's his ruthlessness was known throughout America's underworld. The crimes he committed during this period, the number of hired killings he personally carried out, the beatings and sluggings he inflicted, no one knows. Early in the 1920's, however, he had begun to move into the green plateaus of extortion.

Manhattan's fur trade business was composed largely of small independent companies. To maintain a degree of order and stability they had formed two associations: The Protective Fur Dressers Corporation and the Fur Dressers Factor Corporation. In 1939, Lepke and an associate, Jack "Gurrah" Shapiro, managed by bribery, fear and beatings to obtain enough support from fur dealers and dressers to take over control of these two operations. So many complaints began to pour in to authorities that the U.S. District Attorney in New York started a federal investigation which resulted in Lepke's being indicted, in 1933, for violation of the Sherman Anti-Trust laws.

It was while these cases were pending that Lepke turned his hands and attentions to another field—dope.

This part of the Lepke story the public did not know. The woman who called herself X-2 began to unfold some of the

details to me for the first time in that summer of 1937. I
realized that X-2's life would be worthless if they discovered
how much she had learned in her intimate underworld associations and how much she was spilling in sheer feminine spite.
I assigned one of my men to protect her life at all times during
the investigation, and I turned loose a number of my own
agents to track down every detail of her information on
Lepke's role in narcotics.

I had known for some time that Lepke was deeply involved
in drugs. As an associate of Jack (Legs) Diamond and Sam
Bernstein, both New York mobsters active in narcotics, Lepke
was No. 3 on our confidential list of major suspects. But we
had not been able previously to uncover a shred of actual
evidence. Leads given us by Madame X-2 made the difference.
The jig-saw pattern of facts our agents pieced together presented the following picture:

The drug deal in which Lepke was involved had been started
in January 1935, by three men who lived in the Bronx. Their
names were Yasha Katzenberg, Jake Lvovsky and Samuel
Gross. These three ran a clandestine plant in a tenement, manufacturing heroin from a prepared opium and morphine base.
They sold the heroin to middlemen who supplied the pushers.
One day the equipment they had painstakingly put together
blew up. The three held a business meeting and decided to
find a reliable source of supply for manufactured heroin to
resell to their customers in the Bronx, Harlem and lower Manhattan.

They had a meeting with Lepke, whom they had heard was
anxious to increase his activities in this field. They wanted
him to use his influence to help them get regular shipments of
heroin from China, through a trafficker whom Lepke knew.
Lepke agreed—for better than half the profits—to go along
with the deal.

A multi-fingered smuggling operation was developed, with
world-wide connections, distribution methods and outlets.
The primary source was Shanghai, where carriers working for

the gang made connections with Lepke's man. He put them in touch with two Greek dealers, a man named Janis Tsounias and his partner, George L. Mexis. These two provided large supplies of heroin direct or sent the carriers to a factory in the Japanese concession at Tienstin where orders would be filled.

Carriers recruited by the gang were made up of an outlandish collection of "world travelers." One was a fellow who hung around at an East Side barber shop and was glad to go the world-circling junket for $1,000 plus expenses. Another was an ex-fighter. Another sold frozen custard at Coney Island. In contrast, still another was a woman who posed as a society woman, wore the finest clothes and who later appeared in court wearing a plumed hat and a fur coat.

The plan revolved around the bribery of two Customs officers in New York. At the rate of $1,000 a trip, these two sold to the gang "clearance stamps" used by Customs to indicate that a piece of luggage had been inspected and cleared. The stamps came in eight colors—pink, red, purple, yellow, green, orange, blue and brown. The color used was changed daily. No one knew in advance what color would be picked. Customs thought they had a smuggle-proof plan. But the gang provided their carriers with a large supply of stamps of all colors—supplied by these Customs men, of course.

An elaborate scheme of corruption and bribery was evolved by Lepke and the trio in New York to get their merchandise into the country. As a rich world-traveler, the dope courier would take a leisurely voyage to the Orient, stopping off at Shanghai, where he would fill several trunks full of heroin and morphine, continuing on his way via the Suez Canal. The couriers used only the finest ships: the *Majestic*, the *Aquitania*, the *Berengaria*, the *Queen Mary*. On the pier in New York, when the luggage was brought ashore, the carrier would find the trunk with his "goods" in it, casually perch on it for a moment or two—and leave the proper color sticker firmly in place. The porter would carry the piece through the gates to a waiting car. The heroin was home.

Each trip brought in a minimum of $100,000 worth of pure heroin or morphine, which on the retail market might run as high as $5,000,000.

Of the stories of the underworld double-cross, one of my favorites is that of Yaşha Katzenberg, who, as a leader of the mob, decided to take a couple of trips himself to the Far East. On his first trip to Shanghai he was to bring back two trunk loads of dope. Some of the crowd in Shanghai were afraid he might find out too much about their operations and blackmail them into lower prices. "Shanghai streets are too dangerous," they told him, "you better stay right in the hotel room. We'll bring the trunks here." This required a few days, and Katzenberg began to fume in his hotel prison. "Hell, I'm on a kind of vacation. I want some action," he told his "protectors." The boys said they would take care of that. They had access to a Russian princess. She was—they informed their impatient prisoner—"the highest priced whore in Asia." It would cost $1,000. But to give him a pleasant memory of the hotel and of their service they would provide the lady at no cost to him. They would pay the fee.

When they brought her to the room, Katzenberg took one look at her and said, "Hello there, baby."

The Shanghai dealers looked startled. "Oh, we didn't know you knew Her Highness," one said.

"Sure, I know her," Katzenberg told them. "She was here last night. All night. For two lousy bucks."

This background and evidence we compiled from information furnished to us by X-2. We obtained, for example, from a member of the gang, a kilo of heroin with Shanghai markings still on the package. The next move was to use this evidence to convince some of the people involved to "sing." We learned that Lepke took a stand-offish attitude toward actual involvement in the deals, but still insisted on his cut.

We gathered evidence, witnesses and testimony. Madame X-2 was protected but other insiders talked to the Grand Jury to save themselves. The number of individuals in this mob at that time was thirty. On the basis of the testimony and documentary information, we obtained secret indictments of all thirty. Two thirds of them were seized immediately; half of these confessed, assuring conviction of all. We were thereupon able to obtain additional indictments against others involved. Lepke was named in ten indictments but was not brought in at that time. He was still under indictment and being sought as a fugitive on the charges growing out of Sherman Anti-Trust violations in connection with fur industry extortions.

Katzenberg was in China when this broke. On his return to America he realized that he was "hot." He slipped out of the country, heading for Rumania. We relayed word to Rumania of his background. They didn't want to send him back to us but deported him immediately to Greece, where he was promptly seized by authorities and turned over to us, brought back to America, convicted on the narcotics indictment, given ten years in prison and fined $10,000.

Five others were also convicted and given long terms. Lepke, already a fugitive, now became a fugitive also under the narcotics indictments. A world-wide hunt began.

We received word that Lepke had given orders for extermination of all witnesses who could testify against him. Day by day men would disappear on whom we had counted—or the child of an individual who had information would be found dead. The situation with Lepke had become so serious that Thomas E. Dewey, at that time New York District Attorney, called an unprecedented secret meeting of four high enforcement officials—FBI Director J. Edgar Hoover, New York Police Commissioner Lewis J. Valentine, District Attorney Dewey himself, and I representing the Bureau of Narcotics. "If the killing off of witnesses continues," Dewey told us, "there will soon be no one left to testify when we finally catch up with Lepke."

Director Hoover of the FBI brought up the question of operational procedure. It was agreed that each of us would function independently within our own areas but with a full exchange of all information and leads at the top level, to avoid crossed wires. We agreed to throw all our available manpower into action.

The four of us reached a unique accord: We would pool not only information but also financial resources. We felt that a sufficiently large reward was the bait that worked best in such intra-underworld cases. The FBI offered a reward of $5,000. Dewey increased this to $30,000—for whoever brought in Lepke, dead or alive.

"If the four of us together can't land Lepke," Dewey said, "we might as well turn the job over to the mobs."

Throughout the country we followed up leads, brought in hoodlums, fences, associates, friends and business partners of killer Lepke. Members of Lepke's family were brought in and questioned by the grand jury. Under oath they were asked: Had they seen him? Heard from him? Had he called or written?

His enemies were brought in, men who would be glad to drop a hint if they could without risking their lives. Criminals on the fringes of Lepke's crowd also were questioned. What had they heard? The heat was the hottest ever put on the underworld in a single investigation.

We made it so hot in fact that the syndicate bosses decided they wanted no more of the unrewarding job of shielding Lepke. The word spread over underworld channels: "Tell Lepke to give up or we'll kill him ourselves and dump his body on the steps of the courthouse in Foley Square."

Lepke heard the reports and, tough as he was, realized that he was no match for the entire organized syndicate. With half the police forces of the nation seeking him, and the underworld gunning for him on their own, Lepke, in a dramatic phone call exchange with Walter Winchell, surrendered to the columnist, who turned him over to the FBI.

The federal court's bill of particulars against Lepke—in ten indictments—charged him with bribing Customs officers of the United States government, and conspiring to violate the narcotics laws. We had witnesses able to tell about the original gatherings at which the narcotic ring was formed: Katzenberg, although a defendant, told of the amounts and percentages of the profits Lepke took. All through the trial, Lepke kept making threats and shouting obscenities at one of our agents, who was the chief witness against him in his case. "We'll get you, you son-of-a-bitch."

Lepke was convicted on one narcotics count, pleaded guilty to the others as the best way out and got sentences totaling close to fifteen years. All this time New York State continued its probe into the workings of Murder, Inc. But the facts of that blood bath were still under investigation and indictments were not yet ready.

At this critical point Lepke's family decided to make a major effort to obtain lenient treatment for him by sending one of their attorneys to Washington with an extraordinary story—one of the most extraordinary in the history of modern crime. It involved a highly placed labor leader. The attorney wished to talk with me about it and informed me that the case involved murder. I refused to talk with him on the grounds that murder as such was a matter for the district attorney, not me.

I already knew something of the situation. Two of our witnesses against Lepke had also mentioned to our agent the name of this important labor leader, since deceased, who had known and worked with Lepke, they stated, for more than twenty years. The information provided by one of these witnesses, and substantiated by the lawyer who tried to talk with me originally, ran as follows:

This world-renowned labor leader paid Lepke $350 a week from 1932 to 1937. Fifty dollars of each payment went to one of Luciano's men. Lepke was given $25,000 for his role in winning a strike and paid other sums for activities in connection with labor disputes. Two men acting as go-betweens brought Lepke $1,400 when he was a fugitive.

Lepke also demanded and got more from the leader at these times, the witness told us. The witness said that he himself was handed the weekly payoffs which the two emissaries brought from the labor leader. The witness said he would then personally hand the money over to Lepke. "Once he (the labor leader) gave me $20,000 to give to Lepke," the witness revealed, "so that Lepke would fix a murder charge that involved his industry."

The informant also told us that Lepke owned ninety percent of a clothing business in Baltimore that earned a profit of $250,000 a year. Emanuel "Mendy" Weiss, another hoodlum and dope dealer, owned the other ten percent. One of their associates in this enterprise, Max Rubin, was shot through the head by would-be assassins. The cause, we were told, was that Rubin returned to New York while Dewey was investigating the clothing industry and particularly Lepke's role in it. Lepke had told Rubin to stay out of New York. He was afraid Rubin might spill too much if anyone started asking hard questions.

Rubin, however, did not die and was to pay back his boss for that wound by becoming a key witness against him at his trial for mass murder.

All of this, of course, we reported to Dewey and to J. Edgar Hoover in our "pooled information plan" to get Lepke, Weiss, et al., and break up the narcotics-murder gang. With the narcotics convictions, we had this pair stowed away for long prison terms. Other agencies thus had time to dig for evidence, to piece together the jigsaw facts.

Despite the felonious character of most of our informants and witnesses, there was no doubt on the part of Hoover, Dewey, Valentine or myself that their detailed outpourings regarding the labor leader's deals with killer Lepke were correct; the facts fitted together too precisely for error. Lepke was willing to talk, so far as we could gather, in an all-out attempt to save his neck. While I do not believe any deals should have been made with this mass murderer, I believe his testimony and that of his associates who wanted to corroborate his story should have been taken, the evidence presented to a grand jury, and an indictment obtained against the labor leader.

This phase of the case, however, was entirely out of my hands, as our role was limited to enforcement of the narcotic laws and these were not involved with the labor leader in any way that I could establish. The powers of the Bureau of Narcotics are closely defined; once we have turned over the facts to the proper investigatory and enforcement people, we have no further right to interfere when they put the case down as "still under active investigation."

The truth is that politics with an oversized "p" won that round and prevented what might have been the most explosive murder trial of our age from taking place. The facts were not presented; no indictment was requested. The charges of all informants were placed quietly on a shelf and forgotten.

This was just at the time when William O'Dwyer, later mayor of New York, was running for mayor against Fiorello La Guardia. Democratic backers knew that their candidate needed the labor vote to have a chance against the La Guardia slate. To dig into that cesspool of rotting corpses, seeking to involve a labor leader of national prominence would have turned either candidate's campaign into a political suicide. Neither party dared to take a stand. I feel that they both made an error.

Dewey's investigation of Lepke had uncovered so much violence and murder that a member of his staff called Lepke "A one man reign of terror." In the garment industry, the fur industry, and also in the baking industry hundreds of small owners had been forced to pay tribute under threat of death, beatings, wrecked automobiles and trucks, strikes and fires.

Seven men who were scheduled to tell Dewey about Lepke's activities in the baking industry were killed; others were beaten so badly they were crippled for life.

On counts of extortion and conspiracy to terrorize these businessmen, Lepke was sentenced, on his fourth felony conviction in New York State, to from thirty years to life—after he completed the twelve to fourteen he owed the Federal government for his narcotics operations.

An important part in the New York murder ring was played by still another prominent narcotics figure—Benjamin (Bugsie) Siegel. We had learned that Siegel was a part of the Lepke-Weiss apparatus of hired killers; on the West Coast he acted as a vice president and unofficial "agent" of the mob.

Owner of the multi-million dollar Flamingo Club in Las Vegas, Nevada, Bugsie was shot to death at the Las Vegas home of a woman named Virginia Hill, who achieved a measure of "standing" when she appeared before Senator Kefauver's T.V. Committee. We had known for some time that Siegel was interested in narcotics and we had a conspiracy case against him that was about to be sprung when he was slain. One dealer, Francisco Orbe, told our agents after Bugsie's murder, "He gave me $20,000 to buy a shipment of heroin for him in Mexico City. I made the delivery to Siegel himself. I was to get sixty thousand dollars as my cut out of the profits. He's dead and I'm waiting for my money."

In the spring of 1941 Lepke, Weiss and Louis Capone went on trial for murder in New York. They were tried on an assortment of murder charges. The case against Lepke was built around the murder of a candy store operator, Joseph Rosen. Lepke had feared that Rosen, who formerly drove a truck in the garment district, would spill everything he knew to Dewey. Weiss was charged with being one of the actual killers who pumped seventeen bullets into the candy store operator.

Because of the evidence piled up in the narcotics investigations of these men, we were able to contribute important

5

evidence in the trials of the Murder, Inc. bosses. They were convicted late in 1941 and sentenced by Judge Franklin Taylor of Kings County Court to die in the electric chair. All appeals failed although they dragged on for four more years. All three died in the electric chair on March 4, 1944 at Sing Sing.

Thwarted in his efforts to get an open hearing on the labor leader case, Lepke retreated into monolithic silence about the case in his last hours. It was his one fly-speck of victory. He took the facts to his grave and left behind an indestructible shadow of uncertainty about a man whose name was—and remains, long after his death—a revered symbol of achievement in the labor movement.

5. Baron

With the upsurge of the popularity of heroin in the world markets, an underworld struggle for power erupted. Out of this lethal but unseen knife-play emerged a kid-gloved, gray-spatted, striped-pants Greek-born Parisian who had belonged to none of the contending elements but who sought to hold the entire dope underworld, with its glittering promise of profit, in his well-manicured hands.

His name was Elias Eliopoulos. Elie, his innumerable friends of the international merry-go-round called him. Elie was said to be on a first-name basis with more crowned and uncrowned royalty than anyone else on the French or Italian Rivieras. In the developing international narcotic syndicate operations, Elie was an historic link between the individual network and personalized violence of the 1920's and the deadly and dedicated dominance, in the late 1930's and thereafter, of the dope-running murder-machine called Mafia.

Elie—whose agents in America alone included Lepke, Dutch Schultz, Waxey Gordon, Legs Diamond and nearly fifty others—was the son of a respected Greek business leader. Elie was class. What he lacked was conscience—and the ability to make a living honestly.

One balmy Greek evening Elie was dining in an Athens café with a narcotics trafficker named David Gourievidis. The latter told him of the enormous profits to be made through dope deals in China. Elie became interested; the two took a junket to the Orient so that the persuasive Elie could explore the possibilities.

In Tientsin, China, Elie made a Far East "connection" with a man named Jean Voyatzis, largest importer of manufactured dope in all China. Voyatzis sold his morphine and "treated" smoking opium to millions of Chinese addicts through his native outlets. Increasing restrictions on the international trade in drugs put into effect through the League of Nations, were making it harassingly difficult for Voyatzis to get shipments regularly. "I want someone in Europe," he said, "to represent me and guarantee me large shipments. I'm unable at present to fill my needs."

Elie told him, "We'll ship you all you want. My brother George and I are going into the business."

"Why should Eliopoulos do it, where others can't," Voyatzis countered.

"Because we have the social position," the urbane Greek answered. "We know everyone. They know us. There is no one in Europe's business or social world I can't reach. No door is closed to me."

Elie set up operational headquarters in Paris. With Voyatzis as a customer, he began negotiations for supplies with two of France's important drug manufacturers—the Comptoir des Alcaloides and the Societé Industrielle de Chimie Organique. Elie was in an enviable trading position. Voyatzis provided raw opium shipped from China, which Elie sold to the French concerns—below market prices. Neither firm appeared too curious as to how much of their manufacture went into illegal channels, so long as they stayed technically within the laws. (Both French firms operated on government permits with supposedly limited quotas.) Elie then bought it back in manufactured or "heated" form, for shipment back to Voyatzis. On each transaction Elie made a handsome profit. Voyatzis got his prepared smoking opium to sell to Chinese addicts by the millions; the French chemical firms got large supplementary orders and Elie and his brother George reaped a harvest in francs.

Many of Elie's shipments of raw opium came in legally; controls at that time in international trade were not very tight. Additional supplies, sent in cases marked "tea," Elie sold to the two companies and to other firms as well. Elie purchased not only prepared opium but also morphine and heroin from several chemical companies. His main suppliers were, however, the firms headed by Paul Mechelaere of Paris and M. Devineau, whose plant was located in St. Genevieve, France.

The operations expanded to every corner of the world. He had connections in America with "Little Augie" (August Del Gracio), an East Side mobster of whom it was said he would sell his own sister if the price was "realistic." Little Augie was supplying the New York mob, receiving drugs shipped by Elie into the States in crates disguised as shipments of books, cloth, or farm equipment.

Elie always claimed he himself did not ship anything directly to America but he was quibbling; he shipped to America through "agents." He and his brother sat back and took in more than $50,000 a month profits from Voyatzis alone. In one six month period his take reached 150,000 pounds sterling —nearly half a million dollars.

As his fame spread Elie attracted more business. Runners and couriers offered their services. His connections, sales and purchases, reached into new cities and countries. Within one year after he had started, Elie had agents working for him not only in China, France and America but also in Egypt, Turkey, Greece, England, Germany, the Netherlands and Italy. In the world of dope, he had become the handsome, swaggering, well-dressed baron of the business. In Paris he was the *bon vivant*, a frequenter of boulevard cafés, impeccable, always carrying his gold-topped cane which was a kind of trademark, splashing his money around for champagne parties, race tracks, opera and dinners, and an assortment of women.

One of these was the daughter of a famous French family. She had lived a chaste life until Elie seduced her, after convincing her they were about to be married. The next day he told her that she had misunderstood his supposed promise. The girl later discovered that Elie was syphilitic and that she had contracted the disease from him.

Elie had made an "arrangement" with a high official of the Paris Prefecture of Police. So long as the brothers agreed not to sell their products in France itself, they could continue their vast enterprises in dope unhampered. Elie and George had no objections. They also agreed to turn over to this police officer any information they happened to pick up regarding activities of other traffickers. Elie had outstripped all competitors. He had the police in his pocket. He was a baron without an equal in the history of dope.

So vast was this enterprise by 1930, and so openly was it being conducted in France, that it had become an international scandal. At a conference held in London to work out controls for countries manufacturing drugs from raw opium or the coca leaf, the activities of the Eliopoulos brothers were brought up as a special item on the agenda. The French delegate at once declared that any discussion of M. Devineau, head of the plant in St. Genevieve supplying Eliopoulos with much of his needs, would have to be held in private sessions, with representatives of the public and press barred.

His wish was complied with until the time came for discussion of the international illicit traffic in open plenary session. At that point I announced that I was under no instructions from my government not to discuss the case of the Eliopoulos brothers at this open session. Inasmuch as most of Elie's dealings had to do with the United States, I intended to get some of his more vicious activities on the record.

Sir Malcolm Delevingne, the British delegate, supported me in this insistence on public discussion. The French delegate later drew me aside and expressed his apologies for the whole affair. "I had to request the private discussion on this matter," he explained. "I am under instructions from the French government to clear the name of M. Devineau. He is quite highly regarded by the Premier," he concluded with a shrug of resignation.

In the open discussion of Elie, the story was presented—as much as was then known. The French government could no longer hope to keep the facts behind closed doors. Stringent laws were passed in order to clamp controls on narcotics in strict accordance with the Geneva Convention,* passed in 1930, to which most of the civilized countries of the world were signatories. French authorities notified all factories producing drugs to quit within three months or face pre-emptive penalties. Narcotics for medical and scientific uses could be turned out only in stipulated quantity under rigid government controls.

A few optimistic enforcement officials insisted the new laws would ruin Elie and his brother but Elie had too much invested to quit. At his urging, the plants supplying him with drugs in France packed up their equipment, their machines, and trained personnel and shipped them off to Istanbul. Here—backed by Devineau of Paris—Elie convinced his clients that the production would not only continue but increase. He would be able to ship from Istanbul any amount of narcotics for trans-shipment through the ports of Marseilles, Trieste, Antwerp, Rotterdam, and Hamburg. There was at that time no anti-narcotics legislation in force anywhere in Turkey.

We had good sources of information in Turkey. On my personal orders they kept us informed of what was happening in the new narcotic plants, in the section known as the Golden Horn in Istanbul. As a matter of concern to both the American and Turkish governments, this information was relayed to our Turkish ambassador, again on my instructions.

The day before Christmas—some weeks after I began shipping our ambassador this information—the ambassador decided to have a talk about these conditions with the president of the Turkish state, Kemel Ataturk, also called the Ghazi. The

* For a record of the principal contraband conventions and agreements, see Appendix 1.

ambassador made his plea on moral and religious grounds. "As a Christian," he told the Turkish leader, "I believe in the great power of the prophet Mohammed. You similarly must believe in Jesus Christ, knowing the power Christ had to heal a paralytic arm with only a word."

Ataturk listened respectfully but made no answer. The ambassador continued: "You have the power to shut down these factories that are pouring out poison to our country and other countries as well." He furnished details which the Ghazi may not have known personally, although the facts could not have been a secret from Turkish authorities.

The Turkish president asked, "All that you are saying is confirmed?"

"It is, sir. All of these details are known to many in our government and yours."

After a silence, the president told the ambassador, "I will take care of this myself."

The following day—Christmas morning—he went down to the Golden Horn district and personally padlocked all of the guilty factories "as a Christmas gift to the American people."

But the combine Elie had created, and the huge sums he now commanded, were not this easily overcome. The baron of narcotics found other plants in Turkey and elsewhere to provide his production, and his empire continued to operate.

Because of the importance of this case, I had arranged with the narcotics officials in most European countries for a direct exchange of information. I was able to supply them with the background and activities of Elie's accomplices in the United States. We were faced with a turbulent sea of seemingly unrelated facts. Then a break came for all of us; Gourievidis, who had first put Elie into the traffic, quarreled with him. Going directly to Eliopoulos, he charged him with reporting to the authorities certain shipments of drugs Gourievidis had purchased, resulting in seizure of these drugs and heavy financial loss to Gourievidis. The imperturbable Elie had a dinner date at the home of a leading French politician. Telling

Gourievidis to forget such nonsense, he hurried off. Gourievidis drove to the French police and denounced Elie as a trafficker in drugs, which they already knew, of course.

However, they did not know a number of details Gourievidis provided, including evidence regarding remittances from Voyatzis in China totaling $800,000 for a six-months period. With this open denunciation, the French government had to act. They notified us and other nations that there was a possible break at hand. They brought in Elie, showed him the evidence of remittances from Voyatzis, a known trafficker for many years, and requested Elie to show from what legitimate business the $800,000 was derived. Elie, of course, could not comply and he was expelled from the country.

The critical break in the case, however, did not come through Elie at all, but through Little Augie Del Gracio, who had assumed an international role as Elie's top executive in the American branch of Elie's sales force. We had never been able to link this much-traveled punk with Elie directly. But we knew that he liked to brag to underworld pals about champagne cocktail socializing with the ultra elite during his frequent trips to Europe.

The American underworld mobs, of which Little Augie was a part, were locked in a struggle for control of the rackets, including, of course, the market in narcotics. One mob was headed by Lepke and Weiss; another by Al Spitzer, Abe Stein and "Big-Nose" Fleishman; and there was the Louis Adelman mob and the Newman brothers.

The Newmans—actually their names were George, Charles and Harry Neiditch—had been operating for nearly two decades out of plush offices in New York. Their supplies in drugs came primarily through a man named Louis Lyon in Paris. Lyon was an agent for Eliopoulos. The Newmans in turn were wholesalers to mobs in every part of the United States, including that of Arther Flegenheimer (Dutch Schultz).

Serving as a courier for Elie, and for the Newmans, as a go-between for the big gangsters in America was Little Augie.

In the underworlds of Europe and America, Little Augie was a familiar figure. One of his shipments—it was labeled "woolens" and actually contained $3,000,000 worth of drugs destined for the Newmans—was seized by Customs. The loss was colossal, but it was said that the Newmans merely told Little Augie: "Get us more and get it here fast."

Little Augie did. This patent-leather hood was without question one of the biggest individual smugglers ever to operate in the United States. The total value of the shipments of drugs he sent into the United States may have run as high before he was finished as $50,000,000.

We didn't catch Little Augie or put him behind bars in America—a fact for which I make no apologies. We had a full file on this man and a considerable amount of carefully documented evidence. Several times we went to the district attorney with evidence that we believed would have sustained an indictment against him. In each instance our request for legal action was turned down. And when I tried to keep Little Augie from going to Europe, some of his political connections made such a fuss the State Department issued the passport.

I had compiled in the Bureau an International Black List of the most notorious narcotics traffickers, their background, history, arrest, convictions and other data. Little Augie was Number 89 on that list, copies of which were sent to our consulates throughout the world.

Not long after the list was compiled and distributed I had a message from our able and alert consul in Istanbul, Charles Allen. Allen telegraphed that Number 89 was in his office, trying to get his passport extended, and that he had noticed an alteration on the passport. What did the Bureau of Narcotics want him to do?

I wanted Little Augie but more than Augie I wanted Elie. To nail either we had to have evidence strong enough not only to prove our case but also to overwhelm the wealth and political influence they would seek to bring into play. I cabled Allen in Istanbul: "Report departure and destination." Two days later came the answer: "Simplon Express tomorrow, destination Berlin."

Why Berlin? We had no leads but something told me this trip was important. The timing had to be now. I notified German authorities: Little Augie, international narcotics dealer, was en route. When he arrived, two German secret police walked into his compartment on the train. Augie must have been suspicious at the delay in opening the train doors. As the agents reached him, he was throwing a piece of paper out of the window. It was a scrap of paper with two words. One was "Devineau," who manufactured morphine and heroin for Elie. This was the first definite link between Elie and Little Augie.

The second word was "Atsok." This was found to be the telegraphic address of a woman who was living in Berlin with a man named Saya Moses, a notorious international spy, also rumored to be associated with Elie's ring. Moses was arrested. With him were found papers and account books proving that he was acting as the intermediary in the narcotic deals linking Eliopoulos in Europe, Voyatzis in the Orient and Little Augie in New York.

Papers found on Little Augie enabled German police to seize 250 kilos of morphine in the free port of Hamburg, in a warehouse whose owner stated he knew nothing except that the crates belonged to a man named Karl Frank. The morphine had arrived in Hamburg via Prague from Istanbul.

With Little Augie's arrest, widely separated elements of the syndicate were identified—and smashed. As a result of our international pooling of information on the Elie syndicate, British authorities in Tientsin, China, notified Russell Pasha (Sir Thomas Wentworth Russell) of the Egyptian Anti-Narcotics Bureau that Voyatzis was soon to leave for Greece, by way of Egypt.

Voyatzis was under observance all the way by agents in several nations. We let him into Egypt where he amused himself for a few days gambling on the Alexandria stock exchange. Then he embarked for Piraeus, Greece. Egyptian customs,

EMBRYO   65

tipped by Russell Pasha, searched his heavy luggage. No drugs
were found, of course; Voyatzis was above that. What was
found instead were two additional documents—a list that
turned out to be a "Who's Who" of the international narcotics
traffic—all the big shots and punks the gang used in its global
operations—and a code book that gave the key to the cipher
the gang used in its communications.

The code book was one of the most illuminating documents
ever seized in the international drug traffic. It contained the
names of Elie's group in Europe and Voyatzis' gang in the
Orient. It contained names of firms supplying drugs to the
illicit traffic. Code numbers were assigned to each of these
names. There were code numbers also for opium, morphine,
heroin, cocaine, for apparatus used in manufacture of narcotics,
and for transforming morphine into diacetyl-morphine, which
is heroin. Code numbers were also given for mixtures containing percentages of drugs, and for localities of origin. A list of
shipping lines employed was appended, together with code
numbers for all phases which might be required in relaying
or requesting information.

A net was closing around Elie. Things were too hot for his
comfort. With his usual arrogance, he sent word to Russell
Pasha in Cairo: He knew of the Little Augie affair and he
wished to make a statement in his own behalf. He would like
to meet with Pasha or his representatives in Athens. So important was this development in our eyes that I had an
American official from Paris sent to Cairo to join with Russell
Pasha's man in this meeting with Elie.

Tall, disarming, and carrying the inevitable gold-tipped
cane, Elie put on a spectacular performance. It was his hour
in the Egyptian sun. He was ready to make an open deposition,
giving all the facts, names, dates, addresses, everything. His
chief disclaimer was not for himself but for his brother George
whom he insisted was not involved in any of the major deals.

This was hardly a criminal come to confess. It was instead
a gentleman of magnificent calm, recalling nostalgic details out

of his tempestuous past. He spoke of his family background, his childhood in the Piraeus, his education at Roberts College in Istanbul, his mingling with the social set—and his constant lack of funds. Elie poured out his story not in remorse but because, he said, he was being falsely associated with a shipment of morphine seized in a warehouse in Hamburg following the arrest of Little Augie.

The suave Elie told our people he wanted to clear his name of any taint of connection with this gross example of double-dealing that had begun when Little Augie ordered a $10,000 shipment of morphine cubes from the Devineau-Mechelaere plant in Istanbul.

"Little Augie paid cash in dollars for the consignment," Elie said. "He ordered it specially packed in cases containing machine parts. Paul Mechelaere promised to ship it to him in America via Hamburg." But Mechelaere, Elie added, had no intention of letting the morphine reach America. He sent word to his agent in Hamburg, Karl Frank. "What he really intended to do was to extract the drugs from the cases and send only the machine parts to America, pretending that the stuff had been stolen en route. Mechelaere dispatched the eight cases to Karl Frank at Hamburg, who knew nothing of these plans and was merely instructed by Mechelaere to find American buyers for the drugs."

At that point, Elie confided, a fantastic buffoonery was set in motion. Karl Frank got in touch with an old friend, the trafficker Gourievidis. Would Gourievidis be interested in this shipment of morphine cubes, presently stashed away in a Hamburg warehouse? Gourievidis said he might have an idea. The customer who came to his mind first was Little Augie. He got in touch with Little Augie, who was at that time in Turkey, and told Little Augie of a shipment of morphine cubes in the Hamburg warehouse. Would Little Augie be interested?

"When Little Augie heard the details," Elie said, "he was intrigued because they coincided exactly with the consignment he was expecting from Mechelaere. So he hurried off to Hamburg where his suspicions were confirmed. He was being asked to buy his own merchandise."

Little Augie, Elie related, rushed back to Istanbul to confront Mechelaere. "It was my own goods," Little Augie protested. "Your agent in Hamburg was trying to sell me my own goods all over again."

Mechelaere was the picture of mollifying concern. It was all a mistake, an almost unbelievable coincidence. This was another shipment of morphine cubes, also being offered for $10,000. Little Augie's shipment hadn't even been crated yet.

The gangster knew it was a stall. He made up his mind to go back to Hamburg and get his morphine cubes out of hock if he had to kill Karl Frank personally. But first he had another deal to wind up for Elie in Berlin.

Little Augie's arrest in Berlin, following our tip-off to German authorities, led to seizure of the morphine cubes by German officials—and the bizarre episode became a source of laughter among the underworlds of several countries.

Elie also disclosed details of his own double-dealings. At the Cairo meeting he admitted that he sold four big shipments to an American smuggler but feared that if the fifth got through the smuggler would be rich enough to get out of the business. Elie then followed the routine of notifying a high official of the Paris police about the upcoming shipment. This police official in turn would tip off our own people in the Bureau that a shipment was on the high seas. For details of the ship's name and the location of the narcotics on board we paid the French policeman a reward. (We would dicker about the price but it usually came to $2.00 an ounce. This was a good investment because we turned such seizures over to our strategic stockpile, which cost us $10.00 an ounce when purchased from the manufacturers direct.)

Eliopoulos revealed details of complicated smuggling techniques employed to get the stuff into the States and to other countries, including secret rooms built on ships while they were still in the construction, and hollowed-out masts and storage panels welded into the steel plates of the hull.

One effective method was to send the supplies to New York in the baggage of a man named Carlos Fernandez Bacula, one-time Peruvian chargé de'affaires in Vienna and later in Oslo. Bacula was the possessor of a priceless document—from the smuggler's standpoint: a diplomatic passport. On six trips to New York, via Miami, Montreal, and other points of entry on the American continent, he brought into the United States the incredible total of a ton and a half of pure heroin. Sold uncut at retail in the United States, this shipment would have been worth $37,000,000. Heavy cutting could have built the retail value to well over $300,000,000!

Bacula was a weak sister in this kind of underworld; he was all right as long as others were close by to protect him. But this was not always possible—especially in the jungles of Manhattan.

On one of his trips, Bacula was in a New York hotel with 150 kilos of heroin in his baggage which he was attempting to sell. Even in that day, the wholesale value was nearly $400,000. Through a member of the American mob, Bacula sent out 50 kilos to a prospective customer, holding the rest until he received his personal payoff. The messenger arrived back at the hotel shortly thereafter, his head bandaged and bloody. He stated that he had been held up and robbed.

Bacula was dismayed at his loss—and suspicious. A few days later a visitor showed up at his hotel room. "My name is Jack Diamond," the caller announced blandly. The diplomat had heard of the American gangster but was surprised at the smiling affability of the tall lean young man who asked if he might come in for a moment. "I heard about your unfortunate loss of heroin," Legs Diamond said. "I may be able to help you get some of it back. It's a hell of a load of heroin to lose—fifty kilos. Maybe I can get it back for you. I know a lot of guys."

Bacula listened. He had done business with Newmans. He knew Diamond's reputation as a killer. Even though he suspected Diamond was in on the original hijacking, he told the gangster, in his best South American accent, "I'll be glad for whatever you can do, Legs. I want to get that stuff back."

Diamond's good looking face was shadowed in a scowl. "You got a lousy, stinking deal from those sharks," he said with great indignation.

Bacula agreed.

Two days later Diamond showed up at the hotel room with thirty kilos of heroin in a suitcase. "I had to use the other twenty as a payoff," the gangster explained glibly. He didn't mention to whom the payoff went and Bacula didn't ask.

As Bacula stowed the kilos away in one of his trunks, Diamond watched with an air of professional concern. "This stuff could get knocked off too," he warned Bacula.

Bacula said, "I've got no other place to put it."

"How much do you have, the whole thing?"

"With the thirty you brought, a hundred and thirty kilos."

"You're bats. Somebody'll bust in. You can't leave it here. I'd worry about that. The safest thing to do is to get it to another place. There's a hotel downtown where I got connections. Nobody would touch it there."

Bacula started to raise objections—but Diamond brushed these aside. The stuff had to be protected. "We'd better put somebody we can trust to guard the stuff even down there, just in case anybody on the inside gets itchy."

Partly through fear of losing the entire 130 kilos, partly through fear of this gangster, Bacula agreed to the plan Legs suggested. The man whom Diamond put in charge of the heroin was an Austrian hoodlum sent by the European gang to keep watch on Bacula. Exactly what this gangster thought he was going to get out of this assignment—or what Diamond promised him—will never be known. His body was found the following day at the hotel where he was supposed to be guarding the heroin. His wrists had been slashed to give the appearance of "possible suicide." Whether it was suicide or a particularly cold-handed gangster killing, one additional riddle still remained: The 130 kilos of heroin were missing. What happened to them was never officially determined.

Following Little Augie's arrest and Elie's revelations, I talked to the United States Attorney in New York City about the Peruvian diplomat Bacula. The U.S. Attorney and I called him in for an interview. His answers were glib; he had explanations for everything. A few days later, Bacula sailed for Europe using his diplomatic passport.

Scotland Yard, Rotterdam police, Swiss police, the French Sureté and American, Canadian, and Egyptian enforcement agencies worked on the Bacula case. Peru dropped him from their diplomatic rolls. He was expelled from France. Eventually we caught up with him in Zurich, where he was arrested on a warrent issued in Vienna in connection with the seizure of 300 kilos of opium there. Finally he was convicted and sent to jail.

Another Elie "agent" brought to trial was Louis Lyon, the man who supplied the Newmans in New York. He was arrested in connection with a seizure of heroin following an explosion and fire in the heart of Paris, across the street from the French ministry of Foreign Affairs. Lyon was a racetrack bookmaker who branched out into several questionable operations in Paris and Cannes. Dope was his biggest activity just before World War II when he worked closely with Bacula. At the high point of his criminal career he was one of the largest suppliers for dope dealers in Europe.

Lyon, however, redeemed himself with the French people and government by services rendered in the battle against Hitler. Just before World War II he uncovered an arms cache of the Cagoulard organization, the Nazi-type group seeking to do to France what Hitler had done to Germany. Later, during the war itself, Lyon kept the French Underground informed on the activities of German spies pretending to be anti-Nazis and seeking to infiltrate the Underground itself. As a result many of these spies were apprehended by the Underground and summarily dealt with. Following the war, the French government awarded ex-gambler, ex-bookmaker, ex-dope dealer Lyon the Legion of Honor.

From the outset my main target had been Elie. He was the gold-tipped white whale I had to reach. To get to him I followed a shifting trail that led us around the world and back. We broke through the outer fringes, pieced together the jagged bits of information, uncovered the code and the men just under Elie in the scheme.

In New York, tall, easy-speaking, relentless Garland Williams, at that time New York District Supervisor, launched the greatest investigation in that district's history, bringing in hundreds of witnesses, tracking down a thousand pieces of seemingly irrelevant trivia to smash the New York outlets for Elie.

Elie and his brother George saw their empire crumbling around them as the Nazi troopers rolled over Europe. They fled to Greece. Elie became a Nazi collaborationist and anti-Semite. With the Germans pounding at the Greek frontiers, the defenders of Greek freedom had George and Elie marked for liquidation as traitors; the pair escaped, ultimately got to South America and eventually—as "innocent" refugees—arrived in New York City.

By then, our dossier on Elie was bulging. We had evidence to convict him on a dozen shipments. We knew he was coming; our men were at the pier waiting when the ship came up the harbor past the Statue of Liberty. We were giving him the full protection of our laws. But we also intended to see that he got full justice. To that end, we picked him up as he came down the gangway. He was indicted and ordered to stand trial in Federal court in the Eastern District of New York.

Our case was overwhelming. Elie and his brother were convicted. But our gratification over their convictions was brief. Three months later they were set aside on the technical grounds that the statute of limitations should have excluded much of the evidence. We appealed but were overruled. We sought to have Elie indicted on additional evidence both in New York and New Jersey but again were thwarted. Final decisions in these appeals were delayed by many behind-the-scenes stratagems directed by the defendants through prominent attorneys. A Senate Crime Committee held a lengthy secret hearing seeking to find out why the convictions were set aside.

With some of his profits Elie had purchased bauxite mines in Greece. His Washington attorney tried to get permission from U.S. Immigration officials for Elie to return after the war to Greece so that he could recondition his mines. At that time we were still appealing in his criminal prosecution. As I did not wish to let him slip through our fingers, I opposed any such approval.

Elie was used to whipping governmental "brass" into line. His Washington attorney told me that one of the highest officials of the Bureau of Mines wanted Elie to receive the approval because, the official felt, Elie's presence in Greece was indispensable to the cause of freedom. I took this up directly with the Old Curmudgeon, Secretary of the Interior Harold Ickes. I would like to have heard the tongue-lashing Ickes gave that Bureau of Mines official. I am told it was classic. In any event, Ickes informed me in a letter that the Interior Department disclaimed any interest in Elie, beyond a wistful desire to see him jailed.

Eventually Elie did get back to Greece, after our appeals failed. While he was awaiting those decisions, he lived in Park Avenue apartments, went out with top American society women, gambled in stocks and commodities and in one instance cornered the pepper market, sending pepper prices sky high. As a temporary visitor, he didn't even have to pay income taxes.

With his case dismissed, he decided to stay right on. But if we couldn't keep him behind bars—we wanted him out of here. It was a hard fight, however, before we finally got him deported back to Greece. The moment he got back there our agents discovered that he was in a new business: Selling arms to Israel with one hand, and smuggling arms to the Arabs with the other.

With consummate impudence he tried to get the International Export-Import Bank in Washington to loan him a million dollars to recondition his mines in Greece. One of the directors of the bank, Herbert Gaston, had formerly been Assistant Secretary of the Treasury and had heard me speak often of the Eliopoulos case. He remembered the name and suggested that Elie's American attorneys get in touch with me. When I gave those men the full story, they were delighted to let this Athenean hot potato drop from their fingers.

A few years later I had a call from Elie's Washington attorney. "I thought you ought to be the first to know," he said. "I just had word that Elie dropped dead in Athens."

The empire Elie forged with such misdirected brilliance had long before been replaced by the overriding terror of Mafia gangs. Elie's death was a postscript to the past.

"Too bad," I said.

"You're charitable," the lawyer said. "After all the trouble he caused."

"Not at all, counselor," I told him. "I simply know where he's going. After this, hell won't be fit to live in."

The attorney chuckled and hung up the phone.

PART TWO

INSIDE MAFIA

PORTRAIT PARLÉ

The most powerful of the decision makers of the Mafia murder trust in America are not even known to the public. These names, let me add, are rarely if ever seen in print, for leadership in the brotherhood requires a shunning of the limelight and headlines. The true *Mafiosa* maintains a reticence and humility, an unassailable façade of respectability.

He is the owner of a small business on a sidestreet in a great American city. A kindly man who gives small sums to the needy, who contributes to the church and local charities, a wise and graying *don*, accepted and beloved in the neighborhood.

Tonight he meets with a few old friends in the back of a restaurant. One man is a corporation head. Two others are known figures in the rackets. Two are neighborhood *dons*. One is a man who has served time for murder. They drink red wine and talk in Sicilian dialect. The terms are archaic, the phrases obscure. The meanings and ideas are a mixture of superstition, ritual, fraternal loyalty and cynical ruthlessness.

This is a court of underworld law. A brother has failed to pay a debt as ordered by the council. The defendant is their long-time friend and associate. He has often sat with them as a judge and passed the sentence of death on others. However, he has been unfortunate; he tried to raise the money and failed. They know it is not a willing default; but what you owe, you pay.

The defendant is on the spot. In the society of silence, the word somehow spreads. No one will help him, no one will hide him, no one will take up his cause. The laws forbid.

He is stripped of the protection of the invisible world-wide government. Even his kin turn from him. There is no place to run, no place to hide. Sooner or later hired Mafia executioners find him and shoot him down as he walks a street, or paints his front porch, or relaxes in a barber chair.

In his neighborhood world, the white-haired *don* continues to play his quiet role, an obscure symbol of wisdom and love and charity. The racketeers slip back into their own well-protected circles. Whatever they make, a share goes to the brotherhood leader. The corporation head returns to his board of directors, his civic committees, his political efforts to improve local government and get rid of the rackets. . . .

This is the picture, this goes on, these are the men who control and corrupt whole communities—not a century ago, but in the 1960's, in the United States of America. . . .

6. From the Mafia Files...

I grow impatient with those who—however well-intentioned—persist in posing the question: Does Mafia exist? In the face of all the evidence available in this country and abroad, there seems little room for any serious doubt. The hoodlums, of course, never make any serious denials in this regard, Luciano himself was quoted by a friend as saying, "Is there a Mafia? Sure there is. Aren't there Masons and Knights of Columbus?"

I am proud that it was the Bureau of Narcotics which led the way in exposing the activities of this organization. We revealed the existence of Mafia when many officials insisted that the organization, its rituals and rules and punishments, were largely myths, and that I, personally, was building this distorted picture of conspiracy largely to make an attack on Italians and those of Italian-American descent.

Let me refute here those deliberate distorters of fact who charge that because I have fought Mafia I am anti-Italian. The truth is that many agents in the Bureau are of Italian parentage or Italian background. Ninety-nine percent of the Italians, including the Sicilians, are decent, law-respecting human beings who have contributed greatly to America and the world. They themselves have been terrorized, both in America and abroad by the criminal syndicate called Mafia. The party line put out by the hoods is that anybody who fights Mafia is anti-Italian.

No answer to this smear campaign is called for, in my opinion. Responsible Italian leaders and all informed public officials engaged in war on this criminal conspiracy are fully informed of the facts. I expect and accept attacks on me as a part of the routine of the war against an invisible but closely knit empire.

For instance, the editor of an East Coast newspaper assailed me personally in one of the most vicious editorials I have seen in print. A powerful man, known throughout the country, he was enraged, I was informed, by testimony I dared to give before a Congressional committee on the extent of Mafia control in American cities. Following that editorial, I received calls and letters from many leaders in both political parties. The tenor of the calls was: "Don't back down, Commissioner. We'll support you all the way if he tries to swing his weight." It was reassuring to me to have that kind of backing. I knew the measure of the editor's influence.

He himself ran into a slight embarrassment just after the editorial attacking me was published, when one of his friends, the ex-boss of Mafia on the East Coast, was shot and narrowly missed death; the bullet merely grazed the skull.

The police learned that the editor who continually denied the existence of Mafia—and this ex-Mafia *capo* who had his skull creased—had attended the same lavish dinner just an hour or two before the shooting. The local press played that footnote to the story in soft key.

Our Bureau's Mafia files bulge with material on this "secret" organization, from its earliest history down to the latest clippings, with full backgrounds of members and leaders, with complete dossiers on cases and gangsters, with such a variety of published and unpublished material that one wonders how it could any longer be described as a secret organization at all. Conspiracy, yes. Criminal, yes. Violent, yes. Murderous, yes. But hardly secret.

As a part of these records, I had drawn up a list of eight hundred members of this sinister movement in the United States. This "Who's Who" of Mafia was compiled by piecing together thousands of fragments of information about seemingly unrelated material that suddenly, when dovetailed with other fragments presented a clear picture. The eight hundred *mafiosi* are described with complete histories in each case. Our list was used by the Kefauver Committee in developing its months of hearings in American cities. My assistant, Malachi Harney, who helped complete the list, likens the Mafiosi to a plate of spaghetti: "Pick up one strand and you're tangled up with all the others."

Of the men on that list, we have convicted over three hundred, as of this writing. Most have been deported back to Italy. Several of the top men have been able to postpone deportation by having "special bills" presented in Congress to cancel deportation orders. A few have succeeded in this way in remaining permanently in America. Several have been able to get the courts to pass sentences with the provision: "Not to be deported."

No political party has a monopoly on Mafia. The organization is strictly bipartisan. One of our agents, after an undercover investigation in a New York State city said to be dominated by Mafia influence, reported in part: ". . . uncorroborated reports have it that 30 percent of the profits from organized gambling and prostitution go to _____ (the reputed Mafia *capo* in that city); 30 percent to the Republican leadership; 30 percent to the Democratic leadership; and 10 percent to an unnamed individual. . . ." We have had similar "bipartisan" reports from other communities.

Outstanding men of both parties are dismayed and helpless before the betrayal of a few local politicians. The fact remains that Mafia does not care. It corrupts where it can and where it must. It requires no written guarantees that benefactors will repay favor for favor. Mafia does not take lightly a double-cross or failure to deliver as promised and paid for.

The typical Mafia pattern is apparent in the story of Frank S. This man lived in East Harlem, home grounds of the narcotic mob that dominated American traffic for many years under the reported leadership of Frank Costello, born Francesca Castiglia, who lived and grew up on the sidewalks of East 107th Street.

Frank S. was big in narcotic smuggling. Many knew of his activities; he even had his picture taken with Luciano. He had been given funds by mobsters back in America to bring in a shipment of heroin from Europe. One of our undercover agents working close to the New York mob reported to us, "This is a real big one. Maybe a hundred thousand dollars or more."

"Frank S. will carry the cash?"

"He's got it with him. I don't know how much. It's a big wad."

We kept the gangster under surveillance although there were times abroad when he eluded our own limited coverage or the local authorities tailing him. But we knew—from several European informants—that he was bringing back a large supply of heroin when he set sail for the States after his European "vacation."

When the ship reached New York harbor, we covered the vessel so completely that Frank decided not to run the risk of trying to get the stuff ashore. He had it hidden, we learned, in some secret compartment built into the hull itself. Customs as well as our own agents searched the ship with almost microscopic care but could not locate the hiding place. Some of these secret compartments are so cleverly hidden that they are not discovered for years—if ever. When the vessel returned to Europe, we kept it under surveillance; ships officers were ordered to report any unusual occurrence. We did not believe that anyone had been able to get that shipment of heroin off the vessel.

A week later, the ship cast off from its berth at Marseilles, starting on her return trip to New York. As it edged away from the pier, the ship's captain saw an object thrown overboard. He at once ordered all engines stopped and instructed deckhands and officers to recover the package. The package proved to be a watertight sack. It contained thirty-four kilos—

about seventy pounds—of heroin. The cost in France was approximately $100,000. At $10,000 a kilo wholesale in the United States this would be worth $340,000. The retail value of such a supply would run into many millions.

"As the sack was being recovered," the captain told our men, "I saw a car pulling away from the pier. I could not get the number, but I am sure the occupants were there for the purpose of recovering the sack." The captain turned the narcotics over to authorities at Lisbon when his ship reached that port, and they reported the affair to the United Nations Narcotics Commission.

Frank S., of course, had already collected large sums from his associates in America to pay for this shipment. When Frank returned to America, empty handed, the mob was furious. "Produce the heroin or return our money," the gangster was told.

Frank got a passport—despite protests from the Bureau— and flew to Italy. He put the blame for the debacle at Marseilles on the mob there, composed of Sicilians, Corsicans and Frenchmen. He pleaded with the crowd to let him have some more kilos of heroin, on credit. "All I want," the terrified gangster was quoted as saying, "is enough to return to America and satisfy my friends who put up the money."

The mob in Italy listened sympathetically but showed no interest in advancing either heroin or credit. It was his mission, not theirs. They had fulfilled their part in furnishing the original heroin. What happened after that was not their concern. "Why should we take any financial risk in this business?" they demanded. It was cash or nothing.

Frank came back to America with nothing and tried to explain it to his pals in the East Side Mafia bars. The pals listened in silence. A few weeks later, as he chatted with a friend in a grocery store, he was riddled to death with mob bullets.

His family, I was told, were greatly grieved. He was a

good father and husband. Many of his life-long pals attended his funeral.

One important reason for the public's difficulty in comprehending the facts of Mafia may be found in the word sometimes used as another name for the organization—*Omerto*. The meaning of the term is obscure. Some say it comes from a word meaning "man," others that it stems from a word meaning murder. In the modern Mafia it has come to symbolize silence.

Silence is the great protective wall. Whatever happens behind the closed doors of the councils remains unspoken. The brother who violates the rules is slain if discovered. Some time ago one of our agents was bringing in a Mafia gangster who ultimately was electrocuted for murders committed in association with narcotic crimes. As the agent was taking the man in, the killer whispered to him, "I'll give you fifty grand if you will tell me who told you."

Fifty thousand. Not to save his life, nor as the price of escape, but to find the man who talked.

The early Mafia dates back hundreds of years in differing forms and under various names. It is, in effect, a murder society. It rose to prominence under the name of Mafia about the middle of the last century in Sicily. Mafiosi of that time were members of the poorer classes, banded together for self-protection against those who controlled the government and kept the people in peonage. At the start the Mafiosa bands were small and their acts of violence were directed only against the landowners. The actions were lawless, but many felt that there was justification.

But Mafia's Robin Hood phase was short-lived. As their power increased, the night raiders dropped the mask of selfless "agrarian reformers." Crimes of rape, robbery, arson, extortion, kidnapping and murder were soon rampant in Sicily. Poor farmers who would not pay for Mafiosi "protection" found a barn on fire, grain and hay and animals destroyed.

Sicilian landowners—large or small—were compelled to buy protection. The peasants were terrorized. Large estate owners had to employ whomever Mafia wanted, at the salaries Mafia demanded, and to sell grain and other produce at prices set by Mafia. Mafia thus established—as they have tried to do in other countries on a far vaster scale—a super-government, above all other laws, a law unto itself.

Since 1860, successive Italian governments have tried to suppress Mafia, even going so far as to arrest 152 *mafiosi* at one time in 1892. But this action and many trials did little except to force hundreds of Sicilian criminals to leave the country and come to America or other countries, setting up new branches. One of the nineteenth century enforcement officials who tried to suppress the Mafia was Signor Antonio Cutrera, once a police chief of Palermo. This official wrote a book entitled *El Mafiusi*, published in Sicily in 1900 and regarded as the standard work for scholars on the Italian and European Mafia of that era. Mussolini used another political official, Signor Cesare Mori, prefect of Trapini and later of Palermo, to drive the Mafia out. With dictatorial powers behind him, Il Duce ordered Mori to get rid of the gangsters by all means available to him, no questions asked. Mori was ruthless but effective as far as Italy was concerned. In three years —1924 to 1927—he convicted more than a thousand Mafiosi and forced thousands of others to flee Sicily. Most of these refugee murderers headed straight for the United States.

The early Mafia in America concentrated its main efforts on extortion and murder of its own people. Thousands of Italian families, struggling to get a foothold found themselves forced to pay tribute to this transplanted terrorism. Most of the immigrants were afraid to go to the police. In 1890, when the police chief of New Orleans, David Hennessy, began to look into the ambushing of a group of Italians, allegedly by the Mafia in that city, he was assassinated.

The Mafia could bleed the immigrants only so far. When resistance showed, they began to infiltrate other groups—

ethnic, religious, geographic—wherever there seemed to be a possibility of profits. They seeped their way into the then amorphous underworld in America.

Police Chief Edward J. Allen, of Santa Ana, Calif., in a report on the ancient and modern crimes of Mafia, published in the *Police Chief News*, provides a rationale of the contorted philosophy of the Mafia brotherhood based on personal experience and interrogations of Mafia hoods. Chief Allen describes one interview: "Asked about his illegal activities in various rackets, he retorted, 'I am not the racketeer. You are the racketeer. The mayor, the senators, the congressmen, are the racketeers.' For clarification of this statement, he continued, 'How much salary you get? How much the mayor gets? How much the senator, the congressman? How much more thousands they spend to elect themselves? What for? You think they don't get it back, and more? We not the racketeers, you fellows the racketeers.' "

Allen quotes from Cesare Mori's book, *La Mafia*, to give the Sicilian side of "Mafia logic." Mori insists that this logic is built on a basic idea, expressed in a characteristic Mafia slogan, *"Li picciuotti manno a vivere"*—"Brigands have a right to live, too." The Sicilian Mafia says that since crime will always exist, it is better for the people to join with it and try to minimize its injury to the individual, rather than go to the police. The police may try to find the guilty ones, but in nine cases out of ten, will not return the stolen goods or cows. When the injured party goes to Mafia, writes Mori, the results are far different. In his well-informed view, this is their sales pitch:

"The Mafia compiles no statistics but admits that in 5 percent of the cases it fails. There is an underworld of crime which escapes its control and sometimes there are reasons why it cannot act as it would like. But in 95 percent of the cases the Mafia (in connivance with the authors of the crime with whom it settles matters) recovers the lost property which it gives back to the robbed person in return for payment of

about a third of its value. So that . . . the stolen cattle worth
100,000 lire would be restored by the Mafia on payment of
30,000 lire. . . . Indeed, the Mafia offers a kind of insurance
against future robbery, since in this kind of transaction there
is an implicit undertaking by the Mafia to obviate the possibility of repetitions. . . ."

The similarity between this picture and the "protection
rackets" that have become such a familiar pattern in so many
American cities is no accident.

Everything is denied; everything is silence; there is no
Mafia. That is *Omerto*. There is the Unione Siciliano, yes. In
some districts this is a perfectly respectable organization, but
the Mafia hoods have moved in on this organization precisely
as the Communists moved in on innocent organizations which
they sought to betray to their own purposes.

There are new names used, or no names. There are new
methods employed. The telephone offers great immunity because of the severe restrictions on tapping and tapped evidence. Nothing is put in writing. A man in Boston calls his
brother in Chicago and the brother in Chicago calls a cousin
in St. Louis who calls Los Angeles. He calls the brother or
cousin of the man in Boston. The evidence must be ironclad
and overwhelming. But nobody will talk, nobody will remember. It is elusive, unreachable, an interplay of deliberate
confusions.

Carlo Tresca was murdered in 1942 on lower Fifth Avenue.
Tresca had been editor for twenty years of the Italian newspaper *Martello*. He was strongly anti-Fascist and at the time
of his death was forming an Italian-American victory committee which was to have included anti-Fascist groups in this
country.

Among persons antagonistic to Tresca—as an outspoken
man he had many enemies—was one suspect said to have "important" Mafia connections. Persons suspected of the murder
included one known to have had close association with the
man of important Mafia connections.

The suspect was reportedly seen by a New York parole officer, Fred Berson, getting into an automobile two hours before the murder. The car into which the man was seen climbing, Berson asserted, was the car known to have been used in the murder. The suspect fingered by the parole officer was brought in for questioning and released.

Some time later, Berson was fired. The reason given was that he had made remarks about a superior officer. This allegation was stated in a letter which a fellow parole officer read to Berson.

One week later the man who wrote this letter shot and killed himself in his Manhattan home. A note left behind stated that he was killing himself because of what he had been forced to do to Berson.

Nevertheless, Berson was informed by New York Civil Service that he was denied any job in the service because of these allegations against him that brought about his dismissal.

Nineteen years later, as I put down these words, Tresca's murder remains unsolved.

"Syndicate" in America is a loosely used phrase. In underworld parlance, it may have several interpretations. Nationally, it refers to what others call the "organization," a term that takes in not only Mafia itself but other related groups.

In narcotics, the syndicate refers primarily to Mafia. They have held for many years the dominant position in narcotic distribution throughout the United States. The narcotics syndicate in America came into being about the time Prohibition ended, in the early 1930's, when the gangsters were looking around for new opportunities. Dope had always been part of their operation; now it took on a bigger role. The syndicate put the operation on a businesslike basis. They hired a legal staff, set up a supervisory board, a general manager, a traveling representative and a sales force.

Beginning back in 1934 and 1935, our efforts in the Bureau were concentrated on getting the evidence against members of this syndicate, particularly the leaders, both in the United States and abroad. Hundreds of syndicate hoods and hangers-on went to penitentiaries or were deported because of our efforts.

One investigation centered on the Midwest, where the syndicate had been concentrating its activities. For two years I had been watching and guiding this investigation, my nerves constantly on edge because of the danger of a political explosion with national repercussions. Our agents had to move with the greatest care. When we were ready to close in, I went to the scene of operations to supervise the closing of the case. I checked in at a hotel in a Midwestern city and went to the room where my men were drawing up the final tactical plans. In the room was my local supervisor, a man whom I've always insisted should have been a preacher. He had the tall, drawn, soulful look of a preacher, and he meant it; it wasn't sham. After every "kill"—when we closed in and arrested the culprits—he would go to church and pray for the souls of the criminals he had just helped to lock up.

We held a tactical briefing in the hotel room. We discussed who among our suspects should be our first target. It was agreed that we should seize the detective on the local police force who was selling narcotics to our undercover agent. (The agent had carefully marked each purchase immediately afterwards for later use in court as evidence.) The detective had a reputation as a killer. He slept with a forty-five by his side.

I told the men I would take him myself. They pleaded with me not to do anything so foolish. One of the agents had been a professional wrestler, a big man, all brawn but with the speed of a panther. "If I can just get my foot inside the man's door," he said, "I can pin his arms in a fraction of a second and that'll be that."

This sounded like a good approach to me. I had not been trying to show off; I simply believed that if risk was involved in taking the police official, I should be willing as the next man to run that risk. "All right," I told them. "The wrestling hold sounds like a workable plan. Let's go."

The wrestler-agent and I led the way, with four other agents, to the police detective's apartment. One of the agents was an undercover man who had won the confidence of this gun-happy detective as a slightly stupid, "hillbilly" of a dope pusher, willing to pay the detective for protection—and buy drugs from him in addition.

The hallway in the apartment house was silent. The hillbilly undercover man rapped on the door. After a minute we heard the man's voice inside, "Who's there?"

"It's Ike," the agent drawled through the door.

"Okay."

The door opened. Our wrestler-agent leaped forward onto the bed and pinned down the detective's arms. The entire action took about six seconds.

I saw the forty-five beside the bed. One of our men picked it up. The police detective lay there pinned and helpless. I stood over him, looking down at him, "You'll have to forgive us for taking you this way," I said. "I didn't want any of my boys to get hurt."

He realized he was licked. "What do you want out of me?" he asked. "I'll play ball with you. I'll give you all the cooperation you need."

It was sickening to see this police officer crawl. But he did provide us with valuable information and testimony that helped to convict his associates in the Mafia ring. As a result, a few years were clipped from his own sentence.

We sent some fifty members of this mob to prison with long terms. They included hoodlums, politicians, and police officers. Conditions in the city were in such disruptive upheaval following our raids that there was pressure to give the governor authority to appoint the police chief, instead of leaving it in the hands of the mayor and the "local" boys. The chief of police came to the hotel to confront me. "Why are you permitting all of this criticism of me and the force," he demanded, "when my men are working side by side with yours to break these dope cases?"

"I happen to know," I told this official, "that not a single one of your men has been working on any of these cases in association with my men. I have been directing and supervising these investigations out of Washington for two years." I went on to tell the chief that one of our agents had been beaten up, we believed by a member of the local force; a special employee of the Bureau had reported in detail how he had spent part of his evenings with two policemen, rifling the glove compartments of cars; another special employee was wearing a Hickey-Freeman suit, one of a carload hijacked by men protected by the police department. "This gang uses a tailor as a fence," I said. "The tailor has his shop directly back of your headquarters." Lastly I told him a man on the force had sold narcotics directly to our agents.

The police chief had nothing to say. When he left he looked like a whipped dog.

Several days later, there was a knock at the door of my hotel room, which served as my headquarters for directing the technical details and final steps in preparation for the trials. The caller, a well-dressed man of Italian background, presented me his card. "I shouldn't have come here, Commissioner," he said, "because I am probably being followed. I came in the back way. I want to shake your hand and say, 'Thank God for the Federal Government.'"

This man was the owner of a large company in the city. He sat down then and began to pour out the picture of fear and corruption in which for some years this American city had been living, because of the grip of the Mafia syndicate on the local government. It was the story of many cities where the same force had taken over:

"About two years ago," he stated, "I dared to rise up at a Chamber of Commerce meeting and urge that the rotten conditions in this city be cleaned up. A virtual paralysis had taken hold of this city's business. Insurance rates were at an all time high. New construction had halted. Businessmen were being ruined by the high tribute they had to pay. When they went bankrupt, the hoodlums moved in."

Everyone at the meeting, he added, knew that he was speaking the truth, many of them from bitter experience with the mob and the politicians. "But even though they knew it and even though they agreed with me, not a single one had the nerve to raise his voice. We sat in a kind of deadly silence. It was as though I had just read my own obituary."

He had contracts to supply ice to various hotels. He was an honest and efficient dealer with a fine standing throughout the city. Within a week, every one of his contracts had been canceled. Within a few months his assessments had been raised to a point where his business could no longer survive. "The gang that controlled this place was not a gang but like a government unto themselves. To my mind there was little difference between living in East Germany and living here. Thank God for you and your men, Mr. Commissioner. And for our government."

In our drive on the syndicate we continued our raids and roundups in American cities, concentrating particularly on leads we followed up in St. Louis, New York City, Tampa, and Havana, Cuba. We found that although some sizable shipments for the Middle West branch of the syndicate had come in through New York, the majority of shipments over a ten-year-period had been coming in via a family in Tampa, Florida.

This family, which consisted of the father and two sons, had a long history of criminal activities, bootlegging, dope, alien running and smuggling. They had their own boat, and our information showed beyond question that they had smuggled quantities of narcotics from Havana to the Florida mainland. In Tampa, however, they put on a different front: They owned the biggest night club in the city, hired the top name bands and singing stars and their patrons were the very finest people.

The father made periodic trips to Havana, where he obtained, through a Cuban senator, supplies of drugs to be shipped from Tampa to the Midwest Mafia. On one occasion he took $25,000 worth of heroin into Tampa. When this supply went on to the Middle West, it was found to be "turkey"—it looked like heroin but proved to be a non-narcotic substance. The Midwest crowd sent word to Tampa: "Get the $25,000 back to the boys or the old man will be in trouble."

The father flew to Havana and pleaded with the Cuban senator to make good on the heroin. The senator indignantly denied having made any "switch" of the fake stuff for the real. He charged, in fact, that the father himself must have made the switch.

The terrified father came back to Tampa and talked with some of the crowd from the Midwest, trying to explain to them that he had nothing to do with the switch and that he could not be able for a few weeks or longer to raise $25,000 in cash as the expenses of running the night spot were crushing.

Two weeks later he was sitting at a table in the Palm Gardens Tavern and Dance Hall, on the southeast side of the city, having a drink with a couple of girls, when two gun shots roared out at close range and the man toppled over, dead.

The two girls and other witnesses were able to say only that the gunman wore gloves and had a silk stocking pulled like a mask over his entire face. The murderer was never found.

Control of the business operations passed on to the two sons, Paul and Joe, who were later named in indictments connecting them with narcotics activities and transportation of heroin from Tampa to St. Louis and Kansas City. During this part of the investigation we also uncovered a narcotics organization that included a sales manager, wholesaler, distributor, transportation officer and financial expert. Six men, including Joe and Paul, were indicted by a Federal Grand Jury in this phase of the case. One of the men jumped bail. I heard that the Mafia narcotic syndicate believed this man was "singing like a canary" to us. Later he was found dead in San Francisco with a bullet in his stomach. Paul and Joe eventually met similar fates.

Our investigations and arrests involved more than fifty top echelon Mafia narcotic gangsters, all active in the drug syndicate. We obtained indictments in almost all of these cases. The evidence was good. Yet only half a dozen of the defendants received any substantial sentences. In one case a sentence of four years was later reduced to six months and then suspended because the man helped the government.

We had been warned of a possible payoff in some of these cases. We did not at first believe it but later on we found sufficient corroboration as the events unfolded.

One of the men convicted received three years in a federal penitentiary. He served one year and was paroled, with the usual stipulation "not to be deported." (His attorney was a brother of the district attorney in the case.) The ex-convict then opened a liquor store on the Kansas-Missouri state line, where one side of the street was wet and the other dry. When I informed the Federal Parole Board of this violation, his parole was revoked. But the politicians, backed by the Mafia brotherhood, wanted him sprung. Within three weeks he was free again.

One of our witnesses in this case had been a man named Carl who worked as our special employee and was able to disclose many inside details of the syndicate operations. After the trial he returned to his family in Chicago. Three years later, while he was changing a tire in front of his home, with his fifteen-year-old daughter watching him from the front porch, a car drove up and a shotgun blast tore off his head. We had reports that the neighbors were too frightened to talk. The street had been filled with people yet no one could give a good description of the car, the occupants, the license plate or the number.

We knew it was a Mafia execution, and we had a good lead to the man who had actually done the killing. When we called him in for questioning, he showed up with the police captain of his district. "I'm here to find out exactly what this man is being charged with," the captain told us.

"We want to question him over in the state attorney's office, that's all."

"About what?"

"A homicide. A young fellow was shot down."

The police captain was thoughtful. Then he said, "All right. But if you aren't finished with him in one hour, I'll have a writ of habeas corpus thrown at you."

The solicitude of this police captain regarding a suspected killer was extraordinary. He must have had visions that we were giving the suspect the rubber hose treatment because he called every fifteen minutes to make sure "Tony was all right."

Meanwhile, we interviewed the victim's father. He shook his head dolefully: "My boy Carl should never have testified against these people. This is the second son who has been killed by the Mafia." Then he went on to tell me, "I had a fruit cart peddling business and the Mafia came to me and demanded twenty percent of my profits. I simply could not meet these demands but I was told if I did not pay the money they would kill my eight-year-old son. I could not put together enough through profits and loans to pay what they said I owed them so they killed my boy with a shotgun."

When I read of little kindnesses and charitable donations of Mafia hoodlums in America or abroad I am always surprised to see how easily well-meaning citizens are taken in by the grandstand clowning of the hoods. One Mafia mobster on the West Coast was the friend of politicians, movie stars, church leaders, policemen. Tony, as I shall call him, was always ready to help anyone in need. On the side, he was involved in narcotic peddling, was part owner of a series of bawdy houses and owned and operated a café that was a hangout for the underworld.

One day a police officer pal of Tony's dropped into Tony's place, spotted a wanted crook at the bar and took the fellow down to headquarters. When the chief heard where the officer had picked this man up, he demanded of the arresting officer: "Why didn't you arrest Tony too? He knew we wanted this man. In fact, he promised to let us know if the fellow showed up. You told me that yourself."

The officer said, "All right, I knew it, Chief. I couldn't pull in Tony. I owe him too much."

What did an officer owe to a hoodlum tied into every racket in the state? "It's like this," the officer reluctantly admitted. "You know my little girl broke her leg and the bone wouldn't knit. I spent all the dough we had and we got nowhere. A couple of months ago Tony came to my house. He said he had heard about Elsie's leg. He said he would pay whatever it cost to have that leg fixed up right. What could a guy do?" the officer demanded of his chief. "My kid needed help and there was no way to get her help and then all of a sudden there was Tony to help her walk again."

"Go on," the chief ordered.

"Tony said to me, 'It won't mean a thing between you and me. It's just between me and the little girl.'"

"Was it?"

"Then he gets the best doctors you can buy and the kid's all healed up and walking again. This would never have been possible if it hadn't been for Tony." He paused, then plunged on, "How could I take in Tony, even when I found him drinking with this guy? How could I do it?"

Later Tony was arrested for selling morphine. He and his partners were handed 17-year prison terms and $17,000 in fines.

Tony had a fixer, a tough who began to be big once Tony was behind bars. I had all the reports on him and I began to wonder why he wasn't apprehended. When I asked questions I got replies that he was furnishing us with valuable information about the traffic on the West Coast and should not be interfered with at that time.

I decided to make an investigation of my own. I sent an undercover man of Sicilian background to the coast without notifying the local office. With little trouble, my undercover operative purchased heroin through the fixer, and arrested him.

Our West Coast office was shocked at the arrest. Some of them sent word to me that we ought to protect the fixer because of all he had done for the government. They wanted to go into court to testify on his behalf—against my own operative. I told them to stay out of that courtroom or I'd have them indicted for conspiracy to obstruct justice.

The defense attorney made a fist-pounding effort to impress the court with the "contributions to the government" made by the defendant. The court was so little impressed that the judge, after a personal investigation of the background of this case, doubled the normal sentence he would have imposed.

I had no evidence of improper activity on the part of any of my West Coast staff. It was, let me put it, a matter of simple bad judgment.

Sent to Leavenworth for ten years, the fixer screamed that he would "blow the lid off." He sent word that if I could make a trip to the prison, he could convince me he had valuable information. Most of these threats, promises and cajolements from prisoners mean nothing. But in this case the warden got in touch with me; he thought this might lead to something valuable.

A prisoner must not be seen by other inmates when he is talking to a representative of the law; he is labeled a rat and the men retaliate by devices such as sprinkling ground glass in his food. Therefore I arranged to have him removed to an isolated ward in the prison hospital, where, in the role of a visiting doctor, I was able to talk to him. Most of his information was worthless gossip, but one story was important.

It concerned one of my own agents whom he identified. "He is a spy for the underworld," the Mafia fixer charged. The agent he named had killed several violators and was feared not only by criminals but even by law enforcement agents. He had a split-instant draw that discouraged arguments. His temper was short and he was as fast with his fists as with his gun. Yet as an agent he was the essence of efficiency and performance and in all cases where he had killed, reports showed that his actions were warranted by the circumstances.

I called him in and told him the story as I had heard it from the fixer. I told him also of corroborating evidence I had obtained after hearing it.

He stood silent before me.

"Do you wish to affirm or deny any of these charges?"

He shook his head.

"Then it's true? What he said is true?"

He was a tall agent. Fastidious in his dress. A square-faced man-of-distinction type, brusque and aggressive usually. He might have been a bond salesman. But now he stood mute. After a long wait he said, "Commissioner, I'm all washed up. Who gives a ____?" He turned and left the office. He went out of the building, walked to the curb, drew out his pistol and put a bullet in his brain.

Even this last self-imposed assignment he carried out with proficiency. The undertaker reported that the job was so neat he did not even have to change the man's suit.

Mafia is not moribund. If one side gets too hot, if the penalties get too stiff and the enforcement too severe, they move into another profitable area. As we dried up their activities in narcotics, they began to move in other directions. The mobs already were racketeering in labor unions, trucking and other ventures. Now they began to move also in the so-called legitimate fields. Hoodlum money began to show up in New York in major real estate transactions. Theatres, restaurant chains, movie houses, skyscrapers, department stores, the music industry, and some of the young stars on their way up were roped in.

The now historic meeting of hoodlums at the little town of Apalachin in November, 1957, reportedly considered, among other matters, new areas of operation. When the old boys at

Apalachin insisted that Mafia get out of dope, the "Young Turks"—second-generation American-born Mafia—revolted. They refused to obey any such orders. "We're in dope because it's big money," they said, "and we'll stay in and make more."

It was their own sons in revolt. But the rules remained inviolable. Two of the youthful upstarts have since been murdered, Mafia style, for their insolence.

The result of this brief intra-family warfare was a belated compromise. Dope would continue to be a Mafia product in the hands largely of the young "upstarts"; investments of profits from narcotics would be turned to new fields. By 1961, employing the same techniques of innocent fronts and hidden blackmail that they use in seeking political control and power, Mafia was beginning to obtain a creeping control over some major industries of America and Europe. One group in New York City was reported to have purchased several skyscrapers where some of the nation's outstanding firms have offices. Funds for these purchases were said to have been put up entirely by the syndicate.

While it is not clear to what limits this effort will reach, an increasing criminal grasp on legitimate business and finance poses serious problems in the control of crime, particularly the world-wide traffic in drugs. Continuing relentless war against Mafia's millionaire murderers is our only hope for preventing an accelerating pollution of legitimate business in America and throughout the free world by these killers in gray-flannel suits.

7. Il Capo

One night in Florida, I was attending the annual convention of the National Association of State Racing Commissioners, where I had been invited to discuss narcotic irregularities at the race tracks. As a part of the festivities I had attended a banquet at Florida's Hollywood Beach Hotel. After the dinner we went to a night club nearby, where the ceiling rolled back and you watched the floor show under the stars. Milton Berle was the featured performer that night. I saw Eddie Cantor at one of the tables and a number of other popular celebrities. In one of the inner rooms, roulette and dice games were in full swing, with other celebrities playing for high stakes.

Later in the evening I ran into a couple of newspapermen I knew. They were handling the public relations and publicity for both the night club and the hotel. I asked them, "Have you noticed who is at the table across the dance floor? Or whose pals are inside betting thousand dollar bills on the dice?"

Lucky Luciano was at the table across the floor with some of his friends—among them several of the most notorious hoodlums of the land. I noticed one trigger-happy character known as Machine Gun Jack. Another was a gambling operator who from time to time had provided us with information.

The publicity men were understandably disturbed. "You think there'll be a shooting, Commissioner?" one asked me. "My God, a shooting would ruin us."

"Not a chance," I said. "They've got too many beautiful

show girls with them. I just happen to know one of those fellows over there. I may be able to get a line on what goes on."

I sauntered past Luciano's table, heading for the front door and as I did so I gave the fellow I knew a nod. He got up from the table and followed me outside. I said, "What in hell goes on here, Joe?"

"Commish," he pleaded, "don't get us wrong. We aren't having nothing to do with your racket. It's only a little conference."

"There are conferences—and other kinds."

"It's just that one of the guys got out of line, you know. We thought this would be a good place to meet."

"Where are you stopping?"

"The Hollywood Beach. We got the whole top floor."

"That's all I want to know." I was sure they were holding a Mafia trial.

"Look, Commissioner," he said, "please don't cause no trouble for us. There's nobody going to get hurt."

"You're not holding a trial here tonight?"

"No," he answered, hesitating only a second. "What makes you think that? Nothing like that, Commissioner." He went back inside and rejoined Luciano's crowd. As I came back in he was in animated conversation with Machine Gun Jack.

I returned to the table. "Look, boys," I told the two public relations men, "I don't have anything to do with this but I suggest tomorrow you go to the chief of police and let him know what's going on and then—discreetly—tell Luciano and his friends to get out."

The two admitted afterwards that they lost sleep that night. Early the next morning, accompanied by the local chief of police, they awakened Luciano and asked him to leave—quietly —as they did not wish to brew a storm of scandal in one of the best hotels on the Florida coast.

Luciano obviously didn't want any storm either. "Sure, boys," he told them. "Keep your penthouse. We're getting out." He moved out with his entire gang. Apparently the "conference" was concluded, in any event.

Two weeks later, Machine Gun Jack's body was found in a ditch in Chicago. The story went that he had gotten too big for his hoodlum tuxedo. I never was able to get confirmation, but one informant hinted later that the Florida conference had been called "to discuss Machine Gun Jack's future."

To understand Lucky's bespattered path to power—and his role in crime and political maneuvers—one needs a perspective of uncontaminated facts. Some of Lucky's publicity people have tried to present him as the most misunderstood public benefactor of our times. The records, however, show that he was first arrested—for a narcotics violation—in 1918, at the age of 19. In 1920, he was arrested in New Jersey for carrying a loaded revolver. In 1923, he was arrested for selling heroin. The government had him on two counts of selling the stuff, plus possession of two ounces of heroin found in a basement on East 14th Street. Lucky admitted the heroin was his but agreed to provide narcotic agents with information. This information resulted in seizure of a large quantity of drugs in a trunk in a Mulberry Street basement. Lucky got off with a light sentence on a minor rap; all the main narcotic charges were dropped.

Lucky continued to feed the government information about other dealers in dope. As a result, one by one his competitors were sent away and Lucky improved his own position. Thus unwittingly the American government helped Lucky rise to power.

Here is more of Lucky's early record, before his conviction as the greatest white slaver of all times: In July, 1926, he was arrested again for possession of a revolver; in December, 1926, he was arrested in New York City for felonious assault; in July, 1927, he was arrested for disorderly conduct; in August, 1927, he was arrested on several counts involving violation of the Prohibition laws; in December, 1928, he was arrested for assault and robbery; in October, 1929, in New York, he was arrested on a charge of grand larceny; and in February, 1930, he was arrested in Miami, Florida, for running an illegal gambling game.

At that time, Lucky's power was so great that most of the charges could be quieted before any indictment was pressed. I knew, everybody in law enforcement knew, that Lucky was slashing a path across the rackets. We knew that he had virtually taken over the Mulberry Street mob which proceeded the East 107th Street mob as a major factor in New York and national dope distribution channels. I knew also that Lucky was tied up with prostitution. The extent of his involvement was not clear.

Lucky liked the ladies. He developed his personal technique of "induction"; taking the girls out—young working girls usually, waitresses, manicurists, shop girls, office workers, youngsters eager for a way out of the enslavement of drab routine. Lucky gave them plenty of excitement and love-making, and wound up turning them into heroin users—"for kicks, that's all." But soon they were addicted and to pay for their heroin "ration" Lucky turned them over to his lieutenants who ran the call-girl branch of his expanding rackets.

Lucky's prostitution parade became so big that it was making him more money than the drugs he was feeding the girls—for which they had to pay out of their earnings. Testimony indicated that Lucky at one time took a cut from the daily "ticks" of more than 5,000 prostitutes in cities across the country.

In 1935, racket smasher Thomas E. Dewey brought Luciano to trial on a charge of forcing women into compulsory prostitution. The trial was long and sensational. The government produced a warehouse load of evidence, including the testimony of prostitutes and pimps allegedly employed by Luciano. Luciano was found guilty and given thirty to fifty years in prison. Dewey received national cheers for putting this criminal behind bars for what everyone believed would be the rest of his life.

In 1942, with the United States at war with Germany, Japan and Italy, one of my agents, heavy-set, moon-faced Supervisor George White, received a visitor at our offices at 90 Church Street. White at that time had been loaned by the Bureau to the special wartime intelligence agency, the OSS, directed by General William (Wild Bill) Donovan. White had not yet left for overseas service, and was still helping to carry on executive and supervisory chores at the Bureau. The visitor he received that day was already well known at the Bureau. It was August Del Gracio, the Little Augie whose arrest had started Eliopoulos on the final lap.

Augie revealed that he had come as an emissary of a man who was not as well known at that time as he was to become— Frank Costello.

"What does Frank want from us?" White asked in his soft-spoken way.

"Frank has a deep sense of patriotism," Little Augie said.

"I'm glad. Patriotism is a fine thing."

"He hates the Fascists." He hesitated. "Know who else hates their guts? Luciano. You know he and Frank are close friends for a long time."

This was the first hint White had of where Little Augie was heading. "Sure," he said, "They're old buddies. From way back."

Augie went on in a persuasive tone, "Listen, Lucky's big stuff in this city. What he says goes with the Italians, the Sicilian organizations. Any of that crowd—they listen. They jump. They do what he says. Don't you get what that means? Lucky can help us. Lucky can help America." Luciano still had great influence, even on those who were pro-Italy, Little Augie added. He could prevent acts of sabotage and keep us informed on much that was going on inside Italy.

White listened as Little Augie delivered his peroration on Lucky. A former crime reporter in San Francisco, he had a newsman's directness. "What's he want, Augie? What's the price of Lucky's patriotism."

Little Augie hedged. It was just for America. No ulterior motive. Nothing.

As White refused to play dead for this, the little gangster finally told him with a bland smile, "Well, there is one small item involved." He paused. "Lucky wants out."

"As far as I'm concerned," White informed Little Augie, "Lucky can go to hell."

The gangster's smile was gone. "You want me to report that to Costello—just like that?"

"You tell Costello that I wouldn't lift one little finger to help Lucky get out of jail," White answered.

For a long moment, the little hood sat there, looking across the desk at the even, almost expressionless gaze of George White. Then, coat over his arm, he rose from the chair, turned and walked out.

White reported this at once to his superiors in New York and Washington, and gave me a full account over the telephone of what had happened.

Some time later, wartime Navy intelligence in New York City did launch what became known as Operation Underworld, involving the use of gangsters to provide information to Navy authorities. Enlisted in the enterprise, through the help of gangland figures, was Charles "Lucky" Luciano.

In January, 1946, several months after the end of the Second World War, Governor Thomas E. Dewey, acting on the recommendation of the New York State Board of Parole, commuted Luciano's sentence on condition that he be deported at once to Italy.

Some time after Il Capo landed back in Italy and began establishing his new postwar syndicate, he obtained a passport and set off for Havana. The then Cuban ambassador to the United States came to me and asked my advice after the State Department suggested this course to him. He was a babe in the palm groves regarding organized crime. "What do you think the arrival of Luciano portends for our country?" he asked. "He is making a hit with Cuban society ladies here."

I had received a preliminary report through a Spanish-speaking agent I had sent to Havana, and I read this to the Cuban ambassador. The report stated that Luciano had already become friendly with a number of high Cuban officials through the lavish use of expensive gifts. Luciano had developed a full-fledged plan which envisioned the Caribbean as his center of operations. The Isle of Pines, south of Cuba, was to become the Monte Carlo of the Western Hemisphere. Cuba was to be made the center of all international narcotic operations. We had a number of transcribed calls Lucky had made to Miami, New York, Chicago and other large American cities, and the names of hoodlums who called him. Lucky kept himself busy in Havana.

The ambassador telephoned the president of Cuba with an urgent plea to issue an immediate deportation order for Lucky. The press played the story big. A Cuban senator denounced the idea of deportation. (I had information that this man had already agreed to go into business with Lucky.) The Cuban president announced blandly: "No East Side mob is going to take over our country."

The war of words continued, and no concrete action was taken by Cuban authorities. I decided that our bureau was the only American agency in a position to take direct action without causing too great an international upheaval. "As long as Luciano remains in Cuba," I had our agent in Havana inform Cuban authorities, "America will not send one more grain of morphine or any other narcotics, for medicinal or any other needs. This is to go into effect immediately." Since we were the main and virtually only supplier of medical narcotics to Cuba, and our shipments were essential, the government was forced to capitulate, and Luciano's dream of establishing an underworld headquarters on our southern doorstep ended abruptly.

Lucky went back to Italy and continued operations from

there. He set himself up in a swank duplex apartment in Naples and came and went as he pleased. Everyone came to see him; screen stars, celebrities, newsmen, gangsters and old friends from America. Hoodlums carried narcotics to America and returned to Italy for the next consignment, on orders from Il Capo. His assembly line was in full production: opium from Turkey and the Near East was smuggled into Italy, manufactured into heroin and then shipped across the Atlantic. Heroin shipments poured into the United States, sucking into addiction thousands of postwar adolescents. Our evidence connected him with several other rackets including the smuggling of cigarettes, the counterfeiting of money in Austria and the diversion of gold. When the Secretary of the Italian delegation at the United Nations publicly described Lucky as the new boss of the current international gangdom of the world, he was stating a truth for which men who participated in Lucky's release from prison can take whatever joy or guilt conscience dictates.

Seeking a full picture of what was happening, the chief of our Rome office, Charles Siragusa, on my instructions, launched an investigation into what was happening in the matter of diversion of heroin from legal medical uses (Italy is one of the few countries where heroin is used as a medicinal narcotic under medical prescription). Our findings indicated that hundreds of pounds of heroin were being diverted by men acting in close association with Luciano.

One of these men was a Professor Carlo Migliardi, formerly of Turin University, and head of a pharmaceutical company producing narcotics. Migliardi falsified records and charged up as "codeine" about 200 kilos (more than 400 pounds) of heroin which he diverted into the illegal channels of the mob dominated by Luciano and run by his assistants, chief among whom was Joe Pici. Most of this production went by plane or ship, smuggled by sailors or passengers to France, the United States, Canada, Mexico and Cuba.

Migliardi was indicted by Italian authorities on the basis of evidence the Bureau had collected linking him to diversion of heroin to the Luciano mob. He vanished and was tried in absentia. At the last moment he showed up in court, and cried out, "I wish to plead guilty to the charge." Why he did this was not known. He was given a sentence of eleven years in jail.

Closing in on Il Capo himself has proved a harder task for the Bureau, for the Italian police, who would like to get him out of their hair, and for Interpol, the international police force. The loyalty or fear inspired by Luciano has been a primary fact in the difficulty of obtaining witnesses who have the courage to declare publicly what they almost nonchalantly admit in private.

At one time Lucky was brought in for questioning about his relationship with a company in Milan. It was known that Lucky's friend, Joe Pici, had purchased several kilos of heroin from this plant. It was also known that the Milan agent of another firm was negotiating for 50 kilos of heroin to be sent to Trieste. Joe Pici was involved in these negotiations.

Questioned on all this, Luciano glibly told the Italian authorities, "Why shouldn't I go there? The officials of these companies are my friends."

"But why were you going with these friends from the chemical firms all over Italy?"

"We were looking for something."

"What?"

"I was trying to dig up some chemical for them—acid acetic anhydride. They needed some extra supplies for their business."

The police let this pass. When I heard about this, I realized that Lucky was having his little joke with these investigators. As he and they both knew, this acid he said he was trying to dig up is one of the essential chemicals in the manufacture of heroin.

Luciano is uncannily shrewd in avoiding entangling evidence. He talks to his relatives and intimates on the beach, away from casual listeners, and he avoids any open statements. He leaves no trace because there is no trace.

And still we know he is the man.

8. Aliens Bearing Gifts

The key to syndicate narcotics operations is bound up in two words: violence and secrecy. It is a world of gunplay, vengeance, and death. Only by piercing these walls of secrecy can we hope to reach the root of the problem.

In the spring of 1960, one of the men we wanted was Giuseppe (Joe Peachy) Pici, the lieutenant on whom the aloof Luciano shunted the operational problems of his criminal network. Pici and Luciano were friends in the time-honored Latin tradition; they clasped each other warmly when they met; they and their families dined together and went to the races and the beaches together. Over chianti and spaghetti, Pici reported directly to "the boss." As a deportee from the United States, Luciano chose to stay in the background of any conspiracy and let others front for him. Luciano made Pici the front man for narcotic shipments to the United States, and also for the smuggling of aliens who could in turn be valuable in "importing" dope shipments. The aliens were said to carry narcotics as part of the price of passage.

The alien-narcotic smuggling tie-in was a new syndicate wrinkle developed in the late 1950's. Our reports indicated that the aliens being used for this purpose might number in the hundreds, but the Luciano-Pici operation was so smooth that neither we nor Immigration had been able to uncover a single tangible piece of evidence during months of investigation. Aliens picked up by Immigration were silent when questioned about syndicate narcotic shipments.

Then an operative in New York City picked up a lead in the person of Lorenzo, an Italian short-order cook employed in a restaurant near Jamaica, Long Island. From undercover sources we pieced together the fact that Lorenzo was an alien recently arrived from Genoa, Italy. Immigration informed us that he had entered the United States illegally, via Canada. He may have carried dope. The people who helped him get his narcotic-carrying passage, we learned, were part of the Luciano-Pici apparatus in Genoa. I ordered an investigation of Lorenzo and his background, both on the American side and in Italy, through my agent Charles Siragusa in Rome. Immigration agreed to withhold action pending our investigation.

The probe proceeded swiftly. Three weeks later, I received a long distance call from an undercover man in New York City, assigned to get everything he could on Lorenzo. "The man he worked with in Genoa was G.," the agent told me. "You have the name. The fellow here has had nothing to do with those people back there since he got here. Never writes letters, never gets in touch with them. But anything you do that way it's okay."

This call was the go-ahead for an ingenious but dangerous plan we were about to put into effect. The plan was evolved by the agent who would have to carry it out, a young man of Italian-American parentage. I cannot for security reasons identify him further, nor can I reveal, for the safety of himself and his family to which of our branch offices in America he is attached. The risk in this case was unusually big. We could make no move until we were sure that Lorenzo had not been in contact with the people in Genoa, particularly the man referred to as "G." whom we had heard was Joe Pici's assistant and partner. His name was Giovanni (Johnny) Gioia. Like Pici, he was a deportee from the United States. He now ran a Genoa rooming house as a front for other activities. We believed these to be the smuggling of dope and aliens into America.

Before me on my desk was the typed-out translation of a

letter, the original of which was written in Italian, in scrawled longhand, on a rumpled sheet of ruled stationery.

The translation read as follows:

Dear Giani:

I am very very well. And I hope your family is the same. I had a good trip. About all these things we talked about I couldn't do anything. One of my relatives will be coming to see you soon at Genoa and he is a person you can trust and I think that between the two of you you will be able to organize something good.

Regards from your friend,
Lorenzo.

The letter was a forgery, prepared by my own Italian experts in the Bureau. It was intended to give our agent a lead-in to the Mafia crowd in Genoa.

"Giani" was, of course, Giovanni Gioia. The "relative" whose visit the letter announced would be our agent. He had been schooled in his supposed family background, in the names and idiosyncrasies of uncles and aunts and other relatives, even of neighbors, all obtained for us through our undercover sources in Italy and in America. As an American, it was logical that he should speak English rather than fluent Italian. Both Pici and Gioia spoke English well.

Through the efforts of Siragusa in Rome, the undercover man would have full cooperation from Italian authorities, but meetings and contacts with them would be conducted with extreme caution since the assignment would place the agent on an intimate family basis, in the heart of a high echelon of the Mafia syndicate.

By the time the forged letter, mailed in Jamaica, Long Island, reached its destination in Genoa, Italy, the agent was in Rome. His story was that his name was Tony and he was a nephew of the short-order cook, Lorenzo (who was better known by his Americanized name, Larry). He was to express an interest in narcotics to the people in Genoa, while at the same time indicating that he had his sources for heroin lined up in Palermo, Sicily.

An interim report from this agent, received at our Rome office and forwarded to Washington, stated in part:

"On September 13, 1959, I drove to Genoa and . . . at about 1400 hours . . . I went to this address in Genoa . . . an apartment located on the sixth floor of the apartment building that has been converted into a rooming house . . . a man answered the door who stated that he was Johnny Gioia. He spoke perfect English without any trace of an accent. After I told him I was a nephew of Larry's, Gioia became very friendly and invited me inside.

"Since our information provided us with full details of Larry's background, we spent an hour discussing family members. During this time, I told him I was originally from East Harlem, then had moved to Long Island, that my name was Tony and I was one of Larry's nephews.

"Gioia seemed entirely unsuspicious of anything in my story. He told me he had been deported during the latter thirties, had done 16 years in jail on various charges (in the U.S.), originally came from Mulberry Street and Kenmore. He asked me names of many individuals from the area. A few I acknowledged knowing and others I merely stated that I knew the reputation. Still others, I denied knowing. After talking along these lines for a few minutes, I suggested that we dismiss the conversation since it was dangerous to discuss other people's welfare and activities. He apologized. . . .

"He asked me the nature of my visit and I told him I had business in the Palermo area. I offered no additional information. He asked me if he could do anything for me. I told him no, I needed nothing. I did mention that Larry told me Gioia could be trusted implicitly should any occasion arise. He bemoaned the fact that he had been deported, described his current activities of being involved in sending clandestine immigrants to the United States, stating, 'Sometimes they carry and sometimes they don't.'

"By carry he meant, of course, carrying narcotics."

There was no need to hurry. The word narcotics was never mentioned. Finally, as if by way of explanation, the agent told Gioia, "You see, when I talked with Larry back in New York he thought I'd be doing business with you. But I went to Montreal first and there I arranged to do my business in Palermo."

Rugged, dark-haired Gioia sat across from the agent. The day was hot and they sipped cool beer, provided by Gioia. The gangster appeared anxious and restive. His dark complexion glistened with sweat in the heat of the room. After a long silence, he asked the agent, "When's your uncle going to pay me the cash he owes, Tony? Or send me some business? How does he think I live?"

The agent said quickly, "I don't have anything to do with what Larry owes you guys. I wish I could do something about it, but I got my instructions in Montreal and I've got to carry through in Palermo."

Gioia made a grunting noise. On a table nearby was an Italian newspaper. Gioia picked up the paper, handed it to the agent. "Take a look at the photograph," Gioia said.

On the front page was a two-column picture of Joe Pici. The agent handed the paper back with the comment, "I don't read Italian, Johnny."

Gioia said: "This is my partner, Tony. If you need anything, he can take care of you."

The agent replied quickly, "Sure, I've heard of this Joe Pici, Johnny. But getting his picture smeared like that all over the front pages—that shows how hot he is. I'd be an ass to do business with anybody like him."

Gioia was stung at this. He started to brag about his deals with Pici. They didn't just deal in dope, he told his friend and potential customer. They dealt also in the smuggling of aliens. "See," he added, "the people carry. They sort of work their way over."

"Yeah, I heard," Tony said with mild interest. "Larry said you do it in a breeze."

"By way of Canada," Gioia told the agent. "They just walk off the boat. Just like that. It's all oiled. And getting into the States from Canada is always nothing."

"Suppose I want to get somebody across?" the agent asked.

"To carry something?"

"Could be."

"It costs one grand each man—terms cash." Gioia made a grimace. "That uncle of yours owes me five hundred. The son-of-a-bitch better not forget."

Tony shrugged and sipped his beer. Gioia, still trying to arouse Tony's interest, persisted, "If I send a man, whatever they carry in is none of our business. You understand?"

Tony nodded. "I couldn't decide anything anyway," he said, "until I've had a chance to talk to the people in Palermo."

Gioia decided it was time to drag Tony's oblique implications into the open. "It's none of my business, Tony," he said, "but if you're looking for junk, we have about three kilograms ready at hand and the price would be good. Better than in Palermo."

The agent refused to be rushed. There were several meetings in the next few days. During one, Gioia called Pici. "I want a sample of the material we talked about," the agent heard Gioia tell Pici. This was a sample to show Tony how good the heroin was. It arrived in a few hours. The sample tested as nearly 100 percent pure.

Tony still insisted on going to Palermo. He actually went to Rome and stayed out of sight for several days. The Rome office saw to it that a postcard written by the agent was mailed from Palermo to Gioia in Genoa.

On his return to Genoa, Tony informed Gioia that he had been able to purchase four kilos of heroin—about eight pounds —in Palermo. But he wanted more and wanted it cheap. Gioia reacted. He told Tony, "You go home. I'll see you tomorrow. I want to call a friend."

The moment Tony left for his hotel, Gioia telephoned Pici. We had obtained Pici's number when Gioia made a previous call in Tony's presence. The line was tapped, and the conversation, in English at all times, was recorded on tape. "Listen, Joe," Gioia said, "I want to see you tomorrow morning. You know that thing you gave me about ten days ago."

"Yeah."

"Well, the guy is back here now . . . the stuff was good and now he says he will take three, but you got to come down on the price."

"We'll talk about it tomorrow morning."

"Look, Joe, we should let it go for what he'll take it for. I need the money. He went down south and was disappointed with the way those guys do business. He got four but that's not enough."

"O.K., we'll talk about it tomorrow."

Pici was still suspicious. He warned Gioia the letter from the uncle might be a fake. During one phone call he told Gioia: "Johnny, you ain't very smart. Don't do anything with that guy. . . ."

But Johnny had ideas of going ahead.

While building the narcotics case, the agent was also trying to get additional data on the alien smuggling. Gioia made no secret of the large number of aliens involved and the fact that many carried drugs. In Washington we were working closely in this matter with the Bureau of Immigration.

Through days of drinking at assorted Rome bars, Gioia unfolded to his trusted friend Tony the full story of the shipping operations, including names of ships and what was "carried" by the aliens. Most of them were glad to carry a little junk— "for the chance to get to the States," Johnny said. We passed this information on to Immigration, but asked them to withhold action until we concluded the Gioia investigations.

On the afternoon of September 24th, at Gioia's boarding house, Gioia told Tony of a two-hour argument with Pici about Tony's authenticity. "I told him you were sent by good people and were one hundred percent," Gioia confided. "Pici says maybe Lorenzo had been arrested and is working for the police. Maybe you're from the International police. Or maybe you work for Anslinger."

"The whole deal was your idea," the agent reminded him, "and I'm perfectly willing to walk out on it."

Gioia explained that Pici wanted Tony to purchase the three kilos of heroin one kilo at a time, to prove himself. "If the first sale goes with no hitch, we'll sell you the second the next day."

Tony turned this down. "It's too dangerous," he charged. "I could get picked up or something could happen to the heroin or me while I stuck around for the next load. No thanks."

Of this delicate moment in the negotiations, the agent reported:

"We continued our discussion. The conversation turned to trust in one another. He told me that he had no doubt that I was bona fide but convincing Pici was a different thing. He said, 'You know that kid with the curly hair eating out there? Well, he just came in from South America with 2 K's of coke for Joe. Tomorrow Joe is leaving for Milano with him to get rid of it. Cocaine is worth a fortune over here; up to twenty grand a kilo. Joe had that kid on his mind more than anything else.'

"We had dinner and talked in generalities. . . . After dinner I went aside with Gioia and said, 'What are you going to do, forget it?' Gioia said, 'Let me call Joe again before we call it quits. Why don't you take one kilo first and then I'll get the other two within 24 hours, just as soon as Joe gets back from Milano?' I finally agreed but told him I would not pay for it until I had tested it. He agreed but said I must bring the money for one kilogram with me. I agreed."

Gioia phoned Pici to explain that Tony would have to test the stuff first, before he paid. "Tell the guy to forget the whole thing," Pici said.

In a tone of indifference, Tony told Gioia: "It's probably the best way, if that's how Pici feels."

But Gioia was still going with the deal. "I can talk Pici into it if you'll pay on the first one," he told Tony. "Can you get up the cash for the first kilo by tomorrow?"

Gioia was obviously anxious for the cash. Tony decided it was too soon to walk out; besides the whole operation was nearing a climax and any precipitous move in one direction or the other might be a giveaway.

"So if I do, Johnny?"

"So you show up here like tomorrow afternoon."

The two men grinned at each other.

Barring some unforeseen slip, we were ready to close in. Police in Rome, Milan, New York, Washington and Genoa were alerted. The agent had obtained, in casual conversation with Gioia, the exact address in Milan where Pici and the "curly-haired kid"—actually a seaman from South Africa—would be heading with their two kilos of cocaine. Via the tapped phones, we also knew the scheduled time of Pici's arrival.

About three o'clock the next afternoon Tony called on Gioia. The agent had the money on hand to pay for the kilo of heroin. Gioia told him, "Pici didn't bring the kilo, because he's still scared of the deal." The agent made no comment. Gioia then said, "I've just received a letter from Lorenzo in America."

The agent responded to this with: "Oh? Did Larry ask for me?"

"No," Gioia said, "he didn't."

The agent shrugged. After a silence, the agent stood up and said he had to be leaving. Gioia told him, "Well, I'm sorry. But any negotiations will have to be done with money in advance. Why not pay for the first kilo in advance and I'll have it for you by tomorrow?"

The agent glanced at his watch. Time was running out. Within minutes, police in Milan would be closing in on Pici.

He had no more time for casual conversation with Gioia. A report on this critical moment stated: "I acted perturbed, put on my coat, and started to leave, telling Gioia, 'You asked me, I didn't ask you. I thought I was doing you a favor.' With that, Gioia explained that Pici had let 50 grams there and then admitted he had not received any letter from Lorenzo. I told him I was not interested in the 50 grams.

"He said, 'Listen, do me a favor. Take the 50. When Joe comes back tonight or tomorrow you can have the rest. As soon as Joe sees you've got the money he'll change.'

"After some discussion I agreed to take the 50. He went into his bedroom and brought out a package made up of old newspaper. Inside was a plastic bag. He said. 'Where's the money?' I said I'd pay him after I tested it. With that I took the package to the kitchen and field tested a little with a marquis reagent.* After receiving a positive reaction I returned to the living room and paid him $140. He wanted $200. I told him I'd give him $140 and no more. We talked another ten minutes and I left the apartment."

Once outside the apartment house, Agent "Tony" gave a signal to two Carabinieri officers who were dressed as seamen and who were told to gain entrance by saying "The blond one from the ship sent me." This referred to a blond-headed seaman who not only assisted Gioia with clandestine emigrants but also sent him "clients." The two police officers gained entrance with this ruse, and arrested Gioia. They searched the apartment but were unable to locate the $140. Gioia stated he had flushed the money down the toilet.

Police in Milan completed the roundup by placing under arrest the man we had started out to get and now had landed, Pici, with a full load of evidence to send him away. Other arrests followed swiftly. Among confiscated papers, we found lists of hundreds of names of men associated with Gioia and Pici—seamen, gangsters, U.S. Navy personnel serving on

* A chemical test to make sure the substance is actively narcotic in content.

American warships, associates and "connections" in England, Germany, Denmark, Norway, Spain and other countries. All this information was collated and referred for action to the appropriate agencies of our own and allied governments.

These raids and seizures, in the fall of 1959 and the early months of 1960, led in turn to the arrests of hundreds of smaller fry both in America and abroad in connection with various aspects of this smuggling. Their cases are in various stages of disposition as this is written.

PART THREE

AGENTS AND INFORMERS

PERSONNEL

Over a period of many years, my staff and I pioneered in the development of new undercover techniques of investigation, to meet the special problems our agents must face.

Our agents are of many kinds, shapes, sizes, races and backgrounds. There is no special type of Bureau investigator. One is a lanky ex-librarian or pharmacist, the next a college Ph.D. in philosophy, the third a former football All-American. Some are of Chinese background; some of Italian, particularly Sicilian descent; some are Negroes. Their interests, information, and backgrounds range as wide as the worlds they must investigate. They are picked not only for these special backgrounds but also—even more importantly—for their integrity, their physical courage, their resourcefulness in emergency, their stamina under stress and their mental agility.

What to most men would be the most extraordinary and perilous adventures are to these agents only a part of the daily professional routine job. Temptations are great in the dual role that they play as undercover operatives. The deals in which they are concerned may run into millions of dollars. Bribes and the double-cross by the agent are always a possibility. Yet in more than thirty years only a handful have betrayed their trust. The others have become dedicated to the task assigned, fully aware of its meaning and importance to the public.

In these chapters it is my purpose to picture some of the

123

techniques of these agents on actual assignments, the atmosphere of peril in which they operate, the role of the informer, the range of methods and resourcefulness required, the successes and setbacks—and the failures—in the grueling daily business of the Bureau.

9. A Man Named X

One of our agents in Seattle, Washington, George White, received a phoned-in tip that a crippled white man in the Skid Row section was selling drugs and carrying opium in the top of his crutch. The ubiquitous White—always ready to shake hands with trouble—decided to investigate personally.

I am sure that he had no idea the case would develop into a matter of world-wide implications, nor that it would take him on a nightmarish national tour of dens of depravity. Nor that it would involve him at last in a kill-or-be-killed oath, before the crossed swords and caldrons on an Oriental shrine in an upstairs hall on Second Avenue in Pittsburgh.

As White walked the darkened and almost empty Skid Row streets, he heard in the distance footsteps and a faint tapping noise. He hurried toward the sounds, stopping when he saw, silhouetted in the glow of a street light, a man with a crutch. The crippled man walked a few steps and stood by a wall at the entrance to an alley. White watched from across the street. Another man approached and talked with the cripple, who lifted the crutch, took off the tip, removed an object from inside the tip and handed it to his customer, who turned and walked away.

White then moved in on the startled cripple and demanded a look at this crutch. The tip was empty but the smell of opium was strong. White identified himself as an U.S. narcotics agent. The cripple grew panicky. "I don't want to be arrested," he said. "You let me go—I'll tell you where I got it from."

"Where?"

"My source comes in about an hour."

The man's eyes were bright in the darkness. The agent asked again, "Where?"

The white-haired cripple smiled. "My apartment. You come to my apartment with me. Wait there for him."

The cripple and the agent waited in a shabby, filthy smelling Skid Row room. After about fifteen minutes there was a knock at the door. White opened it cautiously. Outside in the hall was a well-dressed Chinese. He gave a start at the sight of a stranger, and quickly put his hand to his mouth.

White grabbed his hand and smelled the palm where the scent of opium was unmistakable. "You can do nothing to me," the man insisted in shrill tones. "There is no evidence; I swallowed it."

"All right," White said calmly, "I'll take you to a hospital and have them pump out your stomach."

The Chinese decided to be more cooperative. "Look, I can tell you plenty. But if I talk, they may kill me."

"Suppose we promise to protect you?"

The Chinese was silent. The agent went on, "If we can offer you full protection—will you give us names?" White was sure the man wanted to talk, wanted to cooperate, wanted to stay out of jail—but wanted also to stay alive. He kept asking questions. The answers were evasive but eventually White was able to put together the following information, which he relayed to his district supervisor.

Some years earlier this man had been a "hatchet"—paid executioner—for the Hip Sing Tong. "The fellow had a fight with some gangsters years back," White reported, "and was scheduled to be knocked off himself. The Tong shielded his identity. If we take him into court and his identity becomes known, his old enemies will murder him. But now this Chinese would work with us—for a fee—if protected from killers among his own people."

The Hip Sings were involved in nation-wide dope activities

but we had never before been able to get close to the operations. The supervisor telephoned me in Washington, after talking with White and pinning the possibilities down. "He'll work with us, through White," this supervisor told me. "He'll show us all the operation of certain factions of the Hip Sings, and how some of their illustrious members distribute dope in America. But we have to agree to send the Chinese away when his part is finished."

"Whatever he wants—let him have it," I told the supervisor, "I want everything done to nail it down. We'll send him to Tibet, Shanghai, the South Pole, anywhere he wants—afterwards."

Using the name of John Wilson, White set up his cover story: He was the nephew of a successful businessman on the West Coast anxious to develop extra profits in the narcotic business. The uncle was "organizing" a syndicate.

With his new identity of John Wilson, the agent and the Chinese—Mr. X—he had picked up at the cripple's apartment set out on a junket—to buy drugs from Chinese leaders in the Hip Sing Tong.

The first visit of the agent and the informer was Butte, Montana, where they called on one of the most powerful men in the tong, Chin Joe Hip, Chinese "emperor" of Montana. Chin Joe Hip had been a good friend of Informer X when the latter was a hatchet man. He told the informer, "If you vouch for Mr. Wilson, whatever he wishes is his."

There followed a number of fine Chinese dinners. White had learned how to eat with chopsticks and had a gourmet's knowledge of Chinese dishes, so that he could pose as a true epicure. This pleased Chin Joe Hip and his family, who went all out with lavish meals. In the course of talk, discussing how he came to live in Butte, Chin told his guests with disarming frankness: "I like it here. There is much money to be made. I look after the Tong's business all over the Pacific Coast."

"Then perhaps I can get some of what I need for my uncle's operations through you," the agent said.

The Chinese nodded affirmation, adding, "Of course, I am also in close touch all the time with New York. That is where you want to go if you are in need of large supplies of opium, morphine or heroin. You can get all you want there."

"My uncle and I have been doing some business but now we are expanding our ideas," White said. "We already have distributors but need a big supply of goods."

He went on to explain that he and his friend who had brought him here had gone into partnership in this end of the business, as the friend claimed that he could get him all he needed through the Hip Sings.

"Your friend tells the truth," Chin declared. "The Tong itself does not deal in opium but there are many in it who do and they can help you get all you want. They are glad for business."

Chin Joe not only sold a quantity of morphine to the agent—"samples" for Mr. Wilson to show his rich uncle—but also furnished letters of introduction to sources in New York City, and leaders of the Hip Sings. He sent word to all the tongs that a big operator in heroin, morphine and opium was traveling across the nation setting up new sources for his uncle's syndicate. Treat the customer nicely!

It was unusual to use White in this kind of case; he was not Chinese or of Chinese background. In selecting agents for an assignment we usually look for specialized qualifications. Most of our agents in the Chinese districts are of Oriental extraction; they speak Chinese fluently, know the idiom and the slang and can merge into the Chinese community. Similarly in the investigation of Sicilian mobs here or abroad, we frequently use our agents of Italian—preferably Sicilian—backgrounds, steeped in the ancient culture of Sicily, aware of the obscure customs, meanings, intonations, idioms and oaths.

But White had made a speciality of Chinese lore—and this, in any event, was his case from the start.

All of our agents are, of course, schooled in every phase of narcotics: the chemistry of all drugs with which they may be dealing, the physical effects and symptoms of addiction, the psychological and physiological reactions. They must be able to field test narcotics and evaluate the quality and quantity. Posing as a big dealer, they must have as wide a technical knowledge as a big narcotics dealer almost invariably has.

I insist that our undercover agents must be able to "blend" —as completely as any criminal—into their surroundings without a ripple of confusion or doubt. And they must be able to drink with the mobsters without fear of breaking cover through an unwary alcoholic word.

I have known agents to come staggering drunk out of a bar in the company of half a dozen narcotic traffickers and killers. One slip in this condition would not only cost a life but might mean wrecking a case against mobsters who were destroying scores of other lives. But if the agent does not drink freely with all the others, there may be questions in the minds of the suspects. Anything "different" can arouse suspicion. The narcotic hoodlums—with good reason—are the most suspicious and fearful in the world. Our undercover activities are in part responsible for that constant fear.

Wherever Wilson, alias White and his Chinese Mr. X traveled, the doors of the Hip Sings were opened. They dined at Chinese homes and restaurants in the leading cities of the United States. From a number of sources, samples of the finest grade opium arrived—by mail—at hotels where they stopped. The Chinese communication lines were excellent; the narcotics always arrived in time to be picked up by the agent; all such "samples" White forwarded to his supervisor, marked for identification.

At last this curious buying spree took them to New York. Word spread in the city, through the Hip Sings, that "Mr. Wilson" was the biggest customer to hit town in a decade. Many dealers and peddlers tried to get in touch with White at his hotel headquarters.

One of the Chinese peddlers the agent met in New York, obviously anxious to win Mr. Wilson's favor, told him, "I can get you to be a blood member of the Hip Sing Tong yourself. I am very close to the head of Hip Sings in Pittsburgh."

"Don't I have to be Chinese to be a blood brother?"

"Not if we say you can be," the man replied. "It will build trust in you."

Agent White accepted.

In Pittsburgh, he had to get fifty dollars changed into silver, each piece of which was wrapped in red paper. This was referred to as "good luck" money. A special meeting was called at the Hip Sing headquarters. The local "president" and a number of other tong members were present. "Mr. Wilson" was led into a room in which there was an altar where high priests of the Hip Sings lighted incense lamps, while others started a flame burning in a metal container.

Several Hip Sing members, in Chinese robes, stood with their candidate in front of this altar. They bowed several times. White did also. The Hip Sing "president" handed out the wrapped-up silver coins to all present, pocketing what was left over. The leader then mumbled words in Chinese, White was instructed to repeat them. This was an oath of the brotherhood: "I swear to maim, rob, steal, kill or carry out any other act ordered by my superior. I will keep the secrets of the Hip Sings and accept the punishment of death if I violate my sacred oath."

When this was over, the president then announced to the gathering that Mr. Wilson was a full brother of the Hip Sings, entitled to all rights and honors and accepting all responsibilities thereby implied. He was given a card on which his name—John Wilson—was written in a Chinese phonetic transliteration. "This card will open many doors to you that might otherwise have remained closed," the president told the agent. "Everywhere you go, the Hip Sings will trust you and accept you and welcome you into their midst.

"They will help you with your business," he added. "If the police bother you in any city, do not hesitate to let the Hip Sings know at once. Your brothers will see that you get help.

We have many connections and important friends." The president did not understate the power of this card. Everywhere White went he and his friend were shown every hospitality and kindness—and sold supplies of drugs. Step by step, White and the other agents he brought in near the close of this case prepared the final scene. In cities across America—at a predetermined moment—our agents raided dozens of establishments, pulling in hundreds of suspects. Hip Sing headquarters were raided from New York and Pittsburgh to Butte, Montana, and on to the West Coast.

The Hip Sing brotherhood was a shambles. Narcotics, particularly opium and heroin, were the heart of their business. Retail value of seized drugs totaled hundreds of thousands of dollars. Hip Sing leaders who had taken so wholeheartedly to John Wilson and his rich uncle were horrified to discover that Wilson's rich uncle was Uncle Sam.

The resourcefulness of the agent and his associates, his ability to cope with such a melange of backgrounds and criminal activity requires experience over many years—and many cases. The job only begins with the investigation. Reports that follow must be in triplicate and must be exact. Names must be correct, information full and detailed; descriptions not only of the individuals but also of the merchandise must be technically correct and precise, as to the nature of the drugs involved, the chemical content, the exact amounts.

The narcotic agent's role goes far beyond being able to live with underworld suspects for weeks or months, to drink with them, dine with them, become a family intimate; it means also understanding the delicate relationships America has with other nations, with the police departments of individual states and cities, with the agents of Scotland Yard or the British Home Office or the French Sureté, with U.S. Customs and Immigration and the FBI agents who, while not concerned with narcotic law enforcement, are sometimes involved in investigation of the same individuals we are hunting.

Most of our agents must be chosen through Civil Service channels and requirements, which puts a greater limitation on our range of selection than, for example, the FBI, which does not have to do this. Nevertheless, we do have special openings where we can select a man because he speaks a Cantonese or Sicilian dialect.

As the narcotic pushers concentrated more and more on Negro sections in large cities, we found it necessary to increase our number of agents working in these areas. I brought in thirty-five Negro narcotic agents who have ranked with the finest investigators in the United States government, in character, in reliability, courage, and resourcefulness. We employ more Negro agents than all the other Federal agencies combined. Their performance has been magnificent.

Our agents do not count hours. If the agent is the right kind, he not only works around the clock if necessary, but he couldn't be driven from his job with a bull whip. He becomes imbued with the purpose—a crusader. He lives this war against the narcotic hoods.

Whether undercover or not, on assignment or not, all agents throughout our districts are regarded as on twenty-four hour duty, all are subject to call, and the supervisor must know where the agent is and what his assignment is at that hour. An agent is like having a gun in your house. We must know where to reach it when we need it.

Lengths to which our agents go on undercover assignments are sometimes unbelievable. A warden calls; he has a bad situation in his prison; could we send in an undercover man to help? Someone on the inside is peddling junk to the inmates. Only a bona fide prisoner could find out who runs a tight inside-prison-walls dope ring.

We have to play it out all the way. We have to have an agent actually picked up by the police, charged with a crime and sentenced. In one instance, I had the cops nab an agent for loitering around a bank and in possession of a deadly weapon. *The police were not in on the truth;* they picked him up as a suspicious character on the basis of an anonymous phone tip —from us. If an agent in this situation should run into a trigger-happy cop, he might be shot or even killed during the arrest. But the chances are remote because we "case" the situation pretty well ourselves—and our man is instructed to put up no resistance. For security reasons secrecy is essential in such cases. The entire arrest procedure—mugging and fingerprints and lineup and all the rest—is gone through without the police knowing that they are part of an undercover operation.

We usually notify the trial judge of the true situation. The judge will go along with us and sentence the man in open court. Thus the undercover agent comes into the prison with a full set of criminal records and convictions so solid no one could doubt his validity.

Once our man breaks the case and puts the finger on the ring and its method of operation, we get him out of there and the record is fully expunged. Even then, we do not tell the police. We manage to secure the files and get rid of them.

What we are most interested in is the data forwarded by the local police as a matter of routine to the FBI—fingerprints and other personal information and description. From the beginning Mr. Hoover and the Bureau have always cooperated with us on such problems. The records are destroyed.

Our road is not always so smooth. Whether in our country, or abroad, the danger we face is not exclusively from the recognized criminal elements. There are occasions when the authorities themselves present problems.

George White was jailed once because he refused to tell a grand jury the name of an informant who had turned in a narcotics pusher. White explained to the United States district attorney in the case: "If I tell you and the jury the name of our informants, they'll be dead in twenty-four hours. That's for sure. We could just about name the killers."

The United States attorney in the case either did not believe our agent or did not care what happened to our informants. He insisted that our agent answer the question, or be jailed for contempt. On my orders White refused. At the request of the district attorney, the grand jury thereupon held Federal Agent White in contempt.

He was remanded to jail in the city "until such time as he purges himself of contempt." Through his attorney, White got in touch with me. I called the district attorney and reminded him of the number of federal statutes and decisions which held that a federal officer who in pursuit of his duties obtains information from confidential sources is not in violation of the law if he refuses to reveal the identity of the source. I pointed out that within the framework of our system of justice, a judge may throw out evidence from unnamed sources. The court indeed is charged with the protection of the civil liberties of the defendant. But the courts also recognize their obligation to protect law enforcement agencies and agents carrying out their responsibilities.

I patiently repeated our position to the federal authorities. I explained that I would fight the matter all the way to the Supreme Court, and that we would be glad to explore the reasons why this district attorney considered it so important to discover sources of information on narcotic pushers that he had his grand jury imprison one of our agents.

White was released that night and all contempt action against him halted, although for some days we had reports of threats against his life.

10. Oozy: Informer Extraordinary

Oozy was the quintessence of all informers. I have never known a man who was at once so repulsive, so beguiling—or so valuable. Informing was his *métier*, his business and his avocation.

I call this lean broomstick of a man Oozy because, as some of my agents put it, he oozed dope from every pore of his body. I do not know how he stayed alive. He could take heroin, morphine and cocaine all mixed together in one colossal dose, shoot it into any part of his body and show no ill effects whatsoever. How he developed such a tolerance no one knows. I am sure that the same dosages would have killed other men.

Oozy's criminal record was long and varied. Most of the charges involved drugs. He had been in and out of jail many times; usually for possession. Each time we brought him in he would come up with evidence against some pusher or trafficker higher up, and in this way would get himself at least a break on the sentence.

Oozy existed on the police records of his friends. He dressed comparatively well. His face was thin—almost emaciated—yet in spite of that he was not bad looking. One of his talents was his ability to spot another addict, anywhere, any time. How he did it he could not or would not reveal. He would see a man coming a block away and say, "That's one." And he'd be right.

One day Oozy saw coming down the street a mink-coated woman who was obviously what Oozy called "class." He was also aware with his peculiar intuition that the well-dressed woman was an addict and in need of a shot. He was so sure about it that he struck up a conversation with her.

After a little time he said: "You're desperate, aren't you?"

"How do you mean?"

"For something." She realized what he meant.

The woman nodded. She said, "Can you get me anything?"

"I might. I have some stuff. At my place."

In most cases, dope dulls the addict's sex urge, but Oozy was again the exception. Oozy and the addicted lady of society became intimate, needle-swapping friends. They would rely on each other for narcotics when their own supplies ran out. They trusted each other. When funds were down, however, Oozy reverted to his old character. "Listen, I've got a hot one for you fellows," he reported to one of my supervisors, "I can buy heroin from the classiest broad in town. Way up there in the social set. But how!"

This was a new type for Oozy to report on. Our supervisor pressed for information. "She's the daughter of a state supreme court judge," Oozy said. "Her husband is the finest doctor in the city and his clientele is blue blood only."

When I heard about Oozy's report I ordered the supervisor to follow it up. "We've got to find out what this is about," I said. "This is a stratum Oozy doesn't usually invade."

Oozy set the stage for us and one of our agents made a "buy" of an ounce of heroin from the lady in mink. Acting on my personal orders, the agents picked her up following this sale, and brought her to my office. She was a charming, dark-haired, soft-spoken, obviously cultured woman, exactly as Oozy had described her. "How did you get yourself into this filthy mess?" I asked her.

She leaned back in the chair, smoking a cigarette. From her manner and deportment, she might have been engaging in a casual cocktail-hour conversation. It was a familiar story, to anyone who knows the problems of narcotics as they apply to physicians and their wives. Living under great stress, doctors —and their families—often seek various escapes from the daily tensions.

"We go out a lot," she said. "All the time. Every night it's something else. I began drinking, mostly to make up for the fact that I was bored, just the way he was. You get tired of parties.

"We drank and I would wake up with the worst kind of hangovers. I just couldn't move. I would ache all over. So he would go into his bag and bring out a shot of morphine and that would fix me up."

"And the same thing the next morning?"

"Sure. Every day. He was my husband, and he was a doctor. He said it was all right."

That may sound shocking, yet I have heard of many instances in which doctors have used this morphine therapy as a morning after remedy on their wives or friends, or even on business-executive patients who have to face important meetings. Of course, they become "hooked" and of course "withdrawal" symptoms develop—sweating and spasmodic pain—the moment the physician ceases to prescribe the daily morphine dosage.

"Then one morning when I told him I wanted a shot," the woman said "he wouldn't give it to me. He said: 'You weren't out last night. You didn't drink a drop. You haven't any hangover. I'm not going to make you an addict by giving you morphine when you don't need it.'

"I told him he had to give it to me or I'd get it myself, somewhere," the woman added. "He must have seen I was sweating. He could tell I was in pain. He looked at me with horror on his face, I could see it. He said: 'My God, you're an addict. You're addicted to morphine.' When I heard him say that, the way he said it, I felt like I was dead."

The husband sent her to a sanitarium for a cure. She went

through a protracted withdrawal period, given a little less each day until at last she was off drugs completely. "But the minute I was released," she said, "the party routine started all over again. These were my friends, I kept insisting. I had a right to a few evenings of fun.

"Then I started asking him for a shot in the morning and he refused. So I stole morphine from his medicine cabinet. When I tried again I found he had hidden the stuff. So I went out and got myself a peddler. I went to a few barrooms. I asked a few people. It wasn't hard."

This "connection" she made became her regular supplier, she admitted. Oozy was only a spare to fill in when her regular peddler was out of stuff.

I have known a number of women who become addicted and plunged from high positions to complete ruin. I am convinced that sentimental do-goodism is no way to bring these people to their senses. I believe they must be brought face to face with the reality of where they are—and why. "You have sold heroin," I said to the doctor's wife. "This is a serious crime. It means disgrace—headlines for you and your family, plus a stretch in federal prison. You will probably be sent to Alderson. It does some of the finest rehabilitation work in the country with female prisoners."

I could see, in the look on the woman's face, the realization of the terrible trouble she had gotten herself into. I let the silence sink in. Then I said: "You can help yourself, however, and your family."

Her expression softened. "From the amount your supplier gets for you," I said, "enough so you can even sell an ounce or two yourself if somebody happens along—your guy must be big time. He's the one I want."

I felt pity for her. She was beautiful, a graduate of a famous finishing school. Yet I had offered her the only course I considered fair to her, or to the public. "I may be killed for what I am going to tell you," she said finally. "But I'm going to tell it."

She began to talk. When she was in the sanitarium she met the girl friend of one of the biggest gangsters in the United States. "I'm getting out of here," the girl friend told her, "I'm cured. When you get out, if you ever need anything desperately, call me at this number. I'll get it to you, all you need. My boy friend will handle it."

I was sure she was not putting on any act. "How could I be cured with a vulture like that in my brain?" she demanded. "I made the call, I mailed the money. The heroin comes by mail. It is terribly expensive. My husband has spent a fortune to make me well—$50 a day at the hospital. He doesn't know. To this day he thinks—my husband really believes, this very minute—that I am fully cured."

"And you don't want him to know?"

"Oh, God—never. Not after what I have put him through already."

When she gave me the name of the man who supplied her regularly, I was stunned. He was one of the most notorious "operators" of the district; he supplied all the gambling houses with their specially made dice; he served as a wholesale procurer of women for fancy houses; he was known to have smuggled guns into state penitentiaries for use in prison breaks; he owned a hotel in which only bona fide criminals were allowed to register. (A corrupt member of the local police force checked every name for the hotel manager.) Yet for years he had avoided punishment because of his "connections."

This mink-coated addict and I worked out a deal. We fixed up a phony record for one of our agents so that he could get in to this exclusive hotel hangout. The woman agreed to write to her supplier on orchid stationery. Our agent would lounge in the lobby and watch what the desk clerk did with the letter.

Several letters were sent. Each time, the agent reported, the letter was placed in the mailbox used by this untouchable hoodlum, who would come and pick the letters up personally. Also after each letter the lady received her heroin.

Finally we made the raid. Half the guests in that hotel fled as our agents trooped into the lobby. One woman jumped out of a second story window and died in the hospital: In her room were found fourteen valuable fur coats, all stolen from local stores. But we were after only one man; this big shot hoodlum who ran the joint—and supplied dope to customers, as a profitable sideline. In his room we found not only the man, but on the floor, the torn bits of our lady's last orchid letter. We found also crooked dice, burglar's tools, and a supply of heroin worth about five thousand dollars.

We sent this big shot away for a long stretch. The physician's wife went away for a "rest" and when she returned her addiction was cured. This time there was no relapse. Her husband was never told the full story. They are devoted to each other, and to a more leisurely pursuit of their happiness. The past is past.

Oozy did not see her again. But he did brag to the supervisor: "Where would she be now, if I hadn't turned her in?"

It is rarely possible to guess accurately from what corner the informer will emerge. For this reason, a delicate relationship, little understood by the public, exists between law enforcement officials and individual members of the underworld. These men we hunt down are always possible allies who may come over to our side for some consideration of sentence, for some promise to protect their wife or family. My attitude has been to use any means available to cut narcotic violations to a minimum, and where criminals or addicts will cooperate with us to that end I will deal with them.

I take no holier-than-thou attitude. I am concerned with doing a practical job. I play by the rules, which these men, twisted as many of them are, understood and respect. My door is always open to gangster, hoodlum, smuggler, pusher or addict. I insist, however, that they leave their lawyers behind so that we can talk freely.

Whether he comes voluntarily or because he is shown that it is his best way out, whether it is a one-time deal or a source of inside information that may continue for months, the informer provides the solution for ninety-five percent not only of narcotic offenses but of all types of crime.

The informer and the undercover agent are, of course, two entirely separate aspects of enforcement. The agent works for the Bureau and his undercover assignment is a part of the job. The informer—the special employee—comes from within the gang. He remains inside but reports to us.

He becomes a "special employee" when he actually goes to work for us from within the gang—on a regular week-to-week basis. He deserves the special official designation. The risk is high. The payments are never large. Nor do we ever, as some writers have alleged, supply addict-informers with drugs.

I recall a Chinese who helped us in a number of investigations who was also tried by a court of tong members and sentenced to be executed by a hatchet man. I quickly got this "special employee" out of the country. Several years later, from somewhere in the Orient, I received a letter from him: "With money you gave me," he wrote, "I bought beautiful bride and we now have son, name him Hally for you, Godfather."

Most of the people who come to me have something vital to trade—information. But not all. Sometimes they come simply to get justice. I regard it my duty to help them get it. One man complained when he pleaded guilty at my suggestion and got a two-year sentence. I convinced him it was light. He is now in a good business. He also drops in occasionally to see me.

One of the major gamblers of the nation came in to complain bitterly that we had a narcotics charge against him that was a bum rap. He cried profusely in my office. I told him that I knew he had never been in dope, and we had decided to drop the charges. The case was no good. He stopped his sobbing and asked me how he could repay me and the Bureau for treating him fairly. I said, "Give away some of your riches to the poor."

He said he would and he kept his word. But he did not give away all his wealth. He was buried in a solid gold casket.

Getting an informer at the top echelons of a mob is not so difficult as the public—or the racketeers—may believe. There is always someone willing to sell out. We have special employees in places where the hoodlums could not believe an informer would dare go; we have had running reports on the highest levels of organized crime, including details of payoffs, bribe offers, commitments of politicians, plans of the syndicate and—ultimately—the crime for which the top men could be arrested and shipped off to prison.

One of my finest associates and for a long time my second in command in the Bureau, Malachi L. Harney, declared in a treatise he co-authored on *The Informer in Law Enforcement:*

"In the narcotics traffic . . . which comprises as experienced a set of criminals as exists in this country, one of the primary rules is, 'never deal with a stranger.' The attempt is made to extend this rule to 'never deal with any outsider.' This is a policy which cannot always be adhered to, fortunately for law enforcement. Few businesses thrive on inbreeding. The narcotic peddlers eventually find it unprofitable merely to take in one another's washing. But when we approach the narcotic trafficker to purchase drugs, our credentials need to be . . . almost impeccable. Usually considered as good credentials is an introduction by an accepted criminal. . . . In this category the informer can supply the entree which otherwise might never have been obtained."

But where and how the informer comes into the scene—who he is and why he shows up—all this lies in the realm of the unpredictable.

One day a tall, handsome man with black, curly hair and a debonair, pleasant manner walked into my office. "I am going straight to the point," he said. "You probably won't believe what I'm going to tell you. I swear it's the truth. I want you to trust me long enough to send a mob to jail."

This is a beginning I like; it has paid off many times in the past. I said, "Go ahead. Let me have it without any frills. If I nail you with one phony statement, you can peddle it all somewhere else."

He said his name was Maurice. "I have been with this mob for years," he said. "We are big in the traffic. Now I have been marked for the rub-out. You understand? They have decided to kill me."

"Why?"

"It doesn't matter. You can't do anything about that anyway. They don't miss. But before I go I want to get even. I have to stay alive that long. I can trust no one. Even my wife is on their side. She wants them to kill me; it would suit her fine. I've been using planes and trains to shake them. But never for long."

"Do they know you are here?"

"I don't think so. I just escaped being thrown off the train platform when I started down here. I got off the train at Baltimore, ran up the stairs and jumped into a taxi." He drew a breath. "I cannot stand this very much longer," he added.

I said, "Go on."

"We have a setup in France with a mob over there. We get heroin in by using falsely billed merchandise, bonded in transit through New York. It hits the New York pier, goes to a crooked bonded trucker who is supposed to take it to another pier for transshipment to another country, in Central or South America usually.

"What this trucker does is take it to a warehouse where a switch is made. Same boxes, same markings. He delivers the fake boxes. The destination on the boxes reads Bahia, Brazil. But nobody in Brazil ever calls for the boxes. Inside there are usually old electrical fixtures worth nothing. Customs in Brazil finally sells them off with other unclaimed stuff. Simple, isn't it?"

He reached in his pocket, took out a passport and handed it to me. "It's my passport," he said. "You can see how many trips I've made to Paris to make arrangements with the crowd over there."

I examined the passport. It showed a number of visas to France. I said, "The picture is yours but the name is not the one you gave me."

"That's easy," he answered, "I used an alias so they couldn't check on me, the passport people."

"Easy? Honest citizens often have a hard time getting a passport. How come you got one with a false name?"

All he did was have two of the mob swear that he was an American citizen. He was, in fact, a citizen of Poland; he had never been naturalized.

"Sol the Oil is the boss," he concluded. "He lives with the divorced wife of a world's champion prize fighter. I'm going to give you plenty of evidence, documents, the works. You won't need me. Anyway, I don't think I'll be here."

In half an hour he had given me all the facts I needed to smash a New York City mob headed by Sol the Oil.

My "special employee" needed money and drew several large diamonds from his pocket. I gave him the name of a Washington jeweler who gave him a good price for these, enough to carry him for some weeks. I also assigned a man to give him protection while he was in Washington. But in a few days he got restless and ducked out. Two weeks later he was found dead in a vacant lot in Brooklyn. We knew on whose orders he was shot but that was evidence we could not use. Maurice had refused to talk to anyone except me.

We did send Sol and several of his mob to prison for two years on the narcotics evidence, which was solid. After Sol was released he went back into the heroin business in New York. One of the smart young agents in our New York office made a large purchase, following which he led a raid in which we seized enough heroin to satisfy all the addicts in New York for several weeks.

However, in the meantime the New York City Police Narcotics Squad had set up a wire tap in a probe of their own, and heard this young agent of ours giving inside information to a rival New York mob. Our agent, in fact, was playing one mob off against the other, for his personal profit, and looking to receive a citation for turning Sol in.

The head of the New York Police Narcotics Squad reported this to me with a copy of the tape. This is the kind of shock that comes occasionally in our kind of job. The agent had worked his double-cross so cleverly that the only evidence we had was the wire tap.

The New York City Police Commissioner came along with me to view the seizure, however, and afterwards all the agents and detectives involved lined up so that we could shake their hands and congratulate them. In the line was the turncoat.

I asked the Commissioner to follow my actions as we went down the line. When we reached the crooked agent, I deliberately ignored him. He blanched when I gave him a steely stare. Without shaking his hand or acknowledging his existence we passed on to the next man. The agent was out of the Bureau even before he could testify at the trial. He himself could not be tried because evidence obtained by wire tap is not admissible in court.

11. An Agent Named Kip

I write a kind of special citation here—to a dog.

We called him Kip in the Bureau. I doubt that he would have been admitted—for all his smooth gray coat—into the official blue-ribbon canine classes, but he rendered greater service to the public, in my opinion, than all the winners put together.

Kip somehow absorbed the sense of dedication that has marked the Bureau and its agents. The job was more than a job. It was almost as if Kip's canine intelligence grasped—if only in groping outline—the purpose, the concept of crusade, behind the assignment.

The provocative possibility of developing a canine agent came to me some years ago. At a meeting of the international Opium Advisory Committee at Geneva, Switzerland, I heard the Chinese delegate speak of the experimental use of dogs in the anti-opium drive of the pre-Communist era in China. The idea was new and one I thought worthy of investigation. Around the conference table there were some amused smiles. The Chinese delegate abruptly changed the subject.

Later, I talked with the great Egyptian enforcement official, Sir Thomas (Tommy) Russell, otherwise known as Russell Pasha. His government had turned in a report to the League of Nations stating that the value of police dogs in this kind of investigation had been overlooked. Tommy told me that he was experimenting with police dogs.

He described a case in Cairo involving a man who had vanished. Another man—a neighbor—was suspected of having some part in the disappearance, but there was no evidence. Since there was suspicion that the case was tied in with drugs, Russell Pasha's men took a specially trained dog to the room, not of the missing man but of the suspect, who dealt in hashish.

With the smell of the suspect and the hashish in his nostrils, the dog led the police over a puzzling course, out of the city into the desert and the blazing sun, to a spot that was nothing but sand and sky and broiling heat. It was five miles from the house of the suspect to the point where the dog took them. The dog began to dig into the sand. The men watched as his paws finally struck something solid. The police moved in quickly and uncovered the trussed-up body of the missing man.

The dog had followed the scent of hashish from the house to the desert grave. The hashish-dealing neighbor, who might otherwise never have been implicated, was executed for the murder.

This story from a man of Russell Pasha's experience gave me something to build on. I launched my own investigation with several special research men assigned to the project. We explored the whole subject of dog detectives, examining all available material, interviewing police chiefs, dog breeders, "Seeing Eye" authorities, dog show managers, animal trainers and circus performers, both in America and abroad.

All the information obtained pointed to the fact that dogs could be trained, by "rechanneling" techniques, to react to the scent of drugs. Furthermore, they did not have to be bloodhounds or police dogs; what counted was not the breed but the "talents," the reactions and interests of the individual animal—and, very much as with human beings, a willingness to do a good job.

I set about starting a training program. Kip was our first rookie agent with four feet. His breed was police dog—mainly. We kept the whole program top secret. The very existence of a Narcotics Bureau Canine Squad was unknown to the public.

While Kip was being trained, I urged United States Customs authorities to participate with us and perhaps share some of the costs. The dog, I pointed out, could be invaluable in the search of vessels, where hiding places are often impossible to uncover by ordinary means. Two Customs officials dropped into my office and listened politely as I told of the training required, the daily workouts, the potentialities. After the men left, one of my assistants told me that the two men went down the hall shaking with laughter interspersed with simulated barks.

Kip went out on his first assignment only after months of specialized training to make him the first official dog narcotic detective in America. He had been taught to pick out two contraband items—opium and marijuana. In practice he had done well. We took him out for a test run, in a section of the city where we knew there was considerable opium smoking. There was no actual case or tip to follow up; it was just a general look-see through the district.

This "first night" performance started at eleven and went on until just before dawn. The men were weary, and so was the dog. They had meandered aimlessly over narrow, twisting streets throughout an entire night. They sat down at the entrance to a lodging house. The dog lay down on the rough-board flooring just inside the doorway. "Kip looked like he didn't have enough energy to get up for a week," the agents reported.

But Kip did get up the next instant. Some vagrant current of air had given the animal a scent. To the amazement of the thoroughly-bushed agents, Kip was suddenly like a new dog. Tail lifted, nose quivering, he sprang up the uncarpeted stairs of the lodging house.

On the second floor he led them to a tightly shut door. The agents tried it but the lock held fast. They threw themselves against it without success. Kip edged down the hall and halted before a bare spot on the wall. Examining it closely, the agents found it to be a sliding panel into an apartment. The dog had found it by scent; the men got it open and entered what looked like a series of linking apartments.

The place reeked with the odors of overcrowded quarters and Chinese cooking. Kip pulled ahead through crowded little rooms ignoring the protests of occupants. In the last room the dog vaulted across a bed and landed on a rubbish heap in a dark corner. His paws scratched at the pile and his teeth tugged at bits of old rags until he had pulled the pile of rubbish to bits—revealing nineteen pounds of opium, which we learned had been smuggled into New York from a Mediterranean port only a few days before.

Kip's performance was not only the best answer we could give to the laughter of the Customs men but it was also the signal to start a full-fledged dog service training program. Our trainers collected a corps of animals whose backgrounds indicated a history of high intelligence, courage, strength, and a love of hard work. Ribbons were no criteria. We picked animals from both top breeds and breeds considered "unlikely." We wanted performance.

Much of the job, we found, consisted in training certain traits *out* of the dog's background, his natural tastes and instincts: the ordinary smells that attract a dog, for instance. He could not be diverted by the scents of other dogs, of other animals—although some dogs will always chase a cat, no matter what you do—and he could not be interested in doing tricks, begging or other familiar canine routines. He became a detective and—as with the agents themselves—the job became his whole life.

One danger we discovered, in dogs undergoing training as well as in actual field work, was nervous exhaustion. The better trained the dog, the more he was like a temperamental movie star. He lived his part and was emotionally exhausted when it was over. Rest periods and vacations with plenty of sleep, play and relaxation were essential during school and after an actual case.

Kip, however, was always ready to go. One night, I received a tip from a port city on the Gulf. A passenger, sex un-stated, would be taking a suitcase of dope into a train at the El Paso station. I was told the name of the train and the hour of its scheduled arrival in El Paso. We flew out there with Kip and let him mix in with the large crowd around the gate.

Kip moved unconcernedly among the prospective travelers; you would never have suspected he was working. At last he snuggled up affectionately alongside a well-dressed young lady carrying a smart suitcase. The girl stopped to give him a pat. Kip made no move but stayed close.

The agents approached the girl, and identified themselves. "Would you please come with us," they asked quietly.

She looked surprised and started to protest. They warned her, "Don't make a scene. You know what it's about." There was nothing for her to do but go along—with her baggage.

It was packed solid—with twenty-one pounds of opium.

Most of the other dogs we trained for this work—in fact, most detective dogs—are satisfied if they discover one cache on an assignment. They want to call it a day's job. They sit back and wait to be praised. But Kip was never satisfied. Once he turned up a small quantity of narcotics hidden behind a bedroom mirror. While the agents were taking care of this first discovery, Kip sniffed around the next room and located another cache.

In one case a system of shipping marijuana was organized that looked foolproof to the traffickers. New York dealers mailed cash to jobbers in Mexico. The Mexican dealers shipped suitcases filled with dope back as "passenger luggage." The baggage checks were mailed to New York dealers.

The baggage was listed as going along with a passenger on the train but in fact there was no passenger. Customs, making their routine check of passengers at the border, do not examine such checked personal luggage carefully unless they have reason to suspect a passenger's declaration. With no passenger on board to make a declaration, the checked-through luggage simply rolled through unnoticed to the check room in New

York City, where baggage room officials—assuming the luggage had been cleared at the border—handed it to the New York dealers who walked up to the counter and presented the baggage checks mailed from Mexico.

Even after we knew how this check-through racket worked, the job of apprehending the culprits seemed to be walled around by almost unsurmountable legal, technical and physical obstacles and booby traps. We could not, certainly, open every piece of luggage in the baggage room. But there was one way of breeching these walls—Kip. Like a housewife going about her supermarket shopping, Kip went through the endless reaches of the baggage room, picking out piece after piece of luggage.

All we had to do was wait for the characters to show up with baggage stubs for those pieces of luggage.

We once learned that a member of a foreign mission coming to the United States was bringing a heavy shipment of opium with him in his diplomatically immune luggage. He had already made arrangements for the sale of this opium. The situation was delicate. We could not offend the mission or violate diplomatic courtesy. Yet I had no intention of allowing the diplomat to waltz into our country with his suitcase filled with illegal narcotics. All our top Treasury officials agreed. The Secretary himself told me: "I'll be damned if we let anybody, whatever his diplomatic standing, get away with a thing like this. You stop him."

I worked out a plan which I explained to the highest officials of the Treasury, Customs and the State Department. "When the plane lands with this mission," I declared, "members of the delegation will be invited to the Army and Navy Club for luncheon, leaving their baggage behind them. While they eat, Kip can be busy at the airport, and, if he finds anything, we'll report this to the head of the delegation and request—firmly—that the man be sent home, to avoid open trouble." Kip was eight years old by then and not as agile as he once was, but he was flown in for this important assignment.

At the airport Kip collapsed. We called in the two best veterinarians in Washington. They told us Kip was through with active service. He had about a week to live, they said. We had other dogs but none who could perform well enough for this tough assignment. State, when they heard the news, tried a little persuasion by direct negotiation with the foreign nation, just before take-off time, and the would-be diplomatic smuggler found himself suddenly left home.

But by then we were struggling to keep Kip alive. It was no use.

Many dogs in the Bureau since then have carried on Kip's work with efficiency and results—but none have matched Kip in dedication, courage, or performance.

Treasury rules forbid us to memorialize an agent, secret or semi-secret. So Kip lies in an unmarked grave. But there are agents who insist he was worth five armed men in any trackdown of hidden dope. Kip couldn't miss.

12. A Game at Monte Carlo

We have molded unique and extraordinarily successful methods of investigation in the Bureau, and built an unparalleled agent corps of the highest dedication and courage—backed up in their field operations by the painstaking detail and exactitude of our laboratory. But we still have the occasional slip-up, the miscalculation or plain bad luck that is the inescapable burden of every law enforcement agency.

The case in Monte Carlo was certainly one such affair. It provides an example of what can happen, no matter how carefully the Bureau may set the stage. I cannot deny that there were red faces from Rome and Paris to New York and Washington when the case broke in the newspapers. Yet the story did have its lighter aspects. And even its ultimate victory.

It all began in the summer of 1956, when Charles Siragusa received a report from our Nice area: A gang of well-dressed hoodlums were operating in that district, dealing in dope, specifically cocaine and heroin.

Siragusa sent me word from Rome about this case. We agreed that it should be pressed at once with all urgency. An agent was sent into the district, posing as an American dealer, ostensibly seeking to buy a wholesale shipment of heroin. The agent made a "connection" with the gang through a series of seemingly casual meetings in Monte Carlo. He learned that the individuals involved were chiefly French Corsicans. They spoke French, Corsican—"atrocious French" as the agents described it to Siragusa—and faulty, argot-Italian.

In the soft-lighted splendor of a Monte Carlo restaurant, our agent dined with Roger Olivié, alias Olivier, the leader of the bizarre Riviera mob that blended smuggling with the best wine, women, and high-speed motor cars, amid the sea-swept glamor of the Côte d'Azur.

Olivié, who was actually wanted in a cigarette smuggling case in France and was listed as a fugitive, seemed to know everyone in this swank restaurant. How he met them, under what guise, is hard to say. "There is the Countess—you must meet her," he would tell our agent in perfectly good French. "Come along. *Venez, mon vieux*."

Or the young duke at the bar. Or some luscious American heiress on her fourth Riviera honeymoon. Roger seemed to know them all. "Darling, I want you to meet my friend. Andy's an American, but it isn't his fault."

But alone at a table, they negotiated. The agent, in the role of a dealer looking for a big score in dope, explained that he understood that Olivié might be able to sell him some H. Olivié sipped wine and hedged as he tested out this curious customer. "My friends are cautious about even talking this way," he told the American.

"What do they have to be afraid of?"

"American agents, Andy. Or Interpol. You never know."

"But that is fantastic."

"If you like the sample how much will you want?"

"A lot. Six kilos. Over six and a half."

"I think my friends might be interested."

"The price should be good and the quality the best," the agent said.

Olivié shrugged with a gesture of Gallic impatience.

He and his Corsican friends negotiated with the agent for days. Olivié brought associates from Marseilles into these negotiations. Meetings were held in the Monte Carlo district, in the shadow of million-dollar yachts and in the best hotels of Cannes and Nice.

Siragusa was in touch at all times with the developments; so was the Bureau in Washington. There was a full flow of reports on all meetings, preparations and arrangements. The backgrounds, correct names and aliases of the individuals with whom we dealt were compiled for us through the cooperation of the French Sûreté. All involved had records for felonies, primarily for the smuggling of cigarettes and dope.

The negotiations involved six and a half kilos—approximately fourteen pounds—of pure heroin. The price at the wholesale level was to be approximately $18,000, nearly six million francs in French currency of the time.

Our operative—playing the dope dealer role, always distrustful, always haggling for a dollar, always worried for his skin, insisted he would have to test the heroin. He had to have the sample to test. His Corsican suppliers assured him they understood. This was proper. But when he wanted delivery to Italy, not France, because he did not want to take the product across the border to Italy himself, Olivié's two Corsican associates balked completely. It was finally agreed that delivery would take place in France somewhere on the Côte d'Azur in the Monaco district, or possibly Nice.

On the matter of payments, they wanted to know if the American had the actual cash with him.

"I have it safely put away," was his answer.

"In American dollars?"

"Of course."

"It will have to be in French currency," they reminded him. "We cannot make exchanges, besides, it might be counterfeit, and here in France we would have no way of checking quickly."

"If you want it in French francs, that is the way it will be."

"But we will have to see it first," the largest of the Corsicans said. He was a good-looking young man named Pierre. "We will not deliver until we see the money in cash."

Throughout the negotiations, there was an undercurrent of concern on the part of Olivié and the two Corsicans that possibly they were dealing with an agent of Interpol or the

United States. When such hints arose our man ridiculed the idea as preposterous, and the others seemed to accept this.

As the moment for delivery of the dope and payment neared a climax, District Supervisor Siragusa and the agent held a number of conferences. The scene of exchange was to be a hotel room in Nice. The French Sûreté was brought actively into the picture, as well as the police of Nice, Cannes, and Monaco, who were working with us. Plans were completed and detailed. Rarely had a stage been more carefully set. On this the agent's report states:

"Reservations had been made to have two adjoining rooms available. Consequently, I checked into Room 333, District Supervisor Siragusa checked in adjoining Room 334. These rooms were connected by a door. Commissaire Hughes obtained Room 336 which was across the corridor from Room 334. . . ."

"In the late afternoon of October 6, 1956, we concealed a microphone within the folds of a drape in my room (333) with a wire leading beneath the wall-to-wall broadloom carpeting to Room 334. This was totally invisible within Room 333. The wire led ultimately to a tape recorder in the bathroom in Room 334. . . ."

Room 333 was to be the setting for the showing of the "flash" roll of 5,850,000 francs by the agent, the delivery of the heroin and the arrest of Olivié and his two associates.

Our precautions were elaborate. Every word could be heard in the next room, and would be recorded. Police officers were waiting across the hall. And in the room next door, the man whom the suspects were dealing with was our own agent. French authorities, moreover, had the entire hotel under surveillance. Every door was watched, everyone connected with the operation would be under scrutiny at all times.

Olivié kept his meeting with our undercover agent and insisted on seeing the money. "The merchandise is only a short distance away," he said, "But first I have to see the money."

Our agent took him to Room 333 as planned. The money

was there in six packets—five containing a million francs each, the other contained 850,000 francs. From the start of this interview, however, Olivié was apparently prepared to argue every point, to delay. Sometimes he spoke in Corsican, sometimes in French.

As soon as they were safely in the hotel room, the agent handed Olivié the six packets of francs and asked him to count them.

"We will count it afterwards," Olivié answered.

"Afterwards?"

"It will take two hours."

"Not two hours," the agent said. "For that much money it won't take ten minutes."

"But there's so much of it and I don't know, I really don't know. . . ." Olivié's nervousness and delaying antics were obvious throughout this stage of the transaction. Neither the agent in the room, nor the others listening in the next room, knew what it implied. Olivié did finally make a cursory count of the money and found the bills all genuine and correct.

Then they argued about how to make final delivery. Andy refused to take the money anywhere or to leave it unguarded in the room. In either case it could be hijacked, he pointed out. But Olivié said the other two men would not bring the merchandise to the room until they had seen the money.

The agent and Olivié finally went out of the room together with the agent carrying the packets of money which they left in the hotel safe. They were under surveillance by French police all the time. Outside, they met with the other two men, Pierre and Jean, and drove in a car along the French Riviera, arguing over how to make an exchange of the French francs and Corsican heroin.

Pierre and Jean would not agree to make delivery until one of them had seen the money. Unless the delivery was made, of course, there could be no case against these men.

"But Roger here has seen the money," the agent protested. "He is one of you. You can believe him."

"No. We must see it ourselves."

The agent did not like the situation; the danger was that he would be trapped in the hotel room with more than one of them, so that, should they try a holdup, while he was engaged with one, the other could escape with the cash.

In all such undercover cases, the money used for the "flash roll" that we show to the criminals has to be returned. In this case, the funds were put up by the French officials as a courtesy to Siragusa and us.

Faced with the determination of the criminals, that the others had to see the actual money before delivery of the heroin, the agent suggested that one of them come with him to the hotel room.

"I will get the money, take it to the hotel room and show it to the one who comes with me. But I shall not deliver the money until the heroin is delivered and tested."

To this they agreed. Back through the night they drove to the hotel in Nice. The agent and Jean went in. With police watching all the way, the money was removed from the safe, handed to the agent, who then went with Jean up to the hotel room.

The conversation recorded at that time made no sense to the listening officers in the next room. The suspect began jabbering a mixture of French, Italian and Corsican. The sounds coming in over the recorder were confusing. For anyone outside the room, listening, it was impossible to tell what was happening. The agent himself could not follow the Corsican. Then there was a knock at the door and the agent demanded to know who it was. Olivié called out, "Let me in—I have the merchandise with me."

"I opened the door," the agent reported, "and Olivié entered carrying a brown leather bag. As he came into the room, I locked the door. Olivié said he had brought the merchandise. He laid it on the bed and I withdrew a marquis reagent from my pocket, indicating in five minutes I would test samples from a few packages. While I was opening the bag Jean said it was not the merchandise, that it was a maneuver to ascertain if I were a policeman and now he was satisfied I was not. Jean then said, while I was protesting this action, to remain quiet and that he would go downstairs and get the merchandise. While I was protesting with Jean, there was a quick knock at the door and Olivié, as if he was expecting it, quickly unbolted the door, opened it, and admitted Pierre. . . ."

As the agent began to protest about the three-in-one play, the third man pulled out a long pistol from under his coat and indicated wordlessly that he wanted the agent to lift his hands and back against the wall.

It was suddenly apparent to the agent that they had planned the whole deal to steal the money and may very well have known from the start—or suspected—with whom they were dealing. This was to be the play of the year—stealing 5,850,-000 francs from the police of France, and some top agents of the United States.

They must also have known—or suspected—that the police were listening close by. Translation of the recorded tape of the meeting reveals the obviously deliberate confusion of the last few minutes before the holdup and the "stroll out" with the money:

AGENT: I have already been tricked. No. Listen——
OLIVIÉ: I say, look, I guarantee for the two of them——
VOICE: We are through, through——
VOICE: Because if they catch us together, we will take the money——
VOICE: We don't want to take your money——
VOICE: Go on, get in front of the wall. Go on, hop——
AGENT: What is this story——
VOICE: Tell him to come back in——
AGENT: Don't shoot!
VOICE: I'm going to shoot. Don't move, eh?
AGENT: No, that thing——

VOICE: I've been gypped——
AGENT: But, listen, that money——
OLIVIÉ: Come over here with me, come——
VOICE: You go first——
VOICE: I can't do anything——
VOICE: You are leaving——
VOICE: I cannot——
　　　　(Door noises)
　　　　(Several knocks on door)

They spoke in Corsican, or else jabbered incoherently. Under this barrage of Corsican incoherence, with none of the authorities quite sure what was happening, they grabbed up the packets of nearly 6,000,000 francs and walked out of the room—and out of the hotel—under the eyes of several dozen French plainclothes men who knew precisely who the men were but thought this was part of the game.

One instant later the undercover agent was pounding on the door of the next room. French officials across the hall bounded in. Our undercover man tried to explain what had happened, gendarmes on the lower floors blew whistles and police sirens broke the quiet of the Riviera night.

Meanwhile, somewhere along the Riviera a car was making a getaway with six million French francs, which had been provided to us by French authorities for use strictly on a loan basis.

All authorities were put on the alert for the two Corsicans who fled in the car. Olivié, who knew that the agent had his real name and background, did not flee but waited helplessly in the lobby, as if in panic, then telephoned the agent's room. He seemingly did not know at that point that this was an American operative. He said he had not expected this to happen and he was sorry. The agent had Olivié come back to the room to discuss recovering the money. When Olivié walked in he was held for the French police. One day later, the other two men, traced by their car, were picked up in Nice by

French police. Nearly half of the money was recovered. The United States later offered to replace the balance, but the French graciously declined to accept it. It made a great story in the newspapers. The Riviera and indeed all France rocked with the story of the double-cross of the criminals who took the police.

PART FOUR

SCOPE OF EVIL

SURVEY

The scope of evil reaches from the darkest corners to the glittering pinnacles. It is erroneous to think of narcotics criminality as confined to any level, geographical or racial, national or economic. The evil itself—the misuse of drugs—becomes an unseen chain linking together strangers separated by thousands of miles, by time, age, class, background, creed or color. Dealers and users, vendors and wholesalers, growers and manufacturers, couriers and tenement-laboratory chemists—all become part of the international phantasmagoria.

13. Locale: Anywhere

Let me quote from a report taken out of our Washington files on a case in St. Paul, Minnesota. It concerns a certain Wong Chung Sing, alias John Wong, and others whom our St. Paul Supervisor, A. M. Bangs, with Agent Joseph Winberg, had investigated as addicts and suspected dealers.

The investigation, in progress for some weeks, had reached the point where Supervisor Bangs and Agent Winberg went to Wong's apartment and informed the Chinese that he was under arrest. Wong accepted this with seeming resignation and agreed to show the agent where he had opium hidden in the apartment. He started toward a closet door. What followed was reported by Agent Winberg:

"Wong opened the closet door and in a kneeling position, half inside the closet, produced Exhibit 16, and handed it to Supervisor Bangs. Mr. Bangs unscrewed the top of the jar and smelled the contents. It was smoking opium. Mr. Bangs said to Wong, who was still inside the closet, 'This is not all the opium you have; we will have to search the closet.' With these words, Wong produced a revolver and exclaimed, 'Don't move; I've got you now.' Agent Winberg lunged at Wong and was shot in the chest, falling to the floor. Supervisor Bangs grappled with Wong and the two fell inside the closet. Several shots were fired by Wong, at least one of which also struck Supervisor Bangs in the chest.

"In a few minutes Agent Winberg regained his composure and got to his feet. He found that Supervisor Bangs was on top of Wong in the clothes closet and at that time, as he was pulling Bangs, who was then injured, out of the closet, Mr. Bangs drew his revolver and fired at Wong. Both the officers were seriously wounded, but Wong, although shot himself several times, was still firing a pistol. The two officers crawled to the doorway to get out of the apartment and Mr. Bangs was struck again with a bullet in the spine near the waist. After getting into the hallway Mr. Bangs turned left and Agent Winberg turned right and Supervisor Bangs fell dead about twenty-five feet from the doorway. . . ."

In spite of his wounds, Winberg crawled to the third floor where he had a tenant notify the police. From the tenement stairs Winberg prevented any of the suspects from leaving, pending arrival of local authorities. Four men were arrested including John Wong, the alleged killer, who was unconscious with five bullets in his body.

Winberg was taken to the hospital. So was Wong, who was placed under police guard. Both men recovered. Winberg was the main witness against Wong in the trial. Wong was found guilty of what the jury in a bizarre verdict said was only second degree murder. The court gave him life.

A suit was later filed against Bangs's widow on behalf of the incarcerated Wong for $70,000 damages, claiming that Bangs had had no search warrant. The suit was thrown out of court.

The constant potential outbreak of violence with its payoff in a currency of life and death—as in the Bangs affair—is always the unknown factor in every investigation.

Illegal narcotics are by nature international, grown in one nation, shipped to another country to be manufactured, then transshipped still elsewhere to be sold. There are growing nations and manufacturing nations and "target" or victim nations where the stuff is sold finally. The United States has always been in the latter category.

This is why so much of my job and the Bureau's work has

been concerned with, or carried on, at the international level—either in association with authorities of other nations or with the international police agency called Interpol. Only by drying up the illicit product at its source or close to the source can we seriously curtail the number of shipments intended for America.

The scope ranges wide, from the deserts of the Middle East to the tenements of St. Paul, Minnesota. The professionals are businesslike, orderly, with no loose ends. They deal in dope for money and will not allow an addict to be part of the combine, because they cannot trust him. But there is also the case that does not involve the professional criminals, except as an incidental adjunct. Amateur criminals play an important part in the scope of evil with which the Bureau has to deal.

When a case is "made" against an individual or mob, no one can predict where it may lead. Some cases may have international implications. Others fizzle out completely. Others lead into social realms not usually associated with drugs or crime. In such cases it is rare for customer or seller to come voluntarily to authorities. In Narcotics neither is eager to turn the other in.

Sometimes the outsider does step in—a friend or parent of some girl who has been "hooked" or of some youth who is riding for ruin on a heroin roller-coaster.

One serious case was brought to us by a doctor. He insisted he could talk with no one but me personally. In my office he told me that two of the most famous socialites in the nation—whose names were headline news—were using morphine. "I am not talking from gossip," the doctor said. "They asked me to prescribe morphine for them. I told them I wouldn't do it. They offered me a sum of money in the thousands. I told them if they wanted to go to hell they would have to make it on their own."

On the strength of the statements of the physician, I ordered an investigation of this pair. The wife was one of the wealthiest women in the world. She had been married four times. Her fourth husband, who was also addicted, was a Navy Academy graduate who held the rank of commander and was co-author of 32 books, some of them best sellers.

For many years this millionairess had been buying her drugs with no difficulty through so-called ethical and reputable doctors who charged her massive fees for the services—as much as fifty times more than what she would have paid syndicate pushers for the same amounts. But drugs were only one of her indulgences; sex orgies were another. In one of the finest Rome hotels, while her husband was vacationing in the Alps, this woman and a dozen men staged a naked sex binge, with incredible and unspeakable scenes in the hotel corridors. Similar parties were held in other spas and hotels in both Europe and America. Drugs or no drugs, the extent of her sexual aberrations appeared to know no bounds.

We learned also how she had turned her latest husband into an addict. In Yugoslavia he had suffered from an attack of asthma and she gave him morphine to ease the pain. Morphine is the very worst medicine one can give for asthma; it dries up the secretions, freezes the phlegm and may cause the patient to strangle to death. Why he did not die is hard to say, for she continued to give him morphine when his pain persisted. He not only survived; he was launched on the road to addiction.

In quest of new excitements, she and her husband traveled almost constantly, either by private plane or railroad car, always with servants. To amass a supply of morphine for a trip they were planning, she made a connection with a New York City physician who introduced her to a supposed South American diplomat. For $12,500—in cash, in advance—the diplomat agreed to obtain drugs from his country. Once he had the cash, the "diplomat" vanished with the $12,500.

Rich as she was, she disliked being swindled this way. She hired a New York private detective. He failed to find the man or recover any of the money but he did—at her request—purchase narcotics for her. The detective became her main source of supply and was making a tremendous profit out of this one customer when we moved into the picture.

The millionairess, her author-husband and the detective were all indicted on narcotics violations. The man and wife were convicted and given five years on probation. It would have been far wiser and more humane—in my opinion, and in the light of what happened—to have sentenced them to the Public Health Service hospital at Lexington, Kentucky.

After their trial ended and they were placed on probation, the wife hired a nurse to look out for her and help her fight her addiction. The nurse and the husband had an affair. The wife knew about this but did not appear to care.

In the course of this bizarre life, the husband told the nurse that he had been given $4,000,000 by his wife. Half-drunk, he promised the nurse that he would share everything with her on a fifty-fifty basis when the wife died. To prove he wasn't lying, he said he would write a document declaring that he would marry her as soon as his wife died. They did not think it would be too long. She was now existing in a narcotic stupor.

Later, at a time when the husband was sober, the nurse and he became involved in an argument when he attempted to retrieve the document. The pair battled, struggling with each other in an upstairs hall. The nurse, trying to pull loose, gave a wrench and shoved the husband head first down the stairs. He crashed to the landing and lay still, with a broken neck. He died several hours later in a hospital without regaining consciousness. The death was listed as accidental.

For the Bureau it marked finis for one fragment of trouble in the files, although the wife continued to live for some years in her multi-million limbo.

14. Tentacles

In the midst of one of our recurrent world crises, I received word that a flood of morphine apparently was being shipped to top government officials of the United States, including ambassadors and their wives stationed in sensitive overseas posts, diplomats, judges, senators and high-echelon consular aides.

Since, under the Harrison Act, all narcotic transactions must be reported, including details on the manufacture, importation and all the transactions of pharmacists and physicians, we were able to determine without too much difficulty the source of supply for this flood of drugs. The prescriptions, most of them filled through Washington drug stores, were written by one of the most famous physicians on the East Coast, with a clientele of eminent social, business and political leaders in Washington and in other parts of the country.

With this information before me, I realized that either the distinguished doctor was falsifying his records, or half the American diplomatic corps was addicted to morphine.

Among those on the list was an American ambassador who happened to be one of my close friends. He was at that time on duty in a foreign capital. In a letter to my friend, I informed him, "If you are using the narcotics our records indicate you are getting, then you are without question addicted. I can only urge you to return home at once and allow yourself to be given immediate withdrawal treatment."

Back came the ambassador's shocked reply: He had never ordered any such drugs, he never used drugs at all, he could not understand how his name got to be on any such list. He denied completely all of these allegations. I had our agents check on every diplomatic official said to have received these drugs; not a single one, according to their statements, had ordered or received any drugs or had ever used narcotics in such quantities.

I went to call on this physician personally, and was ushered into his inner office where he sat behind his desk. What could he do for me?

"You can answer a few questions about some of your prescriptions, Doctor."

The genial smile faded. For an instant he toyed with an ivory paper cutter on the desk. "I don't get your meaning," he finally said.

"Doctor, we have the full records regarding all the narcotic prescriptions you have been writing for members of the American diplomatic corps."

"I have a large diplomatic practice, as you must know. Some of them—"

"We have talked with all of these patients, doctor. They deny that they ordered drugs from you. They deny that they received any drugs through you. They deny using drugs at all."

He sat back in his chair. He said softly, with a look of unruffled resignation: "So?"

"Either they are all lying, or your prescriptions were written improperly as a way of having drugs delivered to you, probably for your own use."

"Why would I do that?" he countered, as if he enjoyed this verbal fencing. "As a physician I can get all the drugs I want from the pharmaceutical concerns."

"You know if you started using more than normal requirements, our records would show it and we'd make an immediate investigation. This other way—writing phony prescriptions for diplomats—you thought we would never dare to check on."

"You sound very sure of your case, Commissioner."

I brought out photostats of his prescriptions, scores of them, written in his own hand, all for people who denied any knowledge whatever of such prescriptions.

The physician studied them. At last he looked up. "Well, you are entirely right," he said calmly. "I ordered these drugs obstensibly for these patients but actually for my own use."

"How long have you been addicted?" I demanded.

"Oh—months. Years, I suppose. Several years."

He made this admission with a smile, and sought to shrug the whole thing off as of slight consequence. "Doctor," I said, "you are either going to the government hospital in Lexington for a cure or you are going to be indicted."

I had his license to disperse drugs canceled and we got him into the hospital at Lexington. Almost immediately I began to get the reaction. Calls came from important officials in permanent posts, as well as society matrons and wives of high government leaders. Never before had I been subjected to such a barrage. I was shown a list of his pending operations, all of them for wealthy society women—for such things as "removal of breast hair."

One senator tried to reach the doctor, not knowing that he was in Lexington, and was told by someone in the doctor's office that he was in England, attending one of the royal family. And the doctor remained in "England" until the Lexington said he was ready to leave.

The tentacles of addiction reach into many unsuspected areas, often far removed from the organized underworld or its activities. Part of our continuing job in the Bureau has been to keep an alert eye for outcroppings of trouble—and potential danger to the community—in spheres not associated with violence or the underworld. One addict we picked up—I will call him Dr. Howard—had a distinguished record and a lengthy practice in medicine. It was an incontrovertible fact, which our agents checked out carefully, that he had been on the staff of two hospitals in Michigan and one in Canada. All that Dr. Howard lacked was formal medical training. He had never had an hour of it. Everything he knew he had learned from observation and from reading medical texts. In spite of this, he had delivered babies, assisted at numerous operations, including leg amputations, performed autopsies and written innumerable prescriptions. On some of his hospital records he had claimed that he was a former flight surgeon in the Air Force, and had been with the Flying Tigers in Burma. (He was actually classified 4F in the draft.)

From his own statements—later verified—we learned that he had started out as a laboratory technician in a Detroit hospital, left after six weeks at the "suggestion" of a doctor who thought the technician was overstepping his role, and got a job in another hospital, posing as a third year medical student at the Washington University in St. Louis, Missouri. "They took me at my word and never checked up," he told us.

Unfortunately, during the early stages of his "career" he became addicted to the usage of drugs, both morphine and Dilaudid. He continued their use regularly as he shifted from hospital to hospital, always using the third year medical student story and getting away with it. In one hospital he not only assisted at surgery but also took care of all emergencies that came to the hospital at night. In Canada he presented himself as a graduate physician, was accepted and given a job in a hospital as a resident doctor, taking full charge of the most serious medical cases in the hospital, in many of which life or death hung in the balance. Officials in the Canadian hospital were shocked when they learned Howard was not a physician. "He came to us as a newly discharged lieutenant of the Army Medical Corps," they revealed. "He said he needed a little more general hospital work. He seemed to have a knowledge of medicine such as a graduate student without a great deal of practice would have."

"From the first," Howard told us, "when I had nothing but a fast line and a flight surgeon's uniform, it was all easy. You have no idea how easy. I am familiar with most medical terms. My qualifications were never questioned. I had a forged medical school certificate and none of the hospitals ever bothered to check up on me. I feel quite competent to handle most medical cases and I have discovered that there is a good deal of mumbo-jumbo in medical practice."

Howard came back to the States and continued his "practice" as a private physician. His deception might have gone on indefinitely had it not been for an alert druggist whose suspicions were aroused by the heavy load of narcotic prescriptions sent in by "Dr. Howard." The druggist notified us of his suspicions; we checked our records and discovered the "doctor" was not registered as required in order to dispense and prescribe narcotics.

Our agent located Howard and arrested him in the lobby of a hotel. He pleaded guilty to narcotics charges, was given two years in the penitentiary plus two years in a state prison for violating state laws concerning medicine. "And while you are in jail," the judge enjoined him, "don't try to pass yourself off as the prison doctor."

There is no single set way to deal with those trapped in the tentacles. I personally have dealt with many of the individual cases. Each has been different. I am not, for instance, a believer in what the doctors call "ambulatory treatment"—giving a patient withdrawal treatment in his office, with no check on what the patient may do, or how much he may use between visits. Yet in one or two exceptional cases, I have, unknown to the addict, employed this method.

The addict in one case was a Washington society woman. I had known her personally for some years. She was a beautiful, gracious lady. She had become so badly addicted to demerol that no doctor to whom she would go would prescribe for her; her demand was too great.

Word of her case came to me through some of her friends. Was there any way I could help? The woman, I learned, was ready to kill herself. She would not deal with pushers nor would she take a cure or go voluntarily to the hospital herself.

Moreover, if I made a case against her, it would destroy her completely—along with the unblemished reputation of one the nation's most honored families.

I agreed to try to help her, through a trusted physician to whom she appealed for drugs. She was not to know my role. I also learned that she was so afraid that pharmacists would try to cut the strength of her demerol, with sugar of milk or some other non-narcotic substance, that she insisted on receiving only unopened, sealed bottles of demerol from the druggist.

That complicated the business but I called in a pharmaceutical manufacturer who agreed to work with us. Each bottle of demerol, specially packaged and sealed, delivered in routine fashion from the drug store, on the prescription of the physician, contained less actual demerol than the previous bottle.

Within three months, without the woman realizing, she went from a large daily "ration" of demerol to none at all. What she was getting, in the bottles, was not demerol but sugar of milk.

One day this woman was leaving on a liner for Europe. Of course, she had to have her supply of bottles in her suitcase. I was present—as the guest of one of her friends—among those who came to say goodbye. I drew the woman to one side and told her, "You might as well know that I am aware of the whole story and all about it."

She looked at me in astonishment.

"I mean the demerol," I said. Then I added: "I have some news for you. You need never worry about those bottles any more. You are no longer addicted."

Her eyes were wide as she listened, amid the buzz of the crowd. "You mean that I'm cured? Right now? This moment?"

"You haven't had a narcotic at all for a month."

She broke into tears of joy. The others thought it was just the excitement of the farewells.

Ferreting out a new source of drugs, a new operation in the organized underworld, is our continuing job. The hoods try to utilize new groups and individuals we would not normally suspect of being tied into drugs. Early in June, 1960, our agents in the Near East reported to me that they were picking up tips about a major trafficker who was in a combine with Paris as the headquarters. The size of the shipments of morphine base was reported to run forty to sixty kilos. The courier, we were told, was a Spanish-speaking diplomat. He was allegedly using his diplomatic immunity to get the merchandise through Customs. Beyond the fact that he spoke Spanish, I had no further lead to his identity.

I ordered this information forwarded to the French Sûreté in Paris. They were interested also in this case, we heard, and were investigating. We received a report from Europe that the dealer was in Paris. "From there he will fly to New York," our informant said. While this trafficker was in New York one of my operatives picked up an additional item of information: The trafficker had made connections—by phone and then in person—with a man named M. Rosal. A checkup disclosed that M. Rosal was actually Muricio Rosal, ambassador from Guatamala to the government of Belgium.

Rosal and the trafficker—Adolphe Tarditi—flew back together from New York to Paris, on August 17, 1960. In September, Tarditi left Paris, met Rosal in Brussels, returned to Paris and flew from there back to New York City. We learned through sources in Paris, Rome and Brussels that Ambassador Rosal was to arrive in New York on October 2, 1960.

We knew where Tarditi was to stop in New York and we had devices in his room so that we could record anything said there. We also had a taxicab to which Tarditi was "guided" and which he rode into town—with four suitcases—without suspecting that his driver was a United States agent.

En route to the city from International Airport, Tarditi apparently changed his plans, telling the driver that he wished to go not to the Midtown hotel originally indicated but to one directly across the street. Our man—the driver-agent—realized the need for quick action. A second government car with additional agents was tailing the cab, managing to keep fairly close in spite of the heavy midafternoon traffic.

In the thick of this traffic, with Tarditi sitting in the rear seat, the agent-cabby was able to scratch on a piece of paper the shift in hotels. With a perfectly normal driving signal he tipped off the car behind. Then he dropped the piece of paper.

The government car tailing the cab pulled to one side of the crowded parkway, stopped long enough for an agent to retrieve the piece of paper and continued on. When they read the note they raced ahead, pulled in front of the taxi and indicated by braking and other action that they wanted the agent-driver to slow up. He knew what this meant: They wanted time to get a listening post set up in the new hotel. Then they sped ahead, weaving through the traffic heading into the city.

The cab took its time, to the annoyance of Tarditi in the back seat. The driver got himself caught in jams, wedged in behind cars that were turning off or stalled in traffic.

This ingenious piece of detective work, enabled the agents to follow the conversations held in the hotel rooms of Tarditi and Rosal. They were sure that Tarditi's suitcases held the "stuff." Indications were that Tarditi had a very large supply of heroin. The following day we listened to a conversation between these two men, held in Rosal's room in another hotel. This gave us all the information we wanted. They talked in French. Part of the translation of their conversation read:

TARDITI: You will take the suitcases.
ROSAL: Where to?
TARDITI: I will tell you. They are not going to pick them up here.
ROSAL: Oh no. Okay.
TARDITI: Because you knew the fellows. . . . (Not clear). You will go to the corner of 72nd Street and Lexington Avenue. There, there is a car.
ROSAL: Ah. . . .

TARDITI: So at twelve-thirty exactly. I will be standing next to the car.

ROSAL: Ah, good. . . .

TARDITI: You will stop the taxi. You will take the three suitcases, you will put them in that car. There is somebody that sees you, you do not look at him, he does not look at you.

ROSAL: Ah, good. Seventy-second and Lexington.

We had to close in while the evidence was still in their hands. At 12:30 on October 3, 1960, our agents were waiting at the corner of Lexington Avenue and 72nd Street when Tarditi arrived there with another suspect, a steward on an international airline. Ambassador Rosal arrived a moment later in his taxicab—with the suitcases. The agents moved in, identified themselves and put the men under arrest, thereby cutting off one main source of drugs supplying the Manhattan addict trade.

The mute evidence was there in the four suitcases. One contained $26,000 in United States bank notes. The other three were loaded with 100 pounds of heroin worth on the retail market approximately $20,000,000.

Even in such an open-and-shut instance as this, some of our critics took exception. In one of our newspapers the day following the arrests, I was astounded to read a column by a widely syndicated writer attacking us. Regarding this piece of police work which almost certainly prevented the addiction of many thousands of new child-customers in the New York area, the writer's comment was: "All the news stories I read neglected to mention one thing: That the United States is the only country in the world where the amount of heroin would bring that amount of money in, in fact, any sizable amount at all."

Apparently this columnist did not check simple facts as to the high prices of heroin on the retail level in Italy, France, Germany, Greece, Turkey, Egypt or a dozen more other countries. It is remarkable that he would add: "In Britain, where narcotics is treated [*sic*]—as it ought to be treated here —as a medical problem, heroin is legal . . . We have created a vast market for heroin here by making it illegal. . . ."

The truth is that the so-called "English system" has been completely misunderstood here by many who ought to know better. English law does not, of course, permit the promiscuous use of heroin by children or anyone else. Heroin is not sold openly in the stores.

Addiction does not arise from the "forbidden fruit" concept. Before drugs were illegal anywhere, there were millions of addicts in the Orient, the Near East, Turkey, Europe and America. The uncontrolled sale of narcotics has wrecked nations in the past and—if we went back to such a primordial concept—would wreck nations again, including very likely the United States.

Today the cost of drugs varies primarily with the nation and the economic scale of living as well as with the scarcity of the product. Heroin is expensive anywhere in the world, especially in Paris, Marseilles, Tangiers and other cities where demand is strong.

The truth also is that in America, and particularly in the Federal Narcotics Bureau, narcotic addiction is regarded and treated as a medical problem. Our Federal hospitals and other hospitals, the hundreds of doctors with whom we have worked, have devoted a prodigious amount of time, money and effort to the medical aspects of addiction. With all of these we cooperate closely and continuously. At the Federal hospital for addicts in Lexington, we are constantly conducting research programs and studies. In hospitals across the nation we lend our support to such programs; in America and countries abroad we have helped to establish clinics and to train staff officials in the humane and efficient techniques of withdrawal treatment, using a substitute drug such as methodone during the tapering-off period in place of the far more dangerous morphine and heroin.

I recall one case, however, in which I did not insist that the addicted individual be sent to Lexington or one of our other hospitals for treatment. This addict was one of the most influential members of the Congress of the United States. He headed one of the powerful committees of Congress. His decisions and statements helped to shape and direct the destiny of the United States and the free world.

I learned on incontrovertible evidence that this legislative leader was a confirmed morphine addict who would do nothing to help himself get rid of his addiction. It was a delicate moment in world affairs. The situation presented by the morphine-addicted lawmaker presented a precarious problem. There was imminent danger that the facts would become known and there was no doubt that they would be used to the fullest in the propaganda machines of our enemies. Such a scandal could do incalculable harm to the United States and the free world.

I was told by my informants that the congressman was completely intractable. "He refuses even to consider undergoing medical treatment. He says he wants nothing whatever to interfere with him or whatever habits he wishes to indulge."

I called on this lawmaker and told him that I knew exactly what the situation was. "You are an addict and you are using morphine in large quantities and you are presenting a grave threat to this country," I declared.

"Well, that's too bad, isn't it?" was his answer. "But I wouldn't try to do anything about it, Commissioner. It will be the worse for you."

"What do you mean by that?"

"Simply that if you try to stop my source, I will go directly to the pushers, if I have to. I will get morphine somehow, believe me. And if it winds up in a public scandal and that should hurt this country, I wouldn't care."

"You make yourself and your position very clear."

"The choice is yours," he said.

"You are in a position because of your power in this Congress to hurt America gravely," I said. "If you weren't I would throw the book at you. But I'm not going to let you hurt this country—no matter what it costs me."

"And just what can you do, Commissioner?"

"I want your pledge not to go to the pushers—if I see that you get what you need."

He shrugged. "Why not?" he said. "If you live up to your side, it's a good deal for me."

"I'll see that you get all the drugs you need. I can do this legally because of your age. But you are to get them through one store, and one only. You will go to this druggist whom I will designate for whatever you require."

"But my own physician will continue to write the prescriptions?"

"Since you've been with him, it will be all right."

"Then it's okay. I'll go along with your idea and your druggist. Just as long as the supplies are forthcoming I will keep my bargain not to go to the pushers."

I did not like the situation but I felt we had no other course open to us because of the national and international aspects of the problem. As the Congressman tested his supplies regularly for purity, any attempt at gradual reduction would have failed. No one beyond this addicted lawmaker and myself—and an obscure druggist on the outskirts of Washington—knew what was happening. A nationally syndicated columnist got hold of the story through a tipoff from the druggist, and called me to confirm the facts regarding the filing of prescriptions. I warned him that the Harrison Narcotic Act provided a two-year jail term for anyone revealing the narcotic records of a drug store. That ended that.

The lawmaker went on for some time, guaranteed his morphine because it was underwritten by the Bureau. On the day that he died I thanked God for relieving me of my burden.

15. A Girl Who Died

In the early autumn evening, the phone rings in an uptown apartment on Eighth Avenue in New York City. The apartment belongs to a young man I will call A.B. The man calling is named Billy, a Negro who has been associated with a ring of pushers and addicts in the district. Billy doesn't know that his pal A.B. is working for us. Billy is frightened. "Something is wrong," he tells A.B. "Get over to Benny's quick. Something's gone wrong."

Benny is the curbstone pusher in that section of town, and the pimp for a blonde eighteen-year-old addict. . . .

The most sickening—and terrifying—form of addiction in my experience, is that of the teen-agers, both girls and boys. They represent three percent of addicts. They are the primary targets of the pushers, the most easily seduced. Young, unsure, unhappy, maladjusted in many cases, terrified of being called "chicken" by their side alley friends, growing up in homes that are not homes with parents that are not parents and with discipline that is not discipline, they seek escape. Girl or boy, this is a familiar pattern—the dream-flooded highway to extinction.

The kids who get trapped are so sure that they have all the answers. They are so sure that they have judgment and wisdom. They are so sure that "that nice guy" is their friend, their pal, who wouldn't suck a guy or girl into anything really bad. "It's all right, boy, for God's sake don't listen to that drool how the stuff eats you up . . . that kind of jive is for the squares."

When A.B. walked into Benny's apartment, he saw the naked form of a white girl sprawled on the floor beside a cheap iron cot, her reddish-blonde hair disheveled and half covering her face. She lay motionless, apparently lifeless. Benny was bent over her, anxiously slapping her hands and her body, trying to revive her. A.B. told us later that Benny went to a bureau, got a pin and stuck it into the girl's heel but there was no reaction.

"I don't know what the hell happened to her," Benny told A.B. "She seemed all right."

"What do you mean—seemed all right?"

"She was working. Guys kept coming in. Every now and then—while the guy put on his pants—I'd give her a shot."

"How many did you give her, Benny?"

"Who knows how many?"

The girl had apparently been prostituting herself in the apartment all that afternoon with young hoodlums who came in through some of Benny's associates. Benny had been giving her shots of heroin and cocaine to keep her going. "She didn't even have time to put her robe on," Benny said. "It was one after the other." Finally, while waiting for the next customer, the naked girl had slipped unconscious to the floor.

Benny's efforts to bring her to proved useless. Finally, the pimp got a mirror and put it in front of the girl's mouth. No moisture. There was no breath. "She must have died. She must have cashed in," he cried. "We got to get rid of the stupid little tramp. I can't have any cops coming up here."

"You get rid of her, you mean," A.B. said. "I'm not getting mixed up in any business like that."

A.B. returned to his own apartment and talked the situation over with his wife. They decided to call the Bureau but not from the phone in their apartment. A.B. did not want to leave his wife alone in the apartment so the two went out together. The time was ten past midnight.

As they sauntered along the street past the house where Benny lived, they saw Benny and his assistant, a man called Jack, and another man whom A.B. also recognized, carrying a trunk out of the building. Unobserved in the shadows of the darkened street, the special employee and his wife were able to observe that the trunk was old, with a rounded top, and appeared to be heavy. With difficulty the men put the trunk into a small panel truck. Jack drove the truck up Eighth Avenue followed by Benny in his Buick car. The third man disappeared.

All these events A.B. reported to the Bureau. "I saw that girl in the neighborhood a number of times," he told our agent. "About 18 years old. Reddish bleached blonde hair. Came down in bangs over her forehead. About five feet two inches tall. There were plenty of hypo needle marks on her arms."

After hearing the details of his story, the agents decided that the surest way of closing in on Benny was through his assistant, Jack. A.B. was certain Jack would talk once he realized that narcotic charges could and would be placed against him. Jack could then corroborate and fill in A.B.'s evidence. At that time, we did not know the girl's real name or what they had done with her body.

The last was crucial; since we did not have the body they could deny any knowledge of a homicide and we would have no way of challenging their denial. We had to first involve them in a narcotics violation.

For several days following the episode A.B. tried to purchase narcotics from Benny or Jack—with our agents secretly observing—but all attempts failed. The two men, either suspicious of A.B. or aware that they were too hot to commit any overt act, told him they had temporarily suspended operations.

The fact that a white girl had been using the apartment had become known to a number of persons, including, of course, her "clients." When anyone asked what happened to the girl, Benny's answer was a casual, "Some small thing developed. We had to get her to the hospital, that's all. She's coming along okay."

"What was the trouble, Benny?"

"Who knows? Woman trouble, the doctor said. Happens all the time. Doctor said it was good we got her there in time."

The story, as reported to our investigators, sounded so plausible that the agents began to wonder if A.B. had not exaggerated his statements about the girl's condition. The agents decided to clarify the situation before making any homicide report to the New York City police. Meanwhile, Benny and his associate Jack dropped out of sight. A.B. reported that nobody in the neighborhood had seen them for two days.

Then stories appeared in the newspapers about the body of a young girl found in a trunk in Greenwich, Connecticut. Follow-up stories identified her as an eighteen-year-old who had come to New York from Minneapolis, Minnesota. We immediately turned over all facts of our narcotics investigation to New York homicide detectives, explaining our belief that the body found in Connecticut might be that of the girl allegedly carried out of Benny's apartment.

A day after this report, Benny was spotted on the street near his residence and picked up for questioning. He played ignorant. "I never heard of any girl like that. I never pimped for any blonde who died on me."

New York homicide detectives called our Bureau. They had one question: "You have a witness?"

We had. He was our special employee A.B.

The confrontation took place in the office of the New York County district attorney. With Benny standing dejectedly, our special employee described the entire scene in Benny's room that night. Benny listened in silence as A.B. related what he saw and what Benny said. A.B. mentioned the pin that Benny stuck in the heel of the girl. Benny shook his head in a bewildered way, then said finally, "Okay—it's true, but I didn't kill her. She just fell over to the floor dead. I didn't kill that girl; she just died."

He agreed, however, that her death was due to the overdosage of drugs he gave her and signed a paper to that effect. His statement of the facts corresponded in all essential details with that of special employee A.B.

Even with the homicide charge against him pending in the New York State courts, Benny went back to his narcotic activities. We picked him up and brought him to trial. Benny was convicted of violations of the state narcotic laws and sentenced to a state penitentiary for from five to ten years. Homicide charges, despite A.B.'s eye-witness story, could not be sustained. As Benny put it, he didn't kill her; she just died.

Wherever extensive teen-age addiction erupts, as it did in American communities in the years following World War II, we face an extraordinary enforcement problem. Many teenage girls are driven into prostitution to pay for their narcotics. This is standard procedure. The ruthlessness of this business is hard to believe. The boy goes into crime to pay for his habit; the girl sells herself. With the use of heroin, the sex urge is almost obliterated; a girl no longer has any feeling about it, neither desire nor restraint. The sex act becomes an avenue to the money she needs for heroin.

Our agents in New York City—the worst district for teenage addiction in America—picked up a girl named Peggy. She was nineteen. She came originally from Michigan to New York to follow up a number of theatrical offers, but none of them worked out. Meanwhile, she met a musician who became her boy friend. Soon he had her smoking marijuana. Then he introduced her to the habit of sniffing heroin—"snorting" is the word used by the addicts.

We arrested the saxophone-playing boy friend and also brought in the girl. Frightened, only half willing to admit to us or to herself what she had gotten into, she told us a story that eventually unfolded into a full-dress picture of teen-age addiction flourishing in the honky-tonk world of midtown Manhattan. On the basis of the evidence, we rounded up seventy-five persons, all under the age of twenty-one. Some of these teen agers had become thieves, pickpockets or street-walkers at ten, twelve, fifteen. Some told their stories in a few tight-lipped sentences, some with an outgushing of the slang of youth.

Under my direct orders, there began a mass exodus of such youngsters to Lexington. Literally hundreds of them went through the Lexington withdrawal treatment. Many were cured and enabled to begin a new and more hopeful life. During these investigations we developed a new technique in undercover work, making use of intended teen-age victims to bring in the school yard pushers. When the judges and juries began to get a picture of what was going on, they started to give the pushers not the suspended sentences but the heaviest penalties possible under revised laws.

As reports on investigations came in from other cities the tempo of our counter-attack on behalf of youth increased. I ordered all reports of teen-age addiction to come to my desk personally. I issued orders to our district supervisors across the country to halt all outside investigations in any city where teen-age addiction had become a problem, and to concentrate all our manpower on solving this problem, putting the pushers behind bars and getting young addicts into hospitals for treatment with the least possible red tape and loss of time.

Although in various sections local politicians were sounding off about the teen-age narcotics problem and issuing statements, often based on only hazy information, we continued our job with as little public fanfare as possible. I hoped to meet the situation without headline publicity; I wanted to protect our youth from the pushers and at the same time not glamorize the business in the eyes of the youngsters by sensationalized stories in the press.

The hospital of the United States Public Health Service at Lexington was bursting at the seams with teen agers. The figures give some idea of the change. In 1945, less than one patient in thirty at Lexington was under twenty-one years old. By 1955, approximately one patient in six was under twenty-one. We had predicted an outbreak of adolescent addiction after the Second World War and it had come, as it came also after the first war. In the latter case, however, it had ended quickly. The more recent outbreak was more widespread and prolonged and hit at different levels of the population. Most seriously involved were colored children, largely adolescents, of the poorer slum sections in overcrowded Northern cities, living in bad housing with almost unbelievably bad economic and social conditions. Ninety percent of the Negroes and Puerto Ricans are not users—but these groups have been under assault by the mobs.

In parts of Harlem, there are so-called foster mothers, each of whom take care of as many as twenty or thirty children, for which city or state authorities pay board and keep. Many of these youngsters wander the streets, day and night, unwatched and untrained and uncared for, to pick pockets or steal food or cars or join one of the sidewalk gangs. Such children are choice prospects for any wide-awake pusher. Indeed, some candy stores in the Puerto Rican section of East Harlem are purveyors of dope to the neighborhood children.

To cope with such crime-incubating conditions, I needed more men. The operational personnel of the Bureau was only 175 strong, a thin line of combat to spread across the nation. Congress gave us more men and doubled the penalties for those convicted of selling to persons under twenty-one. In addition, I called on the city police departments to lend us their help. Many departments organized narcotic squads as a result of my appeals. A number of these squads were organized under pressure from the American Legion and the General Federation of Women's Clubs.

Contrary to the theories of many social agencies, it is our experience that youngsters who become addicted often begin with other types of delinquency. A boy out of a miserable background seeks companionship with others. At ten, twelve, fourteen, he is meeting with a gang in some basement hideout. It is the embryo of the grown-up gang; these are the neophyte hoods, and hired killers and narcotic pushers of tomorrow. The boy runs errands for older gangsters; he becomes a runner in the numbers business, taking bet slips to pool headquarters and getting paid off in marijuana cigarettes. Some of the older boys are already using heroin. "Try a sniff of it; a sniff can't hurt you, for Chris's sake!" If he holds back, he's "chicken."

Sometimes it is more subtle. Older youths and girls are sucked into the vortex by men or women in their middle or late twenties. This is the age that appears glamorous to the youth of seventeen. What ever the older man or woman says must be right.

A twenty-eight-year-old man named Teddy operated a Bronx "shooting gallery"—slang term for a place where young addicts gather to smoke marijuana "reefers" or to sniff or take shots of heroin, cocaine, or a blend of the two known as "dynamite." Teddy followed the procedure for such places; all drugs had to be administered on the premises; no paraphernalia or packages of narcotics could be taken away. This avoided the danger that the drugs or contraband paraphernalia could be turned over to authorities and later used as evidence.

Teddy would invite a group of youths, most or all of them innocent of addiction or any other crime, to come to his well furnished apartment to listen to his record player. He served ice cream and cake. Gradually he would get them smoking a few marijuana cigarettes and from that to sniffing and then injecting heroin. At first he would furnish the heroin free. Then he would charge $1.50 a "cap"—slang for capsule. Most of them injected the heroin intravenously—this is what is "main lining"; the artery in the arm is the "main line." Teddy furnished the hypodermic needle and syringe.

The light-haired, effeminate Teddy had an additional wrinkle in his setup that made it different from most other "pads" and "shooting galleries." After the youngsters developed their "yen" for heroin—the first stage on the road to full addiction—and found themselves without funds, Teddy did not suggest that they go out and steal government checks or hold up grocery stores. "He gave us a shot or two," one explained, "and then when we wanted more and ran out of money, he would make us 'submit' to him."

"What do you mean by 'submit'?"

"He would make us commit an act of sodomy."

We sent an undercover agent into this setup to make a few purchases, to chat with some of the "clients" and to get the evidence required to send Teddy to the penitentiary. For this agent, of course, we had invented the proper background and recommendations needed to get in. When he arrived, he observed in the living room of the apartment about ten young persons who were under the influence of narcotics. Accepting the agent as a client, Teddy took him into the bedroom and asked how much stuff he wanted.

The agent said, "Give me four caps."

"Do you have the works with you?"

By "the works" he meant the needle, spoon, matches and water tumbler needed to dissolve the heroin for injection. The agent said, "No. I have them downtown."

Because he was so highly recommended and because he insisted that he could not stay but had to get downtown "to avoid suspicion," Teddy allowed him to leave with the four caps, which he handed to the agent from a container holding 20 to 30 capsules.

As soon as he left the apartment, the agent marked the capsules and turned them over to the Bureau as evidence.

He returned a few days later and made a second purchase, following which, our agents arrested Teddy at the apartment. At that time they seized 14 capsules of heroin and 24 marijuana cigarettes. Nine addicts ranging in age from sixteen to twenty—eight boys and one sixteen-year-old girl—were found in the apartment. Some of these were high school students. They were found in varying stages of narcotic stupor. All admitted in signed statements that they had taken narcotics in the apartment that night. Five of the youths admitted that they had taken their first shots of heroin right there in the apartment.

We also discovered that Teddy had been harboring two criminals who had stolen $7,500 worth of jewelry and furs from Westchester country homes. The men had vanished but the loot was recovered in Teddy's apartment.

Teddy was a degenerate who, although apparently not addicted himself, lured young people to his apartment solely for his profit and his perverted sexual practices. Yet he is not unique. There are a thousand of these sub-strata vermiforms crawling in the shadows of any major city.

Because of the laws which I urged upon Congress, this man in 1960 might have faced the death penalty for his corruption of young people who might otherwise have led normal lives.

But Teddy got away with a five-year-term.

As a result of our investigations, raids, arrests of pushers, and the help we were able to bring to literally hundreds of teen agers involved with narcotics many cures were effected in local, state and, most of all, in our federal hospitals. Only a moderate percentage of those cured returned to the hospital for a second time. We know that some who were "cured" did return to drugs and did not get back into the hospital. But the percentage of these is below the average return in such cases.

In some cities, as our agents and local authorities cooperated in the crackdown, teen-age addiction began to wane, and in some of them virtually disappeared. The two most difficult spots were New York City and Los Angeles. Runner-ups included Detroit and Chicago. Because of the contiguous Mexican border, both Texas and California as states presented addiction problems.

In Ohio, Governor William O'Neill launched his own personal campaign against illegal drug usage, marshalling every available police agency in the state and joining with the federal agents to drive dope pushers out of business. He also pushed through a law setting the minimum sentence at twenty years. The result: an almost overnight vanishing act by the pushers, proving that tough laws and rigid enforcement are the main answers on the front lines of this problem.

Congress, in 1956, passed a bill that provided the death penalty for the sale of narcotics to teen agers, provided the jury in the individual case so recommended. They also passed a bill providing a minimum penalty of five years for any illegal sale of narcotics. We at the Bureau have been seeking such legislation for two decades.

In Baltimore, Seattle and in cities throughout the South, relentless investigation and rigid enforcement under these laws have brought the teen-age problem under control. In other cities, as soon as the states themselves enact stiff penalties paralleling and supporting federal laws, they will also begin to dry up the juvenile market in dope that has netted the syndicate such enormous profits—and cost the lives of so many of our children.

16. Stardust

When addictive evil touches Hollywood's hem—or lasso—the reaction is widespread. We have in our records dozens of cases where either a motion picture star flouts addiction or word about it leaks out. It is almost impossible to keep such matters secret indefinitely. And the star-worshiping adolescent demands to know, "Well, if they do it, why not me?"

The evil of Hollywood addiction is a record of the harm that the few do to the many. The number of actors and actresses who fall into the narcotic quagmire is low, but the harm those few do cannot be measured by any normal survey techniques. The effect—and responsibility—of the individual performer is great.

A cowboy hero of the cinematic badlands was picked up for smoking reefers, along with a beautiful actress, also smoking marijuana. All over the country and the world the story was flashed on the wire services and appeared in the headlines. "I'm washed up," the star told the press. "This is the finish." But he was wrong; it was only the beginning. The publicity about the raids apparently made him better box office than before.

Of those stars who are addicted, I must admit—without in any way condoning their own weakness—that some are swept into it by almost unendurable pressures put upon them by the bevy of leeches who, without the public's awareness, often succeed in taking over a star.

I conducted a running battle for months with a famous producer in an effort to save one of our loveliest screen stars. She was in the hands of an unethical doctor who had been in trouble with the authorities on several occasions. Among the cognoscenti in Hollywood he was known as "The Croaker." He had this star on drugs and stimulants almost every hour of her waking life.

She started at six a.m. with amphetemines to get her pretty eyes open so that she could be down at the studio by seven-thirty to begin rehearsing. She would take minor stimulants during the day, but by two p.m. neither her body nor her voice had the strength called for to perform as the director required for his shooting script. The physician would take care of her with a "bang" in the arm, employing a strong narcotic drug. At the close of the day she required phenobarbital to steady her nerves. Then in the evening—because of publicity demands—she had to be seen at various restaurants and night clubs. By the end of her long day her nerves were in such a state that she could sleep only by taking an enormous dose of paraldehyde.

This was her life—the life her loyal, envious public did not guess. I knew what was going on; we had done everything we could to get evidence strong enough to take action against the physician. This was not easy. It was his case; he was handling it as a doctor and as he thought best for his patient.

I knew she was a fine actress. I believed her to be a fine woman caught in a situation that could only destroy her. Inevitably, she collapsed on the set, and the incident was front page news.

Because I knew the story I took action personally, even though we had no legal evidence against the physician. I made a trip to New York and called on the head of the studio for which this actress worked. I told him that the first step in salvaging his star and possibly even saving her life would be to send her to a sanitarium for at least a year. The executive stated that any such course was "simply unthinkable."

"I've got fourteen million dollars invested in her," he said.

"I couldn't afford your plan. She's at the top of her box office right this minute."

"Suppose," I asked, "she takes her life, as she has already tried to several times? Or merely makes a mistake and swallows a few too many of her pills. What happens to your fourteen million?"

"We'll have to take that chance."

"There's one other factor," I said. "In her condition she may blow her top at any time. If she does—there goes your picture and your millions."

That, in fact, is exactly what happened. In a state of almost complete uncontrol, she walked out on her next film as it was in the process of being photographed. Another star had to be brought in and the entire film remade.

I recall a question the producer tossed at me during one of our talks about this star: "Why don't you go after the big peddlers," he demanded, "and let my stars alone?"

"There's no narcotic problem too big or too small, if it affects the public attitude and safety," I told him. And I pleaded with him: "Get her out of the hands of that doctor and under the care of a reliable physician. If you do, you may save her life."

I will never forget his answer: "You can't dictate to these big stars," he said. "They're too emotional and temperamental. Besides, she can use any doctor she damn feels like. Telling her what doctor to use is not in her contract and we couldn't get a clause like that even if we wanted to."

I could see he was serious and his attitude left me speechless. Finally I said, "I've given you every opportunity to cooperate with us, entirely apart from technical procedures and contracts. Now I'll take whatever action we consider called for. It would be inhuman to stand by in a pathetic case like this."

I walked out. He may have thought I was bluffing. I was not.

In the vernacular of the Bureau, we put enough "arm" on that star's physician—letting him know the perilous situation he was likely to be in if he persisted in destroying the woman

—to pry her loose from his control. Eventually the star accepted our advice and secured a good physician who worked closely with her and at the same time kept us informed of the progress of the case. He did not have an easy time with the lady. Her addictions were many and deeply entrenched, but eventually he was able to report to me, "She's out of it—she's on her way back." Ultimately she returned to starring roles.

More than once she has gone out of her way to let me know personally of her gratitude.

There are cases where the addiction of the star has continued for years without the public knowing or guessing. One of the most startling and tragic of these was that of a sword-flashing hero who played the role of a pirate—a gallant adventurer—always battling against impossible odds and always emerging triumphant.

In real life he lost not to a sword but to a needle.

Reports of incidents involving this performer began to reach me from diverse sources. My British associates wrote me: "England is anxious to get this fellow out of here as quickly and quietly as possible. He's besieging British physicians for shots of cocaine, citing as a medical reason his need to overcome an inferiority complex." Fortunately, he left England of his own volition. Later I had a report from Rome. Authorities there were asking the star to get out because of the pressure he was putting on some of Rome's most distinguished doctors.

After he was back in America we had a report from St. Louis: The star had appealed to a physician there for a cocaine prescription for inoperable hemorrhoids. The doctor did not agree that they were inoperable and after some discussion called in an agent from our St. Louis bureau. The agent wanted to know why the star's own physician in Hollywood had not given him such a prescription if it was required. The star said that he did have one but some teen agers broke into his hotel room, took his underclothing and some loose papers including the prescription.

Questioned on other information which we had obtained from sources of complete reliability, the actor refused to admit that he used a cocaine solution in a nasal spray solely for "kicks," or that he used it, as we had also learned, in an unprintable sex ritual.

When Fidel Castro's insurgents took over Cuba, this movie hero showed up in Havana and held a press conference. He was wearing a frayed combat outfit that looked like something he might wear in a movie, and his face was made up with proper smears of dirt plus a beard. His clothes were torn in places and there was a bandage on one knee. His press conference was held in a Havana luxury hotel, and his story was that he had just come through the campaign, side by side with the victorious revolutionaries. He had held an almost identical conference before in a hotel in Madrid just after fighting during the Spanish civil war had ended in that city. Again he claimed he had been fighting side by side with the insurgents in the field.

One day there came to my office a Hollywood producer who had a "proposition." He had refused to discuss it on the phone or in a letter. He started off by informing me, "We both know this actor is badly addicted to drugs."

I didn't make any comment.

The producer said, "Well, I have a problem. I have the son of a bitch under contract. I've got him under an exchange contract. It cost me plenty but I don't want to go through with it."

"You want to break your contract with him?"

"Not exactly. But if I could get out of making that film, I could save myself—net—two hundred thousand."

"And how do I fit—how does the Bureau fit—into your special problem?"

"If you'd throw a narcotics charge at him, I could break his contract—like that."

Hounding this actor a little faster into his grave was not part of my plan. I told the producer to get out.

Not very long after that the news flashed over the wires that this great two-fisted symbol of adventure had died in his sleep. The world lost a good actor, the hangers-on an all-purpose meal ticket, and the pushers a tragic but well-paying customer.

Are actresses and actors, singers and musicians more likely to become addicts than other professional groups in the arts? The answer is—to some degree, yes. When successful, they make fabulous sums quickly, and therefore they become the target of the hoods, quick-money characters, grafters and pushers.

Billie Holliday was an example. The harpies were forever after this talented Negro singer. They not only put her on drugs but would not let her get off. Every time she tried, they dragged her back, and went on selling her drugs, at the highest prices. She paid $100 for a shot that would have cost the average addict $5 or $10. Despite her addiction, she reached and held a high place in the entertainment world. But only a few years after she reached her peak she was dead.

There are other cases—thank God!—of actresses and actors, singers and musicians and many others who seek cure in the techniques developed at Lexington. One famous musical comedy star who became a user of heroin wrote to me:

"I willed to stop my habit, but the claim that will power alone will do it is sheer fallacy. In 24 hours I would take as much as 40 grains of morphine, and 50 grains of cocaine, a dose which would kill 10 normal people, but which was merely an ordinary day's supply for me.

"The taboo associated with drug addiction made it almost impossible for me to find a place where I could be effectively and conclusively cured.

"My final and successful cure was instituted in Lexington, Kentucky. It can't be glossed over with ease for it was an agonizing period. However, in retrospect, with a vivid picture of all the horror to which I submitted, I can honestly say that every moment of torture that I spent was worth the splendid result . . . for I achieved the final cure and with it my dream of being able to help in a crusade to do away with the evil of addiction. . . ."

The Hollywood situation would be bleaker without the job done by one of the Bureau's long-time friends, Kenneth Clark, vice president of the association charged with keeping an eye on the film industry's moral levels. In this spot Clark gets an inside line on what goes on in the picture business. Some of his tips to us as to what mobs are trying to move in on which studios—or stars—have enabled us to save the studios embarrassment—and certain famous stars their careers, even their lives.

17. Western Story

Evil is of one cloth, I find, whether in Shanghai or Istanbul, the Middle Eastern deserts or the western plains. To me the change is only in coloration. The hole-in-the-wall barrooms of East Harlem become the adobe dives of Laredo, Jiménez or Tiajuana; the night club circuits of Rome or Algiers become the chrome-plated gambling joints and fancy houses of Vegas, Reno, or Phoenix. Or Mexico City.

Some cases reflect less of the syndicate type and more of free-swinging bossism that takes over communities at the point of a gun, corrupts or destroys, and reigns as a kind of private czar. "Mr. Phoenix" was one of these bosses. The pose he assumed in the public eye was that of a wealthy rancher with a yen for the soil. "I love nature. I love the herd," he would tell his friends. "I belong to the prairie and the desert." That was the pose. But his business was dope and prostitution.

If anyone had looked into his background, they would have found a record of armed robbery and safe cracking, narcotic possession, pandering and pimping. He even took a couple of prostitutes out to Hawaii and started in business there, turning Hawaiian local talent to drug addiction and prostitution.

We had a full undercover dossier on Mr. Phoenix going way back. Behind the front this man was turning Phoenix into a strategic center for smuggling from Mexico, delivery to West Coast cities, to the East Coast and in Phoenix itself. I learned that the suspect also had a prostitution business in full swing in Phoenix and was even seen driving a ranch wagon loaded with new mattresses for his bawdy houses.

"Our friend from Phoenix," one of my agents reported to me, "has good reason to be interested in the stuff. He smokes opium himself."

"Maybe we can nail him on that," I suggested.

"We've got inside information. But no proof."

"If he smokes, the stuff has to be stashed in his home. Let's try a search warrant."

"And if we find the stuff?"

"Bring him in."

We found the dope. It was opium. Our laboratories tested it to be absolutely chemically certain. Our chemist went into court after Mr. Phoenix was put on trial, and testified under oath that this was opium.

Mr. Phoenix said it wasn't opium at all and he never smoked opium. It was laudanum, he claimed, and it was used only because sometimes he suffered from pains. It was medicinal.

There was no truth to this claim and no proof to back it up, but the jury believed it and acquitted the man. Dope operations, prostitution and assorted other racketeering under his control continued.

Later we made a case against a nation-wide mail-order trafficker in narcotics, who admitted obtaining his supplies from Phoenix. The mail-order pusher pleaded guilty; the big shot from Phoenix was again acquitted. He remained the big shot and rode a fine white horse in civic parades down the main street of Phoenix.

In the northwest United States a man known as Hugo, with a long criminal record, was brought in on opium smoking charges. We knew that he was also a wholesale dealer in dope. He was one of those individual operators—a loner—who just might be useful to the Bureau.

I talked to Hugo and discovered that he was in a desperate plight. "I've got a family to support, Commissioner," he pleaded. "For God's sake, give me a break so I can take care of my family."

"What kind of break?"

"I'll turn the others in. Anybody you want, I'll turn in like that. All you got to do is promise to keep me out of jail and I'm your boy."

He began naming people he said he could implicate in the Los Angeles and San Francisco area. The names sounded impressive. I asked him, "Did you ever hear of Mr. Phoenix?"

"Sure."

"What about him, Hugo?"

"I don't like him. He's dangerous. I wouldn't take a chance on turning him in. You understand? I don't aim to commit suicide."

"He's the one I want, Hugo," I said.

Silence. Hugo was doing some long thinking. I said, "I don't care about the others right this minute. It's either Mr. Phoenix or the penitentiary, Hugo."

"I got to think it over."

"Take your time."

A few days later, Hugo called me back and agreed to help us make a case against Mr. Phoenix. Hugo said he had dealt in the past with Mr. Phoenix through another dealer in Vancouver, known as Elmer. I sent in one of our agents who took the name of Jack V. Talbot, supposedly a Canadian citizen residing in the States, and an old friend of Hugo—but actually Agent Van Trell of our Bureau. With stories of prison terms and service in the French Foreign Legion and association with hoodlums in Canada, Europe, and the United States, the agent completely sold Elmer, who soon was talking openly about his associations with this big shot dealer in Phoenix.

Our undercover man in Vancouver induced Elmer to take him into the States to meet with Mr. Phoenix and arrange a deal. I instructed the agent long distance, "You've got to get Mr. Phoenix out of Arizona—he's got too much influence on the local politicians. Get him into California, make the case against him from there."

They met first in Arizona, at the ranch house, where, behind closed and locked doors, Mr. Phoenix not only agreed to sell opium to the agent at $250.00 for a small tin but also offered him some samples. Negotiations for the purchase of $12,500 worth of opium continued but finally Mr. Phoenix seemed to get suspicious; in any case he backed down. Eventually, they had to go back to Vancouver before Phoenix finally was satisfied by Elmer over the long distance phone, that Elmer's friends were to be trusted.

"You fellows come back here," Phoenix ordered.

Elmer hedged. "We got to meet down south. Near the border."

"Where?"

"El Centro."

"Your friends will be with you?" Phoenix asked.

"Sure."

A pause, then, "That suits me. The way I want to work it, that suits me fine."

They made the arrangements for the place and the hour, and I arranged to have a U.S. Customs agent cover whatever transactions were finally agreed upon.

The agent and our special employees waited a whole day in El Centro. Finally a phone call came in from Mexicali, Mexico. Mr. Phoenix was there with a Mexican partner, who allegedly grew opium. Our men proceeded to Mexicali and met Phoenix and his partner in a bar room.

The Arizona trafficker put it to the agent and Hugo: "I have twenty cans of opium in the United States ready for delivery. But you will have to pay me $5,000 first on the Mexican side."

This was a big sum of money and there was not an ounce of opium in sight. The agent called me to explain the sudden switch and asked my instructions. I had to decide whether to spend $5,000 on what could easily be a complete swindle. I told him to go ahead. "But if you don't get dope for this money," I added, "you can all take a slow boat to China."

The agent went back to Mexico with $5,000. When it was paid, Mr. Phoenix produced a Yale key and told the agent, "The merchandise is in Locker No. 5 in the Greyhound Bus Terminal in El Centro, California." The agent and Hugo proceeded to El Centro and found the opium in the locker, of the proper quality and amount. Phoenix called to make sure that the two men found the opium, and to tell them he would have further merchandise in perhaps five or six weeks.

I wanted to make a second purchase, one that in its entirety took place within the borders of the United States, but Mr. Phoenix hedged and delayed and finally told the undercover agent that his chief source had been taken for a ride in the desert. The killers had put two bullets in his head, cut off a finger to get a diamond ring and left a note pinned to the corpse: "You will not double cross any more."

I knew we could not get any more dope from our man but I kept the case open while we continued getting evidence against his associates. When we had all we wanted we went before a Federal Grand Jury in Los Angeles—hundreds of miles from the heart of his influence—and got a secret indictment against Mr. Phoenix, Elmer, and his Mexican source.

Meanwhile, Mr. Phoenix was involved in trouble in Arizona, where aroused citizens were insisting on action and the houses of prostitution were being padlocked. In the midst of this we arrested him. He was held in $100,000 bail for trial in San Diego. When he had a look at some of our evidence he pleaded guilty to one narcotic charge and drew ten years in jail. So convinced was he that the agent who made the case against him was a bona fide peddler that he called him a "dirty stool pigeon." When he learned the man was actually an agent he congratulated him on the performance.

Elmer was picked up by Canadian authorities on the same day we arrested the one-time big shot of Phoenix. A curious sequence of deaths followed—Elmer's common law wife, Constance, died of pneumonia. A few months after Mr. Phoenix was sentenced, Agent Van Trell died. Through the investigation he had not been well but had stuck with it all the way. He was the only witness, and had he died before Mr. Phoenix was brought in, the man would have walked out free.

Elmer and his associates were brought to trial in Canada, were found guilty and given five and four years respectively. They won reversals on the grounds that they were not properly represented by counsel on the day of their trial, but in a second trial were sentenced to three years in jail.

Just before the second trial, another death occurred—the girl Phoenix had married a few days before his trial. She was said to have been his mistress and the czarina of the prostitutes of Phoenix; reports had it that he had married her so that she could not testify against him.

Her death was followed by the suicide of our informant and special employee, Hugo. Apparently, the difficulty of disentangling himself from his own past and former associates proved too great a challenge. Hugo killed himself by backing into an unused logging camp near Tacoma, Washington, covering his car with bushes and rocks and then turning on the engine, letting the carbon monoxide fumes snuff out his life. He had covered the car so completely it was two weeks before his body was discovered. So ended the life of a man who had done much to help us so he might go on living without going to prison.

18. The Vice President Requests...

I was startled one morning when one of our younger agents, assigned to an eastern city, called our Washington headquarters and insisted on talking to me personally in regard to an urgent case that involved the Vice President.

"I am in this case only because of the Vice President," he told me over the phone. "I am acting on his direct orders." He was obviously agitated and concerned.

I knew that the V.P. lived in the city where the agent was assigned. "How did you get called in?" I asked the agent. "Did the Vice President talk with you personally?"

"Yes, sir. He called me and we had a meeting, he told me the whole story and said it was absolutely essential that we make this case."

The "whole story" was like a piece out of Edgar Allan Poe. The Vice President, the agent revealed, was a member of a secret group—an anti-corruption organization formed in this eastern metropolis by the highest-placed, most respected men of the city. Included were bank presidents, heads of industrial companies, judges, business leaders and ministers. Their purpose was to do all within their power to rid the city of crime and a criminal overlordship that had a death-grip on the city government.

The Vice President had called in our agent with the knowledge and support of the secret band of citizens. He gave the agent facts on alleged narcotic dealings of a man I shall call John Osgood. The Vice President also produced wiretap evidence that backed up these charges. Furthermore the United States Attorney in that district, he said, requested an investigation of the charges.

I learned all of this over the long distance phone. "Did you refer this to anyone at our Bureau here in Washington?" I demanded.

"Mr. Commissioner, it came from the Vice President of the United States. I assumed it was an order from him in his official capacity. I acted. The investigation is under way now. I've been on it for two weeks."

Of course it was not an order. The Vice President should have, in fact, called me directly. The agent should have notified me at once. However, I had no time to debate the correctness of what had been done, or the agent's assumptions or his course of action. The Bureau obviously was already deeply involved. Moreover, I already knew some of the history of John Osgood. It was a lurid story that touched some of the most important financial and social circles in the nation.

"You take the first plane down here to Washington," I ordered the agent. "Bring everything—every scrap of evidence."

"Are you calling it off, Commissioner?"

"I am not. We're in it and we'll stay. But you're going to need a lot of help. You be on that plane."

The image Osgood presented to the world was that of a man of background, money, manners and culture. He wore a Van Dyke beard. He appeared to know everyone of any standing and they seemed to know him. He purportedly was a graduate of two European universities. "It isn't significant," he told one friend, "but I have been decorated several times by governments abroad for my services."

By the time the agent reached Washington, however, we had additional facts about Osgood's background that did not quite fit in with this impeccable portrait. Evidence indicated that he had been associated in Europe with several questionable deals and had actually been arrested and interrogated at length by the police, although no charges were ever brought into court.

The Vice President and his anti-corruption group were concerned with the evidence they had compiled showing Osgood to be a supplier of morphine to prominent people in American society.

On his arrival in America, Osgood had moved into the upper levels of society. One of the richest women in the United States—heiress to an industrial empire, and married to a noted physician—fell in love with Osgood. The pair engaged in an adulterous affair that they made no attempt to keep secret. The physician husband hired a private detective to spy on his wife and her lover; Osgood hired a detective to spy on the physician. This bitter skirmishing had been going on for months below the surface of cocktail hours and elegant dinner parties.

Even the family of the heiress were divided in their opinions of Osgood. Some stood by her husband; others vowed for the seeming integrity and character of her lover. But Osgood had weaknesses the family did not guess. One was the fact that his taste in women covered wide territory. He was not to be satisfied with one woman, even one as rich and good looking as the heiress. Once we picked up this information, we were able to make use of a young woman "informer" who had been a drug addict. We try to help such people when we know they are making a real effort to help themselves. We send them away for cures when they need cures, sometimes half a dozen times or more. In return for our aid, some of these on-and-off addicts help us in ways we do not always put on the record.

This was such an instance. The young woman was still good looking. She was off drugs and not likely to return. But she had other vices and lived a loose life. When I suggested that she might like to meet Osgood and learn what she could from him, her answer was, "If you let me do it my own _____ _____ way, and don't ask any questions."

"What do you mean, Eve?"

"There's only one way to get a man to talk," she said.

"I'm not telling you what to do," I assured her. "I just want facts. We will be glad to have any useful information you obtain."

She had several trysts with Osgood. From one of these she emerged with a token of his affection—a handful of morphine cubes which she turned over to us. It was solid evidence, yet I could not go into court with such evidence from this witness. A defense lawyer could have torn her story—and us with it—to microscopic shreds.

We were tapping the phones of both the wife and Osgood. In fear of the husband, they always talked in code. One conversation had a puzzling implication.

"Do you know when that thing we discussed will be there?"

"It will tie up in a day or two. Two days."

"It will be on there?"

"Unless something has happened. I don't think it has."

We were sure this referred to a shipment of narcotics on some vessel, docking somewhere in the States, probably within the next two days. When customs agents two days later uncovered a large cache of untreated opium concealed in a hollowed out section of the forward mast of an incoming ship—a supply worth many thousands of dollars—I decided this was too great a coincidence to be coincidence at all.

It was time to close in on Osgood and the woman. Our investigation of their activities and connections and the information obtained in the wiretaps linked them closely to knowledge of this illegal shipment and our undercover people had additional information to support this charge.

A five-room suite in one hotel and a lavish apartment in another—both used by this pair—were raided by our agents. A number of arrests were made of individuals in these apartments, but we found no drugs.

Osgood's attorney, on hand immediately after the pair was released, informed reporters, "No charges have been brought against my client, no names can be used without the danger of libel suits and injunctions." He stated further that Federal agents "arrived, searched the suite and took him away without any warrant. He was led to understand that he was in the hands of agents who were on the trail of a dope smuggling ring. It is ridiculous to associate my client with any such organization. His interests are, largely, in plantations."

The Bureau found itself in an uncomfortable corner. Our raids had failed to produce the evidence we had anticipated. It was true that we had enough to get indictments and probably convictions under normal circumstances. But in a case like this we needed double-decked evidence. We were dealing with a woman and a family of great wealth, position and power.

I received a summons to the office of the assistant secretary of the Treasury, my immediate superior in the Treasury Department. The assistant secretary looked at me with unsympathetic eyes. "What about this business?" he asked, "What are you people hoping to do in this case?"

I could almost feel the pressure he was under. I explained to the assistant secretary how we became involved. "We acted on the request not only of the Vice President but also of the United States District Attorney's office."

I also explained some of our difficulties in obtaining conclusive evidence on this pair. "When our agents grabbed Osgood as he entered the apartment," I told him, "he had a box under his arm. The agents opened it expecting to find heroin."

"And it wasn't?"

"It was fried chicken for his lady friend."

The assistant secretary grimaced, "Well, you just toss this whole thing back to the U.S. Attorney's office," he ordered. "They're the ones who pumped for the investigation."

"I've done that already," I said. "It's up to them to prosecute or drop. But I can't seem to get rid of the smell of fried chicken."

Meanwhile, the possibility of going on trial and the tensions, threats and counter-threats in this family feud became too overwhelming for the bearded vendor of love and morphine. The physician husband had let everyone know that there would come a moment of retribution. Osgood was apparently badly frightened. With a brief announcement by phone to his lady love that he had to get away by himself until "the heat cooled off," Osgood climbed into his car and drove off into the protective anonymity of the night.

He drove, apparently at high speed, over narrow, twisting back roads, covering eighty miles in under two hours. It was not fast enough. In a deserted stretch of the unlighted highway a car behind him pulled alongside and forced the machine driven by Osgood into a ditch. Three men got out, opened the door of Osgood's car, seized the terrified man and dragged him out of the car. His screams and cries for help went unheard.

The men carried him to the side of the road, pulled off his clothes, held him on the ground and in a few dreadful seconds, heedless of his screaming agony, castrated him.

They then efficiently stopped the flow of blood, carried the moaning man back to his own car, drove him in the car to a hospital a few miles away and left him parked outside. A fourth man had tailed them in their own car, to which the trio now shifted and drove off.

An intern, starting home in the early hours of the morning, heard Osgood's groans. Mumbling incoherently, Osgood was carried into the hospital.

Meanwhile the gangsters sped for their payoff, carrying with them the bloody evidence of their crime. In a ceremonial bit of evil rarely equaled in crime, this evidence pickled in salt, was presented on a silver platter to the man who had ordered the deed. He thereupon handed the hoodlums their fee in cash: $25,000.

Osgood recovered. The U.S. Attorney informed us, "There are too many conflicting aspects and pressures in the case. We'd have a hung jury if we indicted this castrated lover and his mistress." The heiress was granted a divorce from the doctor. When Osgood recovered, the two left for another country where they were married. Nine months later the heiress died. The family had influence enough to obtain the body and have an autopsy performed, but nothing could be found to incriminate Osgood. Death was apparently due to natural causes.

In spite of objections, he inherited one third of her tremendous estate.

Only when the case was almost over did we learn that the Vice President's niece had fallen in love with the son of Osgood. The Vice President, his brother and the family had wanted the romance broken up; they considered the boy to be like his father, a fortune hunter. The romance had been in progress at the time the Vice President called our agent. We did not learn about that, however, until one of our men stumbled on the information during routine checkups on all individuals connected even remotely with the case.

Love is always an unpredictable factor. Despite the unpleasant facts and publicity, the entreaties of the Vice President and the tears of the girl's parents, the niece refused to set aside her love for young Osgood. She and the youth drove to a village in a nearby state and—without fanfare or publicity—were married.

The marriage worked out well. Later confidential reports indicated that the young couple were living modestly and raising a family in a suburban community where no one could possibly associate either of them with the past.

PART FIVE

EXTRA-
CURRICULAR

SPECIALTIES

Along with our job of bringing murderers and other narcotic criminals to book, we have warred on other fronts in the fight for effective narcotic controls. America is a signatory of many international conventions on narcotics, and I have represented our government in the League of Nations and the United Nations. We have worked directly with other nations —as well as indirectly through Interpol—on the international scene, not only in enforcement but also in trying to get nations and peoples to accept controls, and live up to them after acceptance.

Gentlemanly governmental interchanges are often only a cover for the deadliest kind of cloak-and-bullet diplomacy in modern world councils. And, curiously, our chief antagonist in 1960 was the same enemy I first tangled with as a young diplomat in Hamburg, Germany—the Communists. Then it was only Russia; by 1960, it was also China, and the fingers reached out to Japan, Hong Kong, and Burma.

In addition to international controls, under the Harrison Act and the Marijuana Act, America's control machinery touches on other special fields. As Commissioner, I am responsible for the dispensation of drugs to doctors, dentists, hospitals, for the control of narcotic use by veterinarians, by trainers in famous racing stables, by research laboratories. There are also our collaborative efforts with other agencies in the prevention of illegal importations of drugs. These are special fields and features—extra-curricular in that they are apart from the daily routines—yet important and dramatic facets of the job.

19. Incident at the UN

In 1951 the sheriff of Los Angeles called me on the long distance phone. I did not know him personally but he asked to talk directly to me. "I've got a bird out here," he said, "I think ought to interest your agents."

"Why? Heroin in his tailfeathers?"

"Tailfeathers and all the others. He was carrying enough heroin to start his own private underworld. But it's his *story* I think might interest your agents, Commissioner."

"Where's he from?"

"Trieste."

"What's the source, Sheriff?"

"Well, he's evasive, so far. It could be from behind the Iron Curtain."

That was too important to let slide. "Don't let him out of your hands, Sheriff," I said. "I'll fly a man out there. We'd like to talk to him."

The smuggler was a dark-haired Middle European type, apparently well-educated. He spoke English with only a slight accent. The fact that the case was federal appeared to impress him. He talked smoothly, quietly, and unreservedly. As it turned out, the Iron Curtain was not involved. In fact, there was no curtain at all.

"I can buy heroin in Trieste with no trouble," he informed the agent. "Why should there be any trouble? It is legal in Trieste to buy and sell heroin. There is no law against it."

The moment I received this report, in the summer of 1951,

I sent a man in the opposite direction—by plane direct to Trieste, for a first-hand report. What he found was a narcotic loophole five miles wide with a harbor that opened the gates to trade routes across the world. When the Allied Governments had moved into Italy, they had repealed all the old laws promulgated under Mussolini and no one had gotten around to writing new statutes in regard to narcotics controls in Trieste.

Italy was a part of the United Nations and a signatory of the protocols setting up international narcotic agreements. When I discovered the situation in Trieste, I at once called for the official picture of narcotic production in Italy. I discovered that Italy was legally producing in its chemical factories two hundred kilos a year of heroin, all of it listed on their reports to the United Nations "for medical consumption within the borders of Italy." This figure, compared with the medical consumption of heroin in France and Switzerland, showed that these two neighbor nations used only one-twentieth the amount, on a per capita basis. There was something terribly wrong with the two-hundred kilo figure.

A further probing revealed that the production of codeine in Italy was so enormous that it could not possibly be used for medical needs; and this production figure was in addition to the heroin production. It seemed to me amazing that the narcotics control boards of the United Nations had missed the significance of these production and manufacturer figures which the Italian government had dutifully sent in to UN control agencies, and which these agencies had routinely approved.

It was then that I had Charles Siragusa make his survey of the production at Italian chemical plants, already described in detail in connection with the Mafia and its tie-in with some of these concerns. We asked the Italian government, on a basis of Siragusa's unequivocal evidence, and in view of the large and unaccountable heroin and codeine production, to close these firms that were obviously violating the law, and to discontinue the production of heroin until the hoard they had on hand was used up. It was a long and difficult war of attrition and memoranda in quadruplicate, but the heroin production licenses of the five main culprit plants were taken away and heroin was no longer legally manufactured in Italy. Narcotics control laws were also enacted in Trieste.

The purpose of international control is to set up the procedures and limitations on legal production, manufacture and distribution of narcotics. By production is meant cultivation and harvesting of raw opium, later to be manufactured in chemical factories. Every nation that has signed the international protocols each year submits estimates on its needs, its raw narcotics, its production and manufacture, as well as figures on actual use in the past year. Through these figures and comparisons, it is not difficult to pinpoint trouble spots.

Development of international control agencies has been achieved over long and bruising years, shaped out by complex economic and social conflicts, special interests and politics. In countries where opium has been a major crop of the peasant farmers for centuries, it is difficult and even impossible for local authorities to tell the growers: "Give up your high-grade, high-priced opium and grow hay or wheat instead." There isn't enough profit, the farmers say, in hay or wheat. Because of such conflicting interests, international control came slowly, grudgingly, phase by phase and word by word; but still it came, as a product of the conscience of mankind.

By 1960, controls rested in four organizations. Three of these—The Commission on Narcotic Drugs, the Permanent Central Opium Board, the Drug Supervisory Body—are part of the UN. The fourth group, the Expert Committee on Drugs Liable to Produce Addiction, is a part of the World Health Organization.

At the heart is the Commission on Narcotic Drugs which functions as a part of the UN Economic and Social Council, replacing an earlier advisory committee on traffic in dangerous drugs, set up by the League of Nations. Fifteen governments constitute the membership—each selected by the Economic and Social Council because they are either producers of opium, large manufacturers of narcotic drugs, or primary targets of the international traffic.

In 1959, these fifteen nations were Canada, China, Egypt, France, Greece, India, Iran, Mexico, Peru, Hungary, Turkey, Russia, the United Kingdom, the United States of America and Yugoslavia. An official description of the purposes of this unique international body states:

The Permanent Central Opium Board and the Drug Supervisory Body are closely related and a draft treaty in preparation as this is written would actually combine the two into one agency. The eight members of the Permanent Board are chosen by the Economic and Social Council to serve as individual authorities, not as representatives of any government. The board deals primarily with vital statistics of narcotics, figures on legal manufacture, export or import. Where figures indicate trouble, board experts may seek further information. It may in flagrant cases recommend that all countries cease exporting narcotics to the overproducing nation, if voluntary requests fail.

The Drug Supervisory Body is concerned itself primarily with the estimates. It was this body that should have spotted the situation in Italy before the Los Angeles sheriff called me on the long distance phone.

One man who did a little-known but heroic job in tightening this control was Colonel C. H. L. Sharman, Canadian delegate on the commission who took on the job as chairman of the Drug Supervisory Body from 1952–1958. Formerly a member of the Canadian Royal Mounted Police, the Colonel has fought relentlessly for effective world-wide controls. In many cases—and in many ways unpublicized—the United States owes this man a debt.

Behind the forms, behind the statistics and the procedures, the table and tabulations, is the reality of the deadly war. In the late 1950's, we had a deteriorating "opium for all" situation in Iran. Production of opium in that country amounted to over 700 tons a year—about seven times more than the needs of the entire world.

Through cooperation with Interpol, I sent some of our Bureau people into Iran. These agents reported to me that opium dives were operated openly day and night in Tehran and other Iranian cities. All of the seven hundred tons of opium were consumed by Iranian addicts. One-tenth of the Iranian people were addicted.

We talked with the Shah of Iran, who agreed to curtail Iranian opium production. We then sent our own Colonel Garland Williams, former head of our New York office, to Iran. He reported that complete suppression was the only solution to Iran's near-disaster situation. Some of the UN experts thought we ought to proceed more slowly, with a gradual reduction of production of opium and use by Iran's estimated 2,000,000 addicts. The Williams approach prevailed; he organized the Iranian police to deal with the job of suppressing the production in the fields, the opium dens and addiction. Not only Iranian police but also the army and the Iranian customs were enlisted. The clean-up job was efficient and thorough.

Results were an extraordinary proof of the efficiency of strong methods in narcotics control. Iranian opium, always found in considerable quantity in Singapore, Hong Kong, and many other ports in the Far East, disappeared entirely from the market. The opium dives of Tehran, where Williams saw mothers nurse their infants at the breast in rooms dense with the stench of opium smoke, were closed up. Opium crop production was virtually wiped out. Addiction in Iran went on the greatest toboggan ride in history; within a space of two years, the number of confirmed addicts plunged downward from 2,000,000 to approximately 50,000.

Just as victory appeared certain, a new menace appeared for Iran: opium smuggling from Afghanistan. We countered, through the United Nations, by prevailing on Afghanistan to curtail its large scale production of opium. Opium smuggling from Afghanistan and also Turkey continued. Iranian and Turkish opium members on the commission got together and worked out a policing agreement where, for the first time, Turkish authorities could pursue smugglers into Iran, and Iranian police could pursue smugglers into Turkey. Almost overnight, this smuggling dried up. Iranians and Afghanistans then met to develop similar arrangements.

One development in dealing with such problems is the concept of regional meetings of groups of nations bound together by mutual problems in narcotics and the control of smuggling between these nations. In the late fifties, we in the United States became concerned with illicit cocaine, production and manufacture in South America, particularly in Bolivia and Peru. A regional meeting of North, Central and South American nations was planned to deal with this and other problems.

One of these "other problems" in 1960 was the hammer and sickle—and the narcotic needle—in Cuba. Cuba is loaded with cocaine and uses more cocaine among its addict population on the little island than all the rest of the world put together. Our agents made more than fifty cases against Cuban pushers and dealers in the Batista era. The Batista government did nothing about putting these men in jail in spite of our cooperation in working with their own people to get the evidence, so I sent word to our agents, "Cease cooperating and come on home."

When the Castro regime came in I sent a man to see Castro's secretary and gave him a list of the fifty traffickers who should be prosecuted. Either the secretary or Castro himself, we can't be sure which, lost the list. When Castro visited Washington a little later, he sent his assistant to see me. I gave the assistant another copy of the list of fifty names and the evidence in the case and he solemnly promised to bring these men to trial. Nothing has happened.

Our work in the international arena has been aided by the cooperation of the national and municipal police departments of many countries through Interpol. While Interpol is still in a developmental state, it already serves as an international switchboard of information, as well as the nerve center for investigations carried on by agents of possibly several countries, in association with Interpol and with local authorities. These local authorities always have legal charge of a case; our agents, for example, provide technical and investigatory assistance only when an individual country feels we can be of help.

One key man in the forging of links in this cooperative work is Charles Siragusa. Speaking to a convention of American crime commissions at Dallas, Texas, Siragusa described how our Congress, at the urging of myself and other enforcement officials, had passed legislation authorizing full and formal membership of the United States in Interpol. "We of the Bureau of Narcotics," he said, "as well as other Treasury representatives abroad, have assisted foreign police in many successful narcotic investigations resulting in huge seizures abroad of illicit narcotics which were destined for American underworld markets. Large seizures of counterfeit American dollars have been made. We have worked with just about all of the member Interpol countries, now numbering fifty-eight, on their respective territories. Among the noteworthy accomplishments of Interpol, in addition to tangible contraband seizures, is the effective surveillance of international gangsters' movements." At this point Siragusa told the convention how Interpol watched the movements of the Chicago gangster, Tony Accardo, on a trip that took him to London, Paris, Zurich, Milan, Venice, Rome, Nice, Barcelona, Madrid and Lisbon.

I recall a similar situation, when we learned that Meyer Lansky was planning an extensive trip abroad. I sent word to Siragusa in Rome and through him to Interpol headquarters in Paris. Through Interpol and our own agents operating in various European nations, we were able to keep tabs on everything that Lansky did.

One day in my Washington office I had a call from Lansky's attorney. The lawyer wanted to see me. He came to my office to demand: "What were you doing to my client? Can't any

American citizen take a little vacation trip abroad without having every step dogged by the agents of the Federal Bureau of Narcotics? What kind of persecution is this anyway?"

I reassured the attorney: "I'm just providing Lansky extra international protection, in case any of his old friends we shipped back to Italy take a pot shot at him."

Sometimes they just don't appreciate us.

20. Chinese Red Lullaby

China's narcotic record is an ancient one, going back many centuries. In the past she was the victim, first of the European nations, more recently of imperial Japan. Now Red China has become the dope-vending dragon of the East. But to understand the present, we must explore the past.

For twelve hundred years poppies have been grown in China. But for nine hundred of these years, cultivation was limited solely for medicinal uses. In the seventeenth century, the practice of mixing opium and tobacco for smoking purposes began, and spread swiftly. It was said to have been started by the Dutch in Java and to have been carried from there to Formosa and from there to the Asian mainland.

Importation of opium to China, particularly from India, Turkey and the Near East, jumped to such proportions in the early eighteenth century that the Emperor issued edicts in a futile effort to halt the trade. Ships carrying chests of opium continued to jam into Chinese ports. Each chest held a hundred and fifty pounds of the drug. China in that day was being inundated with dope grown chiefly in the Near East and India and imported on European ships. By 1820, ten thousand chests were coming in annually; by 1830, the rate was more than twenty thousand chests a year—close to two thousand tons of smoking opium in addition to production of China's own fields.

This traffic was a river of riches, and those engaged in it

had no desire to dam it up. In 1839 a fearless Chinese official, Lin Tse-hsu, made valiant efforts to halt the trade. He called the British officials before him and told them that their "conduct arouses indignation in every human heart, and is utterly inexcusable in the eye of Celestial reasoning. . . ."

Inexcusable or not, the British shippers found it profitable and used every stratagem possible to keep on. Lin closed in with his own Chinese forces around Canton, which was an Occidental community, and the British finally surrendered— because they had no choice—20,000 cases of opium. Lin piled them up, lit a taper and started what was probably the greatest opium bonfire in all history. It was said that the stench of the fire reached half way across China.

But the British, and the French and Portuguese, continued to resist all of Lin's efforts to end the traffic. The seething antagonism between British and Chinese authorities erupted into the first Opium War. The British won and obtained a number of concessions, the most important being that Chinese Customs officials hereafter had to allow narcotics into China just like anything else the traders wished to import.

Opium poured into China, resulting in the second Opium War, which the British, with the French, won again. By the Treaty of Tientsin, in 1858, the opium traffic was given an official status. It became sacrosanct.

Not for half a century—until the time when Bishop Brent made his appeal to President Theodore Roosevelt—would action be started against this narcotic aggression of one nation or people against another.

When Chiang Kai-shek ruled over mainland China, the Nationalist Government for several years conducted a campaign against dope that included suppression of the traffic, severe punishments of sellers and wide education as to the effects of dope on the individual.

The campaign, begun at the insistence of Madame Chiang, helped to reduce the use of opium and heroin in China itself by an estimated thirty to forty percent. Then came the Japanese and after them the Chinese Reds.

Red China presents a double-pronged problem. As a part of the United Nations Narcotic Commissions, we are concerned with what this nation, that we do not even recognize, is trying to do to her neighbors, particularly Japan, with the weapon of dope. And I am also concerned with the reports of my operatives regarding Red China's long range dope-and-dialectic assault on America and its leaders.

The standard policy employed in Red China is to suppress addiction *among the Chinese* while encouraging the cultivation, manufacture, export, distribution and sale of opium, morphine and heroin to other countries and other peoples.

Examining confidential background information on the Tokyo riots, and the pictures of the wild-eyed Communist leaders standing on trucks with microphones, urging Japanese teen-age mobs to greater frenzies, I wondered exactly how many of the leaders and followers were high on heroin or cocaine or the new and dangerous Japanese product called hiropon, said to have been used by the Japanese suicide pilots, the kamikaze.

One of the first reports we received about the Communist narcotic smuggling in the Far East came from the United States Armed Forces Supreme Command in Tokyo, just before the new Japanese government took over:

"Investigations, arrests and seizures in Japan during 1951," read the report, "proved conclusively that Communists are smuggling heroin from China to Japan, and are using the proceeds from the sale thereof to finance party activities and to obtain strategic materials for China. . . . During 1950, 10,591 grams were seized which was approximately three times the amount seized in 1949. One of these seizures, 990 grams, in October 1950, involved the Chief of the Communist party in Kyushu who stated he had obtained the heroin from

Kyo Son, a North Korean, who is a Communist committee member in Rashin, North Korea. . . ."

This report was transmitted to the United Nations Commission on Narcotics and denounced by the Russian delegate who charged that our contentions were "false, slanderous, fabricated and baseless." The Russians brushed aside the evidence we presented. "Communist China is resolutely pursuing the policy of strictest prohibition of opium and other narcotic drugs," they insisted.

Our report cited instance after instance—in the most precise detail with names, dates, amounts of seizures, arrests, and confessions, all pointing directly to the Red Chinese smugglers and their political agents. "Of a seizure totalling 3,413 grams of heroin in Japan," our report states, "all information obtained from extensive investigations show the heroin in Japan originated from Communist China. Some amounts arrive from Horai, China, between Tsingtao and Tientsin. The Communists use crews of merchant ships, crews and passengers of aircraft, as carriers, as well as their own Communist couriers and agents to smuggle narcotics. . . ."

"Large quantities of heroin," the report continues, "have reached the United States from Communist China. Emissaries have been sent to the United States to arrange for the details of the smuggling transactions. One of the principals in a case in which 300 ounces of heroin were smuggled in from Communist China is now serving a ten-year imprisonment. . . ."

I continued to present these carefully documented reports to the United Nations in session after session. When cornered with facts the Russians could not refute—the confessions of pushers and smugglers working directly for Chinese Red authorities—the Russian delegate with a sweep of his hand would dismiss the whole matter with, "How can they defend themselves since they are not here?"

It is true that the Red Chinese are not in the United Nations and are therefore not a part of the United Nations Protocol under which the legal manufacture and international shipment of all narcotic drugs is controlled. But whether it would make any perceptible difference if they had been a signatory to this protocol is debatable.

One primary outlet for the Red Chinese traffic has been Hong Kong. Heroin made in Chinese factories out of poppies grown in China is smuggled into Hong Kong and onto freighters and planes heading to Malaya, Macao, the Philippines, the Hawaiian Islands, the United States, or, going in the other direction, India, Egypt, Africa and Europe.

A prime "target area" in the United States was California. The Los Angeles area alone probably received forty percent of the smuggled contraband from China's heroin and morphine plants. The syndicate crowd does not object to dealing with the Reds, as long as the profits are big in terms of dollars.

A story is told in Hong Kong of a Communist functionary who tried to "propagandize" an American airline pilot into smuggling $250,000 worth of morphine from Hong Kong to Bangkok. From there it would be taken by others to America. For carrying out his share of the job, the American was to receive one-eighth ownership of an opium processing factory inside Red China.

The American is reported to have thought about the offer for a few seconds over his gin sling and then replied, "Sorry, but the fact is I already own two opium dives, a house of prostitution and a gambling pad in Hoboken, New Jersey. I don't have a moment to myself any more."

The Communist walked away shaking his head about the ways of American bourgeoise capitalists.

21. Dr. Addison and Others

Dr. Walter G. Addison was a big man in the town of Hope, Arkansas. Big in size, standing well over six feet tall, with mountainous sloping shoulders. And big in the fear his sudden tempestuous rages sent through the little town of Hope. Big also in the range of his criminality.

Our records on Dr. Addison dated back several decades. Reports in the 1920's revealed that he was then dispensing morphine to known addicts. It was learned that he purchased 7,000 grains of morphine and 900 grains of cocaine, all of which he used up without keeping a single record of dispensation. "I used every grain myself," the doctor calmly informed local authorities, "because I'm an addict." He even offered to "take a cure." Later he became involved with charges of accepting as patients unwedded expectant mothers seeking abortions. For this he was expelled from the county medical society.

Still he went on practicing medicine and selling narcotics to local addicts at exorbitant prices. A decade later, the situation became serious enough that we decided it was time to halt his practices for good. Agent William Schaefer, working with District Supervisor Joseph Bell of the Kansas City District, collected sufficient evidence to arrest Addison—full reports on how they purchased morphine openly, without Addison's even bothering to ask a question. The doctor, however, denied everything.

Following a preliminary hearing in Texarkana, Arkansas,

Addison was ordered held in $1,000 bail for action by the Grand Jury. He raised the bond, went back to Hope, continued to practice but sent out word he was carrying a gun and intended to kill the informer who turned him in. Further, putting on the act of the outraged citizen, he strolled in to the Bureau of Narcotics office in Little Rock, to notify us that some narcotics had been stolen from him.

It was Agent Schaefer who took down the doctor's report on the alleged theft. Although Addison knew this was the agent who had made the case against him, the doctor made no mention of his case and seemed friendly and talkative. Schaefer gave Addison the forms and explained the procedure used in reporting a theft. He also told the doctor that he would drop around to Hope in a few days to make a personal investigation.

Dr. Addison thanked him for the kindness.

Intensifying their probe, Schaefer and Bell learned that no drug store in Hope would fill a narcotic prescription for the doctor; all the prescriptions he wrote were filled in other towns nearby. "He's a brawler," the pharmacists told the agents. "He knife-slashed a physician in town he thought was responsible for his being dropped from the county medical society."

On the morning of May 24th the two agents called on the doctor at his office, ostensibly to discuss the robbery the physician said he had suffered, but actually to ask for his records on narcotic prescriptions and to confront him with prescriptions he had written for addicts working for us. The agents were cautious, in view of the man's reputedly explosive temper. They talked about fishing. Then about the "robbery."

"Now, where did you say this fellow broke in?—the one who stole the narcotics."

"Over there. Broke in through that window. Then crossed the room to the safe, where he must have. . . ." The towering physician acted out the reconstruction of the alleged theft.

The agents nodded with apparent interest. They continued

this shadow boxing until District Supervisor Bell asked to see the doctor's order forms and other records that might help in determining just what narcotics were stolen in the burglary.

The doctor said he had trouble opening the safe while people stood over him; would they wait in the other room for an instant? They agreed; the doctor appeared in a good mood and they had him under close watch in any case.

Schaefer bent down to take out some incriminating prescriptions from a brief case he had brought with him. As he did so, the doctor came back into the room, with a .38 calibre pistol in his hand. He rammed the weapon against Bell's chest and said, "None of us will have to worry about this case any longer."

Bell grabbed the gun and tried to divert the aim. In that instant, Addison pulled the trigger. The bullet went through the sleeve of the supervisor but the force with which the doctor jammed the weapon against the supervisor caused such intense pain simultaneously with the retort that the supervisor thought he was shot in the chest.

Nevertheless, Bell continued to struggle with Dr. Addison for the gun. Addison, although in his seventies, had a grip of steel and he was aided by the fact that the prescriptions Bell had in his hand made it difficult for the supervisor to get a solid grasp on the weapon. With a tremendous lurch the old man pulled back, raised the pistol and fired almost point blank at Agent Schaefer, coming to Bell's assistance.

Bell grabbed the doctor's hand again and the two men grappled with each other for the gun, spinning and careening out into the hall. By that time, Schaefer had his own gun out. Bell called to Schaefer, "He's gone crazy. Hit him over the head."

Schaefer hit the doctor on the head with the gun three times. Instead of dropping Addison, the blows seemed to goad him to even greater violence. The two agents continued to battle with the old giant. Schaefer had a hammerlock hold on the doctor but the physician spun Schaefer half way around, hurling him against the wall in the hall with such force that the agent's right elbow was broken and he pitched to the floor.

Again Addison broke away. Schaefer, in agony on the floor, managed to raise his gun and fire three bullets, hitting Addison in the left groin, the right groin and the side. The giant plunged to the ground.

Bell saw that Schaefer was bleeding profusely. He opened the front door. Outside, a crowd had gathered and Bell called out, "Get an ambulance, quick—and call the police station. There's been serious trouble."

Schaefer's condition was critical but he recovered. Dr. Addison was dead when he reached the hospital. Investigation by both local and Federal agencies of this event showed that the officers had acted properly—in fact heroically—in carrying out their duty.

While we discussed medical practitioners—and malpractitioners—in other parts of this book, I want in this chapter to bring into sharp focus the whole narcotic addict-doctor interrelationship. Because of the continual availability of narcotics to a physician, and the life and death strain under which they live, some surrender themselves to dope and become addicts. In most cases these physicians do not involve their patients in any violations and manage to cover up their own usage well enough to avoid suspicion or detection. But physician addicts present a major problem in the medical profession not only in the United States but in many other countries.

Not only doctors but also those on the fringes of the medical profession—doctors' wives, nurses, the children of physicians—represent a larger percentage of the addicts than do most other groups. Professor Dr. H. Ehrhardt, President of the German Society for Psychiatry and Neurology, writing in the United Nations *Bulletin of Narcotics* regarding addiction of German physicians, stated: "While it is true that dentists, veterinary surgeons, pharmacists and members of the other para-medical professions in the aggregate represent a large proportion of the total number of addicts, any one of these occupational groups, taken alone, accounts for a substantially smaller share than does the medical profession proper. . . ." He was writing about Germany but the same general pattern is to be found in other countries both in Europe and America.

Yet even with these figures, we are talking only about one in a hundred. The other ninety-nine not only keep themselves free from addiction, but are constantly on guard against falling victim to the wiles of addicts seeking to use them as a source.

Addicts come to the doctor's office with an ingenious variety of alleged pains, aches, diseases. They bite their cheek and spit blood to make a doctor believe they have tuberculosis: "It is an old case of T.B., doctor. My own physician is miles from here. Can you help me?"

They steal prescription pads of doctors, so that they can write their own prescriptions. Or an addict will go to a pharmacist with a counterfeit prescription, and have the druggist call the "doctor" at the number printed on the pad. The prescription form has been specially printed; the doctor and his address is real; the phone number is that of a public phone where a confederate of the addict waits to play the role of the confirming physician when the druggist telephones to check.

One group of addicts "invented" a woman relative with a full medical history. She lived back in the hills, they asserted, was in terrible pain constantly and obviously needed a full medical check-up and possibly an operation. A sympathetic doctor prescribed narcotics to the addicts for weeks, believing it was for a real woman whom they were arranging to bring to the hospital in the city, as soon as she felt well enough to make the trip.

The addicts even went so far as to reserve a room for her in the hospital. The physician waited all day for her to arrive. She never showed up.

A male addict developed the unique device of using a small

pebble as a kidney stone. He would complain that he had kidney stones and was in agony; when the physician took an X-ray, the "patient" would slip the pebble into a little pocket of scar tissue on his back; it happened to be located in such a position that it would always show up on the X-ray looking like a kidney stone. This method obtained quantities of drugs for the addict until the day when the pebble fell out of the scar-tissue pocket and rolled across the floor as the nurse and the doctor were getting the apparatus set for the picture. They notified us. Shortly afterwards the pebble player was in Lexington working on a cure.

Addicts also resort to holding up drug stores. In Houston, Texas, a pharmacy had been burglarized eight times by criminals seeking dope. The pharmacist was sick of losing cash and costly medical supplies. He waited in the dark one night and when he heard someone breaking in, he fired. The would-be burglar, an ex-convict and dope addict, was pronounced dead on arrival at a Houston hospital.

Many theorists offer schemes for the control of violence and crime associated with drugs. Most of these revolve around giving drugs freely to all who ask. The notion is that then the addict won't steal and so he won't become a criminal. This is fallacious on two points: First, many criminals are criminals long *before* they get on drugs, not after. Second, if we feed drugs to addicts we will only confirm their addiction, make their habit more demanding, spread it to epidemic proportions, and increase the role the syndicate dealers can play, by putting a government stamp of approval on dope itself.

Proponents of the "clinic plan" under which "registered" addicts would be given a daily ration of their drug, at government expense, claim that in this way crime would be curtailed, addiction would be put on a limited basis and the profits to the underworld would be eliminated, thus driving them out of the business. They cite the fact also that a dope clinic plan has been developed with some success within the socialized medical program in England.

I don't think any of this is applicable to the United States. But, in my opinion, they present great danger to the American people: these solutions sound so reasonable that even experts can be lulled into acceptance.

A committee of the American Bar Association and the American Medical Association on Narcotic Drugs, for example, has at least inferentially backed the "English system," in an interim report, on a basis of claims that there is less addiction in England and better observance of the laws by the public.

A committee of experts advising the Federal Bureau of Narcotics explored this interim report and also the entire subject of England's so-called system. One committee expert, M. L. Harney, formerly my assistant, but at that time (1958) superintendent of the Division of Narcotics Control for the State of Illinois, pinpointed what I consider the chief weaknesses of the clinic advocates in the United States: "One can be relatively ignorant of law enforcement and still know that what will produce good law enforcement for England will not necessarily produce good law enforcement in the United States of America.

"Despite our possibly tighter interpretation of the same fundamental philosophy, we nevertheless as late as the 1930's suffered from the outrages of a Ratigan who under the guise of practicing medicine sold in one year four hundred thousand doses in office-administered shots of morphine to addicts in Seattle, several times as much as all the other doctors and all the hospitals in the city dispensed in the same time. . . .

"Perhaps taking advantage of a slightly more complacent interpretation in England and despite the usual rigid English conformity to the law, that country recently had its John Bodkin Adams (whom the press seemed to like to refer to as Irishman). According to press accounts Dr. Adams was investigated when deaths among his patients became a public scandal. He was acquitted of murder, perhaps for the good reason that he may not have been guilty, perhaps again only because there were uncomprehensible lapses in the investigation of his case. In any event he later pleaded guilty to violations of the Dangerous Drug laws and was barred from practice.

"The ironical thing about the "English system" is that Dr. Adams' narcotic deviations were not discovered until there was a charge of murder. Adams apparently made many heroin addicts, most of whom I suggest do not appear in the English addiction statistics, but in the mortality tables."

Included in this exploration by the expert committee was a report by Commander Lynn A. White, in charge of personnel and training in the Los Angeles Police Department and formerly head of that department's Narcotic Squad. White pointed out that the incidence of addiction among English people varies greatly between those who have access to drugs and those who have little or none, and those in medicine or related fields as opposed to non-medical groups. "To summarize," he wrote, "those who can obtain the drug with ease have an addiction rate that is 5500% greater than do those who do not have the drug readily available to them."

A letter from the British Home Office, also included in the Advisory Committee report, states: "Mr. Harney's remarks seem to make a good deal of sense and I hope that the publication of the record of what he said will help to do some good in your country . . . there is not in fact any such thing as a 'British System' which is an invention of certain Americans who wish to prove a particular point of view. . . ."

The Committee concluded that the English system, in most instances, is much the same as that in any country. Their decision was based on the following observations:

1. Per capita narcotic consumption in the United Kingdom is double that of the United States, including both licit and illicit, according to United Nations documents.

2. Heroin consumption in the United Kingdom represents 70 percent of all *licit* heroin consumed in the world.

3. The Crown Colony of Hong Kong has more addicts than there are in the entire United States. The yearly number of arrests in Hong Kong, about 17,000, indicates good police work. . . .

4. Opium smoking addicts are not included in British addiction figures in the United Kingdom, and the advocates of the British system are silent on so-called minimal doses of smoking opium supplied to these addicts by physicians to keep them normal. The British physician would be in serious trouble with the authorities if he wrote prescriptions for smoking opium. According to seizures of smoking opium reported to the United Nations, there are more addicts to smoking opium in the United Kingdom than there are in the United States. . . .

The experts also noted the impossibility of keeping any addict at a given level of consumption of a drug. No matter what point the addict is at when he comes to your clinic, he is going to need more and more of a dose to satisfy his habit; addiction implies an increasing rate of consumption.

A physician whom I rank among leading authorities on narcotic problems, Dr. Charles T. Brown, formerly of the United States Army Medical Corps, wrote to me a private report that I regard as almost classical in the clarity and vision. Dr. Brown has devoted more than a quarter of a century to the study of narcotic addiction.

"You know and I know," he wrote, "that these increasing proposals to legalize the administration of narcotics come from those persons who are lacking in experience, albeit I do not question their good intentions in some instances. . . . Most important is the factor of tolerance. The individual who may be maintained comfortably on one-fourth of a grain of morphine will within just a few days require a doubling of his dose, and so in arithmetical progression he will in a very short time require heroic doses of the poison. . . .

"May I refer the advocates of the so-called British Plan, and in all respect the members of the New York Academy of Medicine, and many others, to the 1906 edition of *The Prac-*

tice of Medicine, by H. H. Tyson, M.D., who casually refers to a patient who started out with *one-fourth* grain of morphine sulphate daily, and ended up with a daily consumption of 800 grains of the narcotic less than a year later. Those enthusiasts of the implementation of 'feeding stations' in the immediate future who would care to go back a little further in consideration of this phenomenon of 'tolerance,' might be interested in the classic, *Confessions of an English Opium-Eater*. Mr. de Quincy tells us that he began with a few drops of laudanum for a minor ailment and in the end reached the mere daily quantum of 8000 drops of the drug. . . .

"The delightful book entitled, *Opiate Addiction*, by Dr. Abraham Wikler of Lexington does much to throw light on this phenomenon of addiction. If anyone is interested, I might cite one of my own publications: 'Morphine Withdrawal,' Vol. 1, Number 3, *The United States Armed Forces Medical Journal*, March 1950, in which my patient for years took a mere 60 grains of morphine sulphate daily. As I remember, he told me that he spent all of his time trying to get *more* for the reason that even 60 grains of morphine sulphate daily failed to satisfy his 'habit.' "

In an interview in *Modern Medicine*, in 1957, I pointed out that when clinics were tried in 1920 in the United States, addiction rates soared to a point where one person in every four hundred was addicted, and worse than that, corruption took over in many dealings of doctors and druggists, who in addition to selling through the clinics were selling to special customers and friends on the side. The whole plan bogged down in a welter of vicious after-effects and had to be abandoned. In an era of highly organized profit-wise criminals I consider the clinic plan an open bid for disaster.

One of the worst criminals I ever met was a so-called physician who believed in the clinic-for-addicts idea. In an eighteen-month period he administered hundreds of thousands of shots of morphine at $1 each. His profit in that period was over $300,000 net.

He had a clinic operation—come on in, the morphine's fine! Shoplifters, prostitutes, burglars, bums. No embarrassing questions asked. "He is running a Hypo's Paradise," one addict wrote in his diary. "His diagnosis is to the point. 'How long have you been at it? How much do you need?' "

The clinic was his private office; he gave the shots himself. The crime rate in his locality soared to an all time high. The public were alarmed, authorities moved in to try to put this thing down. Because no addict took the drug out of the office to administer elsewhere, the doctor felt we could never make a case against him. He was wrong. I tried a new method: Our agents located an addict willing to cooperate with us. We took him to the city medical officer. The addict's urine showed a positive reaction to morphine when tested after he visited the clinic. Using the urine-test method, we obtained evidence of several unlawful sales. We brought the doctor into court, where he shouted: "No power on earth can stop me, no power in heaven wants to stop me. I am merciful." He was found guilty.

He appealed. While the appeal was on, he continued giving out his mercy to hundreds of unfortunates who instead of being cured were being driven down a road to death.

He got supplies from a mail order drug company and we convicted this company on conspiracy charges. We notified the company that they were selling to addicts and they continued such sales nonetheless. Fifty-five of their customers, all so-called physicians, were also convicted. The United States Supreme Court upheld us unanimously in what is called the "Direct Sales Decision."

The minute we see a manufacturer or wholesaler or pharmacist supplying narcotics where the need is obviously not medical, we send along a copy of that decision to give them warning: *This is what the Supreme Court decided. You are on notice.*

I put this doctor on our narcotic blacklist and informed all wholesalers that we would prosecute them for supplying addicts, if they sold him narcotic supplies. This time it stuck. He couldn't even get a prescription filled. We brought in the addicts he had been making and shipped them off to hospitals.

One day the physician showed up at my office. I had been informed that he had lost his sanity and was telling people that he was "coming to Washington to get Anslinger." I knew he was tough; one of our agents who tried to get his records had an arm broken by this benefactor of mankind. But he was waiting outside my office and I let him in.

"When are you going to take me off that blacklist?" he half shouted.

I walked to the back of his chair, and deliberately avoiding the term doctor, I said, "Let me take your overcoat, it is rather hot in here." He looked at me curiously but did not object.

When I took it from him, I reached into the side pocket where I had noted a bulge, and drew out a .32 calibre pistol. Quickly I put the weapon on my desk. "Unlawful possession of a gun," I said, "is a felony. I could blow the whistle on you. You ought to know better. You couldn't hit me through that pocket and even if it struck a vital spot I have a Magnum within reach. I could be on my feet long enough to make a sieve out of you. You don't know how lucky you are to be rid of that suicide pistol!"

Regarding the blacklist I told him that he could have an attorney file an injunction against me in Federal Court. The doctor did this, asking the district court to restrain me, so that his narcotic orders could be filled. The injunction was denied. The court ruled that since I had authority to limit to medical and scientific uses narcotics imported into America (the raw material for all opiate drugs and their derivatives is imported) and since the doctor's use for drugs did not fit the defined limitations, on a basis of his past record, I was within my rights in refusing him the authority to get drugs.

The Supreme Court refused to review the doctor's earlier conviction for selling drugs to addicts. He was sentenced to eight years in prison and the state medical board revoked his license to practice.

In prison this advocate of clinics for bigger and faster profits turned to the Bible and announced that he intended to become an ordained minister. I do not know if this repentance is genuine or only another performance. If it is not real, I can only pray that God will have mercy on the man's congregation.

22. H Is for Horse

Our goal has been to end the misuse of drugs. But the victims of drug abuses are not always people. I personally directed one extra-curricular drive that may even have saved the thoroughbred racing horse from heroin-hypoed extinction in America.

There are fourteen drawers in our files filled with the records of this investigation which culminated in a series of nation-spanning racetrack raids by our agents. The first document in these files is a letter that appeared in a magazine called *Blood Horse*. "Some of the trainers of today are using a concoction of heroin, cocaine, strychnine and citrate of glycerine in capsules," the letter stated. "Others are using just straight heroin even on two-year olds. This is destroying the thoroughbred horse in America and if the Turf's governors in all sections do not enforce the rules against the use of drugs, then the Lord only knows what is going to become of the thoroughbred horses.

"Old timers owning and training thoroughbreds had some love and thought for the horse and did not believe in this brutal practice. . . . But things have changed very, very much and it seems that the men who have come into the business in the last twenty-five years, or I should say the majority of them, have come in through 'hop' prescriptions tucked away in their pockets."

I have a loathing for the scum who misuse animals or inflict suffering on them wantonly or for profit. This graphic letter depicted a situation which I knew had reached greater proportions than the public had guessed. But to what degree narcotics were being employed nationally on horses we could learn only by an investigation.

I made a few phone calls to some top sportsmen, to double-check this letter. The answers were varying—some evasive, some frankly concerned, some disarmingly frank: "Oh, yes, these things happen. We do what we can to keep it under control."

"You agree with the letter then?"

"I wouldn't go that far."

"But your stable managers must know what's going on. Don't they report to you?"

"I leave it in their hands. But you do hear talk in the paddock. Plenty of talk."

I did not press my questions too sharply at that time. Instead I sent two agents to a nearby track to make a quiet survey and report back. They came back three days later with bruises and black eyes. They had decided to pose as publishers of a race track tout sheet and a rival tout had gathered a few of his friends and ambushed our men. I could not resist telling them to use their heads for some better purpose. "I can't be out there with you," I said, "and from where I sit I can't send you diapers with instructions how to fasten them."

I was half serious and half joking. This was a tough assignment because it was new ground. The race track underworld is not regularly a part of our beat. We were moving into it only because of the narcotics angle. Under the Harrison Act we control the importation, manufacture, distribution and sale of narcotic drugs whether they are used on humans or beasts. Apart from its brutal, inhumane aspect, misuse of narcotics with horses—either for stimulation or "slowing up" purposes—is a federal crime.

Our men tried next at a track in New Orleans. I knew that this district was controlled by Mafia syndicate gangsters. Outsiders are not welcome. Our agents showed up posing as Eastern racketeers looking for new fields. Once inside the race track gates they were picked up by the police, thrown into jail and beaten daily by the authorities trying to find out who they really were. Nevertheless, our agents did not break their "cover"—to do this would have alerted too many people that we were about to launch a probe.

As soon as I heard my men were in jail, I hired a criminal lawyer in New Orleans, through an intermediary, and the lawyer "sprung" my two agents without revealing who they actually were. Through the media of several special employees working for the Bureau, word was spread in the New Orleans' underworld that the two men were genuine hoods. They were accepted. The probe went on in New Orleans and at other tracks in the South without any further "incidents."

Some weeks later I had word from my agents on this case, this time from Chicago. They wanted to set up a better "cover" picture for their probe. Would I come at once to talk with a man who had been in racing all his life, who now owned two horses and who wanted to tell some of the terrible things he knew were taking place on the tracks in the United States.

I found this old-timer was bitter over the situation. He wanted to talk to someone in authority. "I want to win with my horses," he told me, "but not with the 'shot-gun prescriptions,' like they call 'em."

Shot-gun prescriptions were also called "speed balls." They were massive shots given to horses just before they went to post. The shots included heroin, cocaine, coramine, carbolic acid, strychnine, caffein and any other stimulants available. As one stable hand put it, "The idea is, one of them damn things is got to work."

I hired the old-timer and his horses. With this horseflesh and blanket "cover," our men could go to any track without causing an upraised eyebrow. As a start, we decided to look over every track in the South, the Middle West and the East.

Coast. We found brutality, corruption and shame. No important stable was wholly exempt. Not a single great name in racing was excluded. Every track visited was involved in this slimy business. Outside of every stable our men picked up and marked for evidence bottles and vials containing traces of heroin, cocaine and other drugs. The general practice was to use the needle or what is called a drench syringe, a long, curving nozzle that is shoved down the horses' throat so that the "shot" can be administered.

These shots, I learned, were usually administered about half an hour before post time, to have the maximum effect when the horses went into the track for the actual race. This was one reason why so many horses bucked and reared at the starting gate.

While our agents were covering every track and compiling a record of documentation and statements as complete and as revealing as any investigation in the Bureau's history, I received a call from one of the finest racing horsemen in America. "Will you put one of your men secretly into my stables?" he asked me.

"For what reason?"

"Some of my good horses—good runners—are coming in last or next to last. And they're bleeding from the rectum. I want to know what is happening, who or what is causing this."

I thanked him, and told him I would put a couple of our best men on it at once. I sent in the pair who had already been on the investigation for months.

We discovered that hoodlums were using a slow-up drug— heavily coated somnifacient sulphonal. The horses couldn't win. They could hardly run.

The stable boy was bribed, our agents discovered. The night before a big race, hired hoods would slip into the stall and put a capsule of this drug up the horse's rectum, using a long rubber glove. Usually this was done when the favorite was going into a five-horse race the following day. If the two top entries were drugged in this manner and the gamblers bet heavily on the other three "long-shot" horses—which they did —the take was often astronomic.

The result was that horses coming off the tracks into retirement, if they recovered at all, took six to eight months just to get the dope out of their systems. Fine horses with great records proved to be "burned out," with glands gone when they went into retirement. Mares were found in many cases to be sterile. The foals of such horses—when there were foals —proved to be weak and without stamina of the thoroughbred quality. As incredible as it seems, the American thoroughbred horse was actually in danger of extinction.

During the course of our investigation, I called on one of the great figures in American racing, Joseph Widener. We discussed the problem openly and he admitted that our indicated findings at American tracks were correct.

"I tried to get a saliva test for all tracks," Widener told me, "but the Jockey Club said it was an unwarranted aspersion on the owners."

The saliva test was coming—that was inevitable—but a lot of trainers were preparing to fight it all the way to the wire. There were many others who fought us as if we and not the hoods were the enemy. The experiences we encountered were unbelievable. One of my agents remarked to me, after some particularly brutal episode, "Man's inhumanity to man is certainly mild compared to what he does to fine horses."

Our agents reported watching the technique of "freezing" used to deaden pain when a horse gives signs of lameness before a race. The bottoms of the pant legs of a pair of overalls are sewed up and the horse's front legs placed in the overalls; the straps are fastened around the neck. Then ice is poured into the pants legs and the horse stands in the ice. It is a common practice at all tracks; since it does not involve narcotics we cannot halt it. And the gamblers are interested only in winning the next one.

One sadistic, leather-booted trainer made a practice of kicking his horse in the stomach when it misbehaved. The brute literally hated this horse with a demoniac kind of fury. Observing him in their undercover role my agents had difficulty restraining themselves. I warned them to hold back; I had seen enough myself. When the time for arrest came, this big boy was mine. I was wrong about that, but I didn't know it then.

The horse was a beautiful 18-months old, which put him in the two-year old class. He would run with the best, but the trainer gave all his horses a "shotgun" when they went to post. He called it insurance. The prescription for this insurance was: 14 grains of cocaine, 3 grains of heroin and sufficient doses of nitroglycerin, phenol and the carrier, kola nut, to kill six oxen.

Through powerful field glasses, we watched this trainer give the horse one of these shots. It took five men to hold the animal. To me it was like watching a gang hold a six-year-old child and pour whiskey down its throat. "I hope he kicks their brains out," our agent muttered.

Eyes wild, flanks sweating, this poor creature went to the post and when the starting gun sounded he burst to the front, running like a foal of fury. Veering and twisting, he threw his rider and plunged on ahead of the pack, one length, two lengths, ten lengths as he went over the finishing line.

When the trainer went into the stable to see his horse after the race, no one was around. The trainer apparently decided to punish the animal for throwing his rider. In any case, the high whimpering agony of the horse could be heard above the normal noises of the track and the paddock. Stable hands rushed in. They saw the trainer holding the horse with one hand and beating him with a heavy board held in his other hand. Suddenly, as we watched, the trainer gave a cry. The two-year-old had edged him into a corner. Then the animal reared. Before the stable hands could reach him, the horse kicked and trampled his tormentor to death.

I felt that the time had come to close in with raids and arrests. I personally participated in a number of them. Federal narcotics agents at racetracks across the United States pulled in owners, trainers, grooms and racetrack hangers-on—anyone against whom we had evidence of narcotic violations.

Many of the racetrack characters we brought in during the raids were given prison terms. A judge in Detroit, passing sentence on one of the country's best known trainers, told this man:

"You have engaged in the most cruel racket ever to be divulged in this courtroom. Your horse would have rejected dope had you placed it before him in a bucket but you forced it down his throat to win a few filthy dollars. I am sending you to the penitentiary for ten years." The man who owned this trainer's stable said he no longer wanted to remain in such a vile business and sold his entire stable.

One prominent horseman I arrested demanded angrily, "Why do you pick on us, Commissioner? Everybody in racing has been doing the same thing."

"And everybody who does it," I informed him, "is going to the penitentiary."

The old timer and his two nags who provided our agents with the front they needed to make the probe was never uncovered nor did he have to testify in court; the evidence we had piled up with his aid was overwhelming.

Almost crushing political pressure was brought to bear in some cases—by top breeders and owners caught in our net. A national figure tried to force the White House to intervene on his behalf. The White House referred the message to me with the curt command: "Give him the works."

One question kept coming into my mind during the investigation: Where was the Society for the Prevention of Cruelty to Animals all this time, before, during and after our battle? Did none of their people have any idea of what was going on? Did none of them care? Did none of them have enough interest to seek the facts? I do not ask these questions merely to point a finger. While there has been much improvement, and the full acceptance of the saliva test, as a direct result of our investigations and convictions, there are still many practices that ought to be eliminated. The "freezing" technique is only one example. The ASPCA has the power and, I believe, the obligation, to take action.

Another point: it is perfectly legal and common practice in most states to grant licenses as trainers to men with criminal records. I made a personal plea to the Racing Association to establish a new rule forbidding the granting of licenses to persons convicted of narcotics charges. I was greeted by a stony silence.

At the time of all the horse drugging, one outstanding horseman, George P. Mahoney, a building contractor who was chairman of the Maryland State Racing Commission, set up what was called a "receiving barn." Here horses about to race could be looked over, given saliva tests, blood tests, urine tests, even a mouse test (the saliva of the horse is injected into the mouse; if the mouse's tail goes up in a question mark, the horse has been given some kind of stimulant).

This brought the expected anguished reactions; trainers announced they would go on strike if the receiving barns were not removed. I attended one meeting of the racing commission on this subject at which owners and trainers stood up to denounce Mahoney and his receiving barn. We had experts there to rebut them on every point, and the meeting ended with the commissioners affirming Mahoney's program to protect the horses of Maryland from the dope merchants. But the next day Mahoney came to me and told me that he was going to be ousted. Some of the owners had had a "chat" with the Governor.

There was a meeting shortly after that of the National Association of State Racing Commissioners, of which I am an honorary member. (This association was organized after our raids, to restore confidence in the tracks on a national scale. They have done an outstanding job and the public owes them a debt.) Mahoney, just before the meeting began, learned that the telegram informing him that he had been removed as Maryland Commissioner had already been written and was ready to go. "It's time to hit right in the middle of the meeting," Mahoney informed me. I was sure, however, that in view of all Mahoney had done to clean up racing, the National Association of Racing Commissioners would have to honor him with a vice-presidency.

It happened as predicted. The announcement that he had been fired came over the Associated Press in the middle of our meeting. George went back as vice-president of our association, however. He ran for governor also—and got the popular vote statewide but lost because of the unit rule in Maryland. He tried again and also ran for senator. Both times he narrowly missed.

After Maryland bluebloods had gotten rid of the receiving barn, they realized they had to do something to show the public how upright they were. They and other racetrack owners and operators across the country agreed to chip in half a million dollars to set up what is called the Thoroughbred Racing Protective Association. This organization was founded to keep all illegality, including all illegal use of drugs, out of the racetracks. Yet in the years from their founding to this writing they have never called at my office or asked us for a look at the fourteen drawers full of vital information about individuals, stables, methods of doping and other important data. Occasionally, one of their men will call in a Bureau branch for special information on some local individual; this is the extent of their curiosity.

It costs the racetrack people half a million dollars a year to keep the TRPA operating. I am sure it does some good and I know some such organization is needed; I only wonder why in all these years no one in the organization ever bothered to drop in.

We did make their task easier. With few exceptions, the drugging of thoroughbreds with heroin, cocaine or other narcotic drugs has virtually vanished. This is true also at foreign racetracks; we have given guidance and suggestions for controlling this business to officials who came to us for help from foreign tracks.

But does this mean all types of stimulation and depressives have been eliminated. In 1953, *Blood Horse* had another report: "Lipo-Adrenal Cortex and other hormones have replaced heroin and cocaine on all race tracks. Sales zoom at drug stores in communities where seasonal races take place. They do not show up in the saliva test. Breeders are alarmed. Mares coming from racetracks are hard to get in foal. Indiscriminate hormone administration to the young horses at tracks is interfering with the oestrous cycle. Young stallions are also being affected. It is now called Hormone Hopping. Horse trainers found it convenient to ignore Federal Narcotic laws until the Federal Bureau of Narcotics convinced them that it was more convenient to be out of jail. The thoroughbred is again in danger through infertility caused by hormone administration just to win a race. The stuff is also used on slow horses. As one expert puts it, 'They get high as a kite on this dangerous stuff.' "

Hormones are not narcotic and our Bureau is without jurisdiction.

PART SIX

PORTFOLIO

CHARACTERS IN A BOOK

Behind all the rules and procedures, the reports and forms and techniques of investigation, behind the daring and the danger, behind the formalism of the Bureau—we are human beings who must deal with other humans. Some of these others are killers, some are preachers, some are great figures of literature. Some stand out from the group for assorted reasons; a depth of despair or depravity they have plumbed, or a taste of the heights of power.

In this section, I cite the facts on several of these beguiling characters who stand out in my mind and memory as heros or villains. Knowing which is which is not always easy. Or even possible, in some cases.

23. "The White House Calling . . ."

A call from the White House does not, of course, mean that the President is on the line, or even one of his assistants. In this instance it was not even a member of his staff. It was, however, one of the most famous ministers in the United States. "I am calling you from the White House now," he announced. "We have been discussing the case of a friend of mine in which you and your agents are involved. I am going to see my Senator about this. I will then come direct to your office. At what time will you be able to see me today?"

His tone was arrogant and rude. It was hardly the approach a man of the cloth is supposed to take. But in the interests of amity between the Executive Mansion and the Bureau, I set a time in the late afternoon.

Pressure and the attempted use of it is one harassment enforcement officers battle unremittingly. Pressures come from many sources; officials, businessmen, criminals, social workers and agencies as well as from the highest positions of power. Sometimes they are justified; and in any case, a measure of pressure is normal and expected. Criminals and suspected criminals are human beings and have friends who stand by them; it is natural for friends to speak a word on behalf of a man in trouble.

So far as the Bureau is concerned, pressure has little effect except where we feel it is in the public interest to give a man a break. This has been my invariable rule. Not pressure from above, but what the man has to offer the public, through us its agents, in terms of information, facts, testimony or leads that can smash a gang.

But there are other kinds of pressures the public office of self-respect finds repugnant and loathsome.

The nationally-known minister who showed up at my office from the White House was the pastor of one of the largest churches in the United States, with a membership in the thousands. I had read about this man and seen his picture often in the press. The name of the underworld figure in whom the pastor was interested was also familiar to me; he was on our list of Mafia hoodlums we hoped either to lodge into jail or deport. The gangster was a big dealer in heroin. Everything I knew about him and his background was bad.

The minister described this gangster as an intimate friend, referring to him by his first name. "The arrest was a disgraceful business," he asserted with vast indignation. "Your men beat him without mercy. I have never heard of such brutality before. His civil rights have been ignored. I've talked with the President and my Senator about it. They are both launching immediate probes."

"In that case," I inquired, "why do you bother to come here?"

"The White House suggested I talk with you and report back to them."

I knew intimately the facts of this case in which he had injected himself. Frankie was one of the high wires in the East Coast narcotics syndicate, handling importation of heroin and distribution throughout the United States. Our agents had risked their lives to get evidence against him. When they had gone in to arrest him, they had to push the man's son out of the way and restrain his wife from beating them over the head with pots and pans.

The minister half smiled. I inquired if he realized that his good friend Frankie had jumped bail of $75,000 and gone into hiding and was now a fugitive from justice.

"Yes," he answered, "and if he is killed as a result, it will be your fault."

I am respectful of clergymen, Protestant, Jew or Catholic. But in this instance the man before me, prominent as he was, was betraying everything that the church he represented stood for. My feelings had reached the thin tearing point. "You are wearing the cloth of a minister of the gospel," I said, "but you represent the Devil. You should be defrocked."

He did not answer me. I stood up. I said, "Your gangster friend is not of your flock—you are Protestant and he is nominally a Catholic. But not a good one, I can tell you. He doesn't even live in your state," I continued, "but he comes into your state and kills some of your own parishioners with dope—he even makes a dope addict out of his own son, so he can use the boy to deliver his poison to the customers.

"I don't need to ask you why you didn't go to the Senator from the state where Frankie lives. You would have been run out of the office. The Senator you went to is the one all the hoods go to when they need help in legislation, or to halt a deportation." I knew the Senator to be a kind-hearted man who in the past had been "used" by hoodlums because they could appeal to his sympathies.

Drawing himself up like an angel of judgment, the minister said: "I shall report your calumny directly to the President."

I answered very quietly: "The White House will not call me about this case. The Senator will not launch an investigation. This whole story and your whole pompous act doesn't quite come off."

"You dare accuse me—a man of God—of lying?"

"If you're not," I said, "pick up the phone and call the White House—or the Senator's office—and tell them about your reception here and my reaction to your pleas for this hoodlum."

I pointed to the phone. The minister stared at it as if hynotized. "What a forked-tongued phoney you are," I told him, "coming here and trying to put the arm on me for the Mafia. If I hear any more of this bilge, I'll throw you through that door by the seat of your pants. Then you'll have a real civil rights case."

I waited. Without one word more he picked up his expensive hat, turned and walked out.

As soon as he was gone, I called the White House. I knew that they would never intercede in such a case; we never have calls from the White House involving dope peddlers. The late Louis Howe, in fact, Franklin D. Roosevelt's chief advisor for many years in the White House, on one occasion told me, "The President hates dope peddlers. If you send a letter recommending pardon for any of these characters—send along your resignation at the same time."

Indeed, only a day before his death, FDR penned in his own handwriting, on a petition for pardon (not recommended by our Bureau incidentally): "Denied—dope peddler—FDR."

I talked with one of the President's secretaries, explained that this minister had called to me originally from the White House and told him what had ensued. The secretary informed me that the minister had been there regarding problems of minorities. Nothing discussed had anything to do with the case of the gangster, in which the White House had no interest whatsoever.

I called the Senator's office and talked with him personally. He said the minister had called him on the phone about the case. He said to forget about it; he was planning no investigation of this or any other matter involving our Bureau.

The hoodlum Frankie defaulted on his bail, slipped out of the country with his wife and family and fled to Italy. Because of technicalities, he could not be extradited. The same minister dropped in to see me, some months later, "I have come to ask your forgiveness," he said calmly, "I was used by that man. I did not know his true character."

I repeated what I said to him before: "You should look

after your congregation instead of Mafia gangsters who make blood-money contributions to the church to salve their conscience."

It is, of course, a routine syndicate gambit to play for the sympathy of the clergy, of social workers and individuals who lack sufficient experience in professional crime.

In a Midwestern city a dealer in dope and other vices actually ran the city, elected officials and told them what they could and could not do. We had the man indicted but could get nowhere; all prospective jurymen from whom the panel was called were working for him, either directly or indirectly. We finally brought him to trial in another district—but lost. Preachers, rabbis, priests and others interested in social service all came forward with hosannas to paint him as the city's great benefactor, giving thousands of dollars each Christmas to their various causes.

This was all entirely true. But it was also true that his benefactions came out of the millions he made in dope, crooked gambling and whoremongering.

It is my opinion that the church could do more today—infinitely more—than they are doing or attempting to do. Our churches and their leaders could—and must—do better in combating illicit drug peddling. There is need for more active interest and knowledge, for more effort. This is particularly true in backing the government—before legislative committees—for tough laws to curtail the illegal sale of narcotics.

An inspiring role in this direction has been taken by one church—the relatively small Seventh Day Adventists. They have, in fact, given us strong support and expert testimony —in the state and national battle for realistic legislation. More active support by all faiths would be a godsend to our country and especially its youths.

24. Literary Lion

In 1958 and 1960, an ex-convict, a former addict and self-admitted forger of medical prescriptions "by the bushel," authored two books; one was called *Mine Enemy Grows Older*, the other *May This House Be Safe from Tigers*. Both were national best sellers for many months. Both were the products of a man who called himself Alexander King.

What Mr. King, alias Alex Rosenfield, alias Myron Klein, thinks of me personally, or of the Federal Narcotics Bureau or the Public Health Service Hospital for addicts at Lexington, is not important. It is his privilege to think and say or write what he wishes. What is important is that this author, whose works reached millions, stands as an example of why there is so much misinformation and misunderstanding about narcotic controls, why so many people attack controls without even knowing what they attack, or the facts at issue.

I cite the case of Alexander King because he makes no pretense about his own record. If what this former addict says is correct, everything that I have striven for, every effort of the Bureau to control dangerous drugs, every effort of the United States to stem the traffic in illicit drugs, is wrong.

I believe that Mr. King has done harm with his attacks on the Bureau, the hospital at Lexington, and me personally. I believe his assault should be answered. For like so many of those who assail our enforcement procedures, King owes his own cure, his whole chance for success and fortune achieved since that time, to the very people and methods and institutions he now derides.

What are the facts about Mr. King himself?

A native of Vienna, Austria, he was brought to the country in 1914 as a youth. In 1930, under the name of Alex Rosenfield, he was sentenced to Elmira Reformatory on a forgery charge.

Following his release from Elmira his career appears to have been that of mingling with all the world, the great and the phoney, black and white, good and bad. A main reason for the interest in his books, in fact, appears to have been his wide range of subjects, associates and interests.

In 1947, King became addicted to narcotics. The record shows that in 1950 he was arrested for his first narcotic drug violation.

"His offense," the record states "involved writing and passing of nineteen (19) forged narcotic prescriptions for a total of 380 tablets of Dilaudid. He stole prescription blanks from a physician's office and forged the doctor's name." The U.S. Attorney permitted King to enter Lexington for treatment.

There can be no doubt that the activities of King during the years of his addiction called not only for legal action by the authorities but also for compassion and pity. Nor is there any doubt of the efforts our Bureau and its agents made to rescue this man from himself, his own weakness, and to send him back cured and able to meet the world on its own terms.

In 1951, for example, after his arrest, King made the following statement to Federal Narcotic Agent John E. Tagley at the Federal Bureau of Narcotics in New York City: "I, Alexander King, make the following statement of my own free will without threat or promise of immunity, with the knowledge that anything I may say may be used against me.

"I have been addicted to narcotic drugs for the past three and a half years; I am fifty-one years of age, and started using narcotics due to medication having obtained same from different physicians. I have been shown approximately 50 prescriptions, each prescription for Dilaudid, $\frac{1}{16}$ of a grain, 20 tablets each, dated from May 31, 1950 to March 23, 1951 and state that I wrote these prescriptions myself and passed them and obtained the narcotics called for at the various drug stores.

"I have been shown specifically 2 prescriptions dated 3/23/51 calling for 20 tablets of Dilaudid $\frac{1}{16}$ gr., written in the name of Alexander King, 180 Riverside Drive, on the prescription blank of Harry Shilkret, and presented in the name of Alexander King, 180 Riverside Drive, on the prescription blank of Dr. Harry Shilkret. I state that I wrote these prescriptions and passed them at the ——— Pharmacy, ——— Broadway, where I obtained the narcotics called for. I had these blank prescriptions of Dr. Shilkret for some time. I had taken the prescription pad from the office of Dr. Shilkret without his knowledge approximately one and a half years ago. At that time this physician was treating me.

"I am anxious to obtain treatment for my addiction and wish to go to Lexington, Kentucky, as soon as authorities will permit."

This was his second arrest on narcotic charges within a year, and on his conviction for those scores of forged prescriptions, a key notation of his record reads as follows: "Judge Sidney Sugarman suspended imposition of sentence and placed Alexander King on probation for 3 years on condition that he surrender to the U.S. Marshal for transportation to Lexington, Ky., to remain there until released as cured." King surrendered to the U.S. Marshall on April 4, 1951.

In 1954, while still on probation, he disappeared and was declared a fugitive. Late in that year the following report was turned in by our agent:

"On November 12, 1954, the reporting officer, in attempts to locate the fugitive Alexander King, visited the premises, 64 W. 9th Street, NYC. . . . The writer interviewed the building superintendent and learned that Alexander King was apparently still living there in Apartment 5-N. The writer went to 5-N. Alexander King was not found in the apartment but a search of the fifth floor found him hiding in a hallway toilet. Mr. King stated he is now earning a good living in that he just signed a contract to write an autobiography of his life. . . ."

King was taken to the office of the U.S. Probation Officer and then turned over to the custody of the U.S. Marshall. The records show that he was sentenced to eight months in a federal prison for violation of his probation.

He himself admits it took four stints at the Lexington Hospital to do it, and mixes his statements with considerable vitriol directed at me personally. But the fact remains that it was at Lexington, during his last stay, that King was cured.

What kind of place is this hospital in Lexington that Mr. King assails? I have mentioned it often before in this book in general terms; here I wish to be quite explicit.

It is a hospital run by the federal government and dedicated to giving drug addicts the benefit of the latest available treatments, medical, psychiatric, and psychological, to help effect their permanent cure.

It is true that the underworld has tried to infiltrate Lexington, sending in "voluntary" patients who have proved to be peddlers connected with the mob outside; it is true that the mob has pushers staked out in Lexington hotels and motels; this too is part of our struggle.

Patients at Lexington are of four basic types: Those who come under federal sentence, those who come under federal probation, those who come voluntarily and those who come as "bluegrass patients."

This last type are volunteer patients who, unable to fight the narcotic habit, walk out after a few days or a week. Authorities, of course, can't go on wasting time and taxpayers' money on this type of in-and-out patient. So, a few years after the hospital opened, in the early 1930's, Kentucky passed a law making it a misdemeanor to be an addict. Now if a patient desires to come back after walking out, he has to surrender to Kentucky authorities, he is found guilty of the technical offense of being an addict, and he is sentenced to Lexington for treatment. His treatment inside is no different from before. But this time he must stay until he has completed the treatment and can be released as cured.

Some addicts seeking help request this "bluegrass patient" status voluntarily—to protect themselves from their own weakness.

Therapy technique at Lexington has been evolved over many years by specialists in this field. Treatment begins with a complete examination, physical, mental, emotional. The tests are as thorough and complete as can be devised. Deep psychological disturbance is found in the majority of patients.

Following the tests, withdrawal treatment is begun, using a substitute narcotic known as methadon, a drug developed by the Germans in World War II. The withdrawal rate varies with the patient, his age, his physical condition, the number of years on drugs and other data. Stage by stage, the dosage is reduced, until, usually within about two to three weeks, the patient is off of drugs entirely.

Treatment for marijuana users is different: Total abstinence is used here, since no bodily withdrawal symptoms develop with this drug; but much emphasis is placed on the psychological and emotional treatment and support phase of therapy.

The addict patient often has additional physical complications, brought on from the abuse of his body in the very processes of addiction, the lack of food, rest, and other factors. These must be treated medically along with the addiction itself.

The purpose of this program is to rehabilitate the whole individual. There is a continued treatment program following the withdrawal stage in which the individual patient is readjusted so far as possible to living without drugs. He is given occupational therapy in his own profession.

This phase is almost as important as the medical and psychiatric. If it is a writer or potential writer, there are facilities for him to write, there is even a newspaper at the hospital on which he can work. There is an orchestra. Plays are produced. If a man or woman has no special talents and training, there are programs for development of manual skills, agricultural techniques, even dressmaking.

Voluntary patients are charged at a rate of $8.50 a day, and required to put down a nominal deposit in advance, if they are financially able to pay. But no patients are turned away because they lack funds.

Such is Lexington, a place of salvage. Alexander King was critical of his first two trips, but he hardly gave himself a chance to get well; his only idea was to get out as fast as he could, back to Bohemia and dope.

Writing of his third experience in his book *Mine Enemy Grows Older*, he reports candidly:

"But all this is really beside the point at the moment, because what I originally intended to tell you about was the time when I was finally arrested for passing a forged prescription in a drugstore up on Seventy-first Street and Broadway.

"I had, as usual, gathered an indiscriminate armful of cosmetics from the display tables and, loaded down with this debris, had stepped up to the counter and placed my phoney scrip before the attending clerk, when a tall, gangly, country-type gent quietly stepped alongside me and flashed his goddamned badge.

"Well, I'd been expecting something like it for quite a while, because for almost two years I'd been flooding the town with hundreds of forged drug prescriptions. But still, when Uncle Sam's boy suddenly stood there beside me with that bronze onion in his hand, the jolt of it nearly knocked me on my can. . . .

"Well, he was a narcotics agent, all right, but, I tell you, he looked and acted less like a cop than some of the doormen I've seen around town. He looked like a sort of untalented

Lincoln, and I also noticed that he had a very nice, quiet voice.

" 'Why didn't you go back to Lexington?' he said to me. 'Why don't you go down there and give yourself a chance?'

" 'I've been there twice already,' I said.

" 'But you just stayed a month each time,' he said. 'A month ain't enough. Why don't you go back there and stay for a while?' "

A few paragraphs later, King reports: " 'Just a minute,' I said. 'You mean, you'll let me put all this stuff in storage and let me go down to Lexington by myself, without handcuffs?'

" 'Sure,' he said. 'You're not a bad guy. You're just in a jam. One of your doctors told me that you *are* pretty sick. So go on down. Only, don't take too long about it. Let's see, today is Friday. Why don't you get off the beginning of next week? By the way, you didn't cash your scrip this evening, so how are you fixed for stuff?'

" 'I'll need a shot pretty badly in a couple of hours,' I said.

" 'Okay,' he said. 'You go to any doctor in this neighborhood and if he doesn't want to write for you, just tell him to call me up. I'll give you my home number and I'll see that he puts you straight until you can get out of town!'

"In short, he was an absolute prince.

"And how did I react to this prince? Like a typical drug addict. I sold all my furniture the very next day and took it on the lam. I moved over to Brooklyn, and for the next six months I scraped and cheated and scrounged and finagled. And then, when I was at last completely strapped and couldn't even raise a quarter, I finally landed down at 90 Church Street, with the narcotics squad.

"I'll say one thing for those boys, nobody reproached me, nobody was disappointed in me, and nobody had a grudge against me."

Further on, he writes:

"When I landed at Lexington for my third cure, great

changes seemed to have taken place down there. For one thing, the psychologists and psychiatrists were high in the saddle, and the tough custodial forces were definitely on the defensive. It didn't last very long, but, while it lasted, it was possible to demonstrate that doctors, and only doctors, could ever achieve any worthwhile and effective methods of coping with the problem of drug addiction.

"For instance, I attended innumerable meetings at which group therapy was practiced, and there was no question in my mind that individuals otherwise inaccessible to any form of social approach or coordination became, in the course of these sessions, voluntarily cooperative and even self-critical to a really astonishing degree.

"I saw no miracles performed, but I witnessed the next best thing. I saw and heard drug addicts who, finally, freely confessed to themselves and to others that their addiction was just an inadequate but desperate cover for their failure to accept the responsibilities of grown-up men. Now, then, this admission is so grimly basic a requirement for any reformation, that no conceivable cure can ever be achieved without it.

"They had some damned good psychatrists at Lexington during that short spell of purposeful rehabilitation, and the best of these, a Dr. James Thorpe, has since become one of my very dearest friends. In fact, he is the only psychiatrist in the country to whom I would dare to disclose the shaky state of my mental equilibrium, if I ever decided to do such a thing. . . ."

Both of King's books were written after his cure. Yet in his second book, he decided to take a far different tack. You might think that he would have some gratitude after his cure. Instead he writes in *May This House Be Safe from Tigers:*

"That's why, of course, there are hardly any cures. I've been off the stuff now over five years, but the people that were down there with me, the ones I kept in touch with, are all back on junk again. Every last one of them, excepting me.

You needn't bother with any of the silly, fraudulent statistics —you're getting it straight from the horse's mouth. And, what's more, there isn't going to be any change for the better until the whole narcotics business is taken out of the hands of the numskull cops who are administering it now. The head of the Narcotics Bureau is a bonehead in my opinion, and so he's hardly the man to suggest any substantial improvements in this bitterly neglected territory. He wants tougher judges and stiffer sentences, and he particularly wants no interference from nosy doctors and psychiatrists. His name is Harry J. Anslinger, and I believe that his name will eventually go down in medical history as one of the major stumbling blocks to an enlightened policy in the field of human rehabilitation.

"I do not know a single physician who is familiar with this subject or a really conscientious penologist who thinks any differently than I do about Anslinger. And I've got him down for a lard-brained cop who knows exactly how and when to cash his pay check—and with this concession to his talents I've just about exhausted everything laudatory that I can say about him. Of course, he didn't invent the monstrously benighted policy of the Narcotics Bureau, he just seems to do his god-damndest to perpetuate it. In this he had certainly succeeded. There is no aspect of American life that is more hemmed in with sinister medieval taboos, more burdened with lurid, rancorous prejudices, and more encumbered with morbid, shrivel-hearted self-interest than the law enforcement end of the narcotics business.

"I say 'business' advisedly. Remember that most of the cops in this game, the wardens, the keepers and the endless guards and shamuses all over the country have a vested interest, by the very nature of their jobs, in keeping the whole slimy narcotics racket going as long as possible.

"Just have that in mind for a moment and you'll understand the whole bastardly setup a hell of a lot better than you ever did before. It pays a lot of people, and pays them damned well, that somebody, somewhere, is permanently hooked on dope.

And many of the guys that find it so profitable aren't gangsters or drug pushers, either.

"Anyway, that's the general picture, and so it stands to reason that the narcotics hospitals can't really do a hell of a lot for you. The guide word is, predominantly, Penology and not Reclamation, no matter what you may have heard about this whole messy theme. There are always two or three decent doctors at Lexington who try their best to be of actual use, who sincerely believe that drug addiction requires a medical and not a punitive form of treatment. Indeed, lip service to such a posture is given in all crappy literature gotten out by the responsible jobholders in this field, but in actual practice it's just a lot of horseshit. Every louse who makes a living at it has a staggering moral ascendancy over the drug addict, and, what's more, he never misses a chance to let him feel it. And that's how it all stands as of this moment, I'm sorry to say."

One wonders about the tall agent of our Bureau who gave King such a break, only to have King walk out on him. One wonders, too, why King changes his tone in the second book, and if he found it more profitable to write in this vein, striking back at those who tried and ultimately succeeded in helping him.

This, after all, is basically all we want to do with addicts: Help them get well. And when we have done it through such facilities as the Public Health Service hospitals, we feel a sense of achievement.

A memorandum from one of my staff reads: "It is clear that Alexander King, alias Alex Rosenfield, alias Myron Klein, was saved from utter ruin by 'those very idiots' whom he now berates at every opportunity."

To borrow Mr. King's apt words: "That's how it all stands at this moment, I'm sorry to say."

25. Pirates, Derelicts and Con Men

Some of the characters in our portfolio strut their way across the stage like ego-maniacs. Still others have the arrogance of anonymity and existence seemingly beyond the reach of laws. The chimerical figure of a California shipowner was one of the latter variety.

At some early stage in his beclouded career he became the owner of a Polish vessel *Przemysl* (pronounced *She-me-zul*), which was devoted to carrying narcotics and other contraband products destined for the United States. The goods were delivered to California.

This man came to be known to us as the "Black Pirate." He was never personally involved. He had a fine home in San Diego on a promontory overlooking the Pacific. His name was never connected with any actual act of smuggling; he was in fact, within his community, respected and looked up to as a law-abiding citizen. If there was trouble an attorney or some underling appeared for an obscure firm which had an interest in this vessel. But the man himself remained a mere shadow in the background.

We first got word about this business when the German captain who had signed as master of the *Przemysl*, came to the American Consul at the German port from which she was to sail, and informed the Consul of the nature of the voyage. The captain said he was under orders of the owners to navigate the ship to a pre-designated point off the coast near San Diego. Fast motor launches would then ferry the California-bound contraband ashore, landing at isolated spots.

As payment for such a tip-off the captain would receive, by law, a percentage of the seizure. The cargo was worth hundreds of thousands of dollars. The captain stood to reap a sea-going harvest for double-crossing the Black Pirate. Such rewards are standard government procedure. The surest way to smash smuggling is to make it worthwhile for somebody to turn the smugglers in.

The *Przemysl*'s German captain was given specific directions; he was to anchor off San Diego at the designated point and wharf. The Coast Guard would take over at the moment when the motor launches showed up to take on cargo.

After the vessel put out to sea weeks passed with no word. Then the ship suddenly showed up not off San Diego but at a dock in New Orleans. Customs spotted her and sent word to Treasury in Washington. Before a decision could be made the German captain strode into Customs to announce he was turning the ship over to them.

Admiralty lawyers showed up within a matter of hours; a little man from Vancouver, British Columbia, also arrived on the scene. Technically, it appeared he was "the owner" of the *Przemysl*. The actual owner did not appeal at all. But the argument was very clear; the court found that the owners were completely within their rights. They had not smuggled in anything—how could they when the ship was taken from them by their hired captain and put into New Orleans. Taking a ship in such a way was simple piracy; the vessel and its cargo must be returned to its lawful owner.

The captain kept pretty much to his New Orlean's hotel room for the next few days. "I am afraid those guys in California might show up and put a hole in my head," he told a hotel bartender. We gave the captain his fare back to Germany. When he got there he was arrested and tried for piracy himself. The German court gave him five years.

The German captain had not understood that we live in America by the rule of laws. Coast Guard could take over within the twelve-mile limit—but only after an overt act. The vessel itself was finished; everyone knew her and pretty much what she was carrying. She went up to Canada, got herself a buyer for her legitimate supplies, threw the rest overboard. The Black Pirate owner in San Diego took a heavy loss.

For some months we heard no more of the Black Pirate. Then word came from one of our most experienced Customs agents in the Far East that a craft was being built with great secrecy in Shanghai. False bottoms were being put in, concealed cabins for carrying opium and Chinese slaves. The name of the vessel was the *Marabella*. She was a 135-foot, two-masted schooner. She would be flying the Panamanian flag. Her engines were reported to be new and very fast. The reputed owner was the Black Pirate of San Diego. We sent the consul a terse message about the *Marabella:* "Cable departure."

The following week came the word: She had departed with a load of opium, heroin and an unknown number of Chinese girls to be sold as prostitutes in the United States. The Coast Guard admiral informed me: "We do not have sufficient ships to cover the entire Pacific or to keep up with a ship reportedly as fast as the *Marabella*. I suggest you ask the Navy for their help."

The Washington Navy officer in charge of the Pacific operations was in favor of participation, but another officer on the West Coast, on receiving the orders to hunt down the *Marabella*, called Washington and told the Navy Secretary: "The United States Navy must uphold its traditions. We are a fighting arm, not an anti-smuggling unit." The Navy Secretary called the Secretary of the Treasury. He was apologetic but the Navy couldn't get involved in this sort of thing; the Coast Guard would have to handle it alone.

The Coast Guard tried. They threw as many of their limited number of cutters as they could muster into the San Diego area and they did, finally, spot the *Marabella* and put at least one shot across her bow before she got underway and with her powerful engines wide open quickly outsped the cutters and lost them.

Sometimes you have to know your way through the channels in Washington, especially in the State Department, to get results. You have to know the people you can rely on. I went to one of these friends who must remain unidentified. On several occasions he pulled us out of international tangles. I explained to him that this ship was of questionable registry. She actually belonged to the Black Pirate but she was registered under the Panamanian flag. "We can't catch her in territorial waters," I told him, "she's too fast. Outside the twelve-mile limit, she feels safe; she travels leisurely. I think we could slip up and surprise her out there."

My friend in the State Department gave me a sidelong look and said, "Pull her in and let's see what happens. She has no status."

I went to the Coast Guard admiral and asked him if he would do it. "Will you take the consequences if it boomerangs?" the admiral asked me.

I told him I had talked with Customs and the State Department. He said he would go ahead if I could assure him that he and the Coast Guard would not be on the hook. I agreed.

The Coast Guard located the *Marabella*, seized her and pulled her in. The Black Pirate of San Diego let out a roar when he heard the news and went into action. The Panamanian Ambassador in Washington called on the Secretary of State and declared that the Coast Guard had committed an act of war. The Secretary of State called the Secretary of the Treasury and demanded an explanation for this outrageous conduct. The Secretary of the Treasury called Customs, the Coast Guard, the Federal Narcotics Bureau—and me.

The burden fell on me. I was called to the office of the Secretary of the Treasury and asked to explain. I protected my friend in the State Department and the admiral in the Coast Guard. I told the Secretary of the Treasury, "Sir, when I asked the Coast Guard to bring this ship in, I exceeded my authority."

Everybody understood what the *Marabella* was and what had happened. The Secretary of the Treasury's reply to my confession was an elaborate wink. And as soon as the Panamanian ambassador realized the nature and history of the vessel, he very quickly decided to drop this complaint.

The *Marabella* was released. From then on she was a marked woman. When she went into Mexico waters, she was fined for changing masters without a license. The captain who had come over with her the first time returned to Shanghai, a haunted mariner. He drank heavily and told anyone who would listen of his voyage on the *Marabella* and how one night the Coast Guard fired a shot across his bow. He had quite a story to tell—no wonder he was haunted. He had turned and fled to sea, he said, and had thrown a hundred Chinese girls overboard to drown because he did not want to be captured with human contraband on board. A few weeks after he began to spread this story in Shanghai bars, he committed suicide.

The *Marabella* never went back to Shanghai. The Panamanian government revoked her phony registry. She succeeded in unloading her cargo at last in lower California and Mexico. Then she put into the Mexican port of Ensenada.

Bill Smale, an old friend and colleague of mine when I was consul at Nassau, was American consul at Ensenada at that time. He kept a close watch on the *Marabella*. All attempts to get a Mexican registry or any other registration was blocked —chiefly through the efforts of Bill, who followed every move the owner and his lawyers tried to make. Finally, the Black Pirate of San Diego ordered the lawyers to have her engines taken out and sold them.

I was in Ensenada not long afterwards, and Bill Smale took me to the coast and pointed to a rotting hulk of a derelict schooner, sticking out of the water. "There's your wicked old girl friend, *Marabella*," Bill said.

"Don't malign her, Bill," I said. "She wasn't old—only misguided."

The *Marabella* and her San Diego owner represented a legendary and elusive kind of evil, a kind of modern flying Dutchman with high-powered engines. An exactly opposite variety in character and case is seen in the brash and self-assured saga of Dr. Fritz.

For us this began on a day when a Polish count came to the Rockefeller Foundation in New York with a proposition; he was seeking backing for a man I will call Dr. Fritz who had discovered, he said, a way to produce synthetic morphine that did not cause addiction. This is, of course, the *sine qua non* that scientists have sought for centuries, an analgesic or pain-killer that does not also produce, if used steadily, habituation, tolerance and dependency, the tripod of addiction.

Scientists still do not know why pain-killers produce this tripod. For a time it was believed that there was something in the opium plant itself, but this theory was abandoned when it was found that the synthetics—there are more than sixty of them at this writing—also produce addiction.

It was not unnatural that the Rockefeller Foundation was interested enough to ask me to check on the Polish count's proposal. The count was happy to give me all the information. "Dr. Fritz is a scientist whose eminence in Europe is unquestioned," the count asserted in our interview. "He's at present in New York."

"And has equipment to produce this drug?"

"In Europe. He is returning to Europe shortly. But he will ship all of it here—at his own expense—if this goes through."

When Dr. Fritz left for Europe, the following week, we discovered after his departure that he had left behind a couple of unpaid hotel bills. Our report to the Rockefeller Foundation on Dr. Fritz was not ecstatic.

Not long after he left, I learned on good authority that the bill-jumping Dr. Fritz was himself addicted to morphine. However, on his arrival in London from New York, he convinced the British government that they ought to back up his experiments. They were ready to let him work with Sir Robert Robertson but when he learned they would not let him use actual morphine or hand any of the drug over to him for personal experiments, he backed out. Then the British authorities found he had obtained morphine with forged prescriptions; they jailed him briefly and deported him to Germany.

Dr. Fritz and his wife returned to America on business, registered at one of the best hotels in New York and began negotiations with a major American pharmaceutical firm on his process for producing non-addictive morphine. He disclosed that he had sold his patent to a Swiss company but now was a major stockholder and official in this firm. The Swiss company entered into contracts with Fritz under which he and his wife agreed to carry out actual production of the new non-addictive narcotic at our American pharmaceutical concern. The American firm agreed to furnish the laboratory and the morphine.

The American company was too eager, too cautious and too secretive. Had they come to us we might have saved them a large sum of money and embarrassment. We knew nothing until we received word through our own channels that Dr. Fritz had been turned loose—with virtual *carte blanche* access —in a plant with a million dollar stock of morphine.

We put some of our agents on this case and found that Fritz and his wife had in their hotel room quantities of liquid containing morphine, plus a syringe and other hypodermic equipment. However, we held back, to let their "experiment" reach a conclusion. We were as anxious as the pharmaceutical firm to see the product; we did not, however, share their expectations.

Fritz and his wife finally produced their "neo-morphine"

and turned it over to the company; the firm's officials asked them to remain for a week to ten days while they completed some clinical tests. Dr. Fritz said he would have to get permission to remain from his firm in Switzerland. On the pretense of seeing these associates, the couple left hurriedly for New York—so swiftly that our agent was caught off guard and lost the quarry. They registered under false names at a hotel in New York and checked out a few hours later. We heard they had boarded a liner for Europe.

The firm had given the Fritzes 965.5 grams with which to experiment. Dr. Fritz reported that he lost 500 grams in preparation of his neo-morphine through breakage. Even if this were true, analysis of his product indicated a 23 percent additional loss of morphine; approximately 224.4 grams simply could not be accounted for—except that the doctor and his wife took them for their own use.

Like strange, narcotic contorted clowns, Fritz and his wife began popping up in odd corners. We received information that the undaunted Dr. Fritz was posing as a "Privy Commercial Counsellor" of the former German duchy of Lippe-Detnold. Authorities in Jerusalem reported that he had come into that city and rented a shop across from a big hotel, presumably "to open a scientific laboratory." Once they checked into his record, he was hustled out of Jerusalem and went to Alexandria. Customs officials arrested him on arrival for possession of two and a half ounces of heroin, enough for about a thousand shots. As a German citizen he was fined $500 by the German Consulate court and kicked out of Egypt.

Dr. Fritz was next arrested in Zurich for passing forged prescriptions for drugs, and kicked out of Switzerland. He went to Panama, was denied a visa to the United States, got himself an Honduras passport which purportedly showed him to have been born in Appledorn, Holland, and to be now proceeding to the United States on official business for the Bolivian government.

Our consul checked on the claims and after an exchange of

cables rejected his visa application on the grounds that he was a fraud traveling with a false passport. He remained in Central America, posing as a professor from the University of Berlin and fooling a great many people. Even the president of one of the Central American nations was taken in. Dr. Fritz was given a large financial grant by this Central American nation to work on a radio beam that could be pointed straight at Hitler and destroy him.

During the Second World War, Fritz and his wife made a suicide pact. The good doctor somehow gave himself a much smaller dose of veronal than he gave his wife; he awakened and recovered; she never awoke. The authorities confined the doctor to an asylum for the insane.

Near the end of the war he showed up in New York City. No one seemed to know how he got there; no one would admit to letting him in. But he was there, traveling on a false French passport under an assumed name, buying chemicals for French laboratories, so he said. He was picked up and interned as an enemy alien. One day an Army colonel called on me. He explained that the Army had discovered that it had interned a famous German scientist who claimed to have an invention that would end the rubber shortage. He had discovered a powerful hormone that could be injected into a rubber sapling and latex would flow within a few months.

The Army was interested, the colonel said. It could be a great thing for America and its allies. The Army was, in fact, ready to build an experimental laboratory at the cost of several millions of dollars. They wanted to give this man his freedom so he could start to work. But they had heard a rumor that he had also done some experimental work for a big American company in the field of morphine. The Army decided to check with us.

It was, of course, our old antagonist, Dr. Fritz. "Colonel," I said, "let me tell you a story."

When I finished, the colonel, somewhat pale, agreed that they could start looking elsewhere for rubber-tree hormones.

I have heard nothing from Dr. Fritz or about him since that day.

Yet the truth is that we are all characters, with a certain measure of duplicity in us, whichever side of the governmental fence we may be on. I am always reminded of this by an episode of my early 20's.

When I was American consul at Nassau, I received word from the captain of a fishing boat that a number of American yachts were being held at Nassau in quarantine, in the blazing heat, and that the owners and operators of these yachts were literally boiling mad. The owners of the five yachts included J. P. Morgan, Vincent Astor, the Vanderbilts and others of similar position and wealth. In addition, five or six schooners of fishermen were also being held.

I went out and investigated personally in the early evening. At the quarantine point, about ten miles from Nassau, all the yachts were bathed in floodlights. The people on board were angry. The quarantine was supposed to last thirty days. I went back and talked to Nassau's governor. He sent me to the health officer, who stated that there was smallpox in Florida and all these ships had come from Florida. I checked with the U.S. Public Health Service. They reported only normal incidence of alastrim, a mild form of smallpox, practically never fatal.

In this kind of situation, the only step is a counter-move. My counter-move was to call in Black Dan, who ran a fleet of smuggling ships and whose information was said to be the most accurate in the Caribbean. I asked him if there were any cases of contagious diseases in the Bahamas.

"Only alastrim—on Andros," Dan stated.

The following day a large passenger liner about to leave for its home port of New York asked for a bill of health. With Black Dan's report on Andros I felt secure in putting down as prevalent diseases in the general area of Nassau and outlying islands: "Leprosy, and alastrim, a form of smallpox." Shortly afterward a group of Nassau steamship agents and local officials stormed into the American Consulate. "This is an irresponsible outrage," one of the men roared out. "You can't have this liner quarantined. The publicity would wreck the tourist trade in Nassau. You can't do this."

"All right," said I, "Lift the quarantine against the American yachts here and I'll remove the notation to which you object."

The Governor sent word he wanted to see me. I found him greatly disturbed. I told him the full story of the so-called smallpox both in Florida and on the islands. I reminded him that they did have an isolation house on the island and on the day before police had discovered a girl with leprosy in the store next to my apartment.

Quarantine for the tied-up American crafts was lifted. The bill of health for the liner was cleaned up.

The millionaire yachtsmen were delighted. They called at the consulate and invited my wife and me to dinner on the biggest yacht out there. After dinner, the men went into the salon for a game of poker. I always have played a careful game. I didn't ask them about the stakes.

Throughout the game, they talked stocks. Any deal smaller than ten thousand shares of American Tel & Tel simply wasn't worth even mentioning. That night I couldn't win no matter what kind of cards I held. I lost with a full house on one hand and a flush on another. Nothing stood up. I began to get a queer feeling in the pit of my stomach, as I realized I was the only real loser and I was losing big. I decided in my mind that I had no course except to give each of these men an IOU for what I owed and spend the next few years of my life paying it off.

As the game ended, one of the millionaires gathered up his chips and added up the damages. "You owe $4.85," he informed me after considerable computation. "We always play penny-ante here, you know."

I have often wondered about it.

PART SEVEN

PERSONAL
TO AMERICA

MEANINGS

While I do not believe that any public official can be an objective judge of his own role, his own work, his own accomplishments, his failures or triumphs, I have tried to give here some picture of the job we have done in the endless war against those I call "the murderers."

One of the charges leveled at me by some extremists has been that I have been too zealous, too anxious to convict. I do not believe that any fair appraisal of my work would bear out such charges.

But I would like in this concluding and personal section to give some picture of a role not generally known to the public—the role not of putting criminals behind bars but of working to keep or set innocent men free.

And I would like also in this personal sense to sound one small warning about tomorrow—and the day after that.

26. For the Defense

For many years the Bureau and I personally have been the subject of attacks. They come chiefly from the left wing. The fuzzy thinkers sound off whenever the issue of civil rights is raised, justly or not. Some of the critics are well-meaning, some merely vicious.

I have been pictured as a czar or bureaucrat without concern or understanding. Some of these critics state that I am unwilling to treat the addict as a sick person. They write that I treat all addicts as criminals, throw them all into prisons and toss away the key. That this is in complete variance with all the facts, that my record of fighting for hospitalization for addicts is known, my support for better hospitalization at federal, state and local levels—that all of this is on the record for anyone to see does not deter the holier-than-thou critic.

In February, 1960, the weekly magazine, *The Nation*, carried an entire article of abuse, distortion and attack against me. In view of all that I have done to help addicts find a road back and to help youngsters in trouble, some of which I have written about here in detail, it is hard to understand how this publication can write: "As America's first and only Commissioner of Narcotics, he has spent much of his lifetime insuring that society stamp its retribution into the soul of the addict."

This statement is a lie.

Apparently to this publication all addicts are alike and should be treated alike. Rapists who are addicts and murderers who are addicts, thieves who are addicts and psychopaths who are addicts are all lumped together. But addiction cannot be treated as a single disease like measles or chicken pox; addicts are of many types. Would the editors of *The Nation* who assail my policies let rapists and murderers run loose, merely because along with these vices they have also picked up addiction?

Even with all their invective, the editors had to include the fact that my record as a law-enforcement officer "may be far from a poor one," as they so circumspectly put it, and they even quote a description of me as "an honest, hard-working cop."

Every policeman has to take his share of abuse, of course. It is part of the business. Yet it is unfortunate that there are those who distort both our methods and our objectives. Such distortions confuse the public and make the job we are trying to do—the effective control of narcotic drugs—more difficult to achieve.

Even in the midst of running a Bureau I have always tried to protect the rights of the individual. The addict, criminal or victim, is a human being. His rights are as important as my own. If he is guilty of pushing dope, I want him taken out of circulation, thrown behind bars or sent to a federal hospital for treatment if he is also an addict, but at any rate taken out of the public byways where he can do no more harm.

If he is innocent I will fight to help him, and in many cases I have turned loose as much effort to get the facts to free a man as I would to secure the evidence to convict.

Here is a man we called Sloppy Joe, high on our list of Who's Who among the hoods. He was on our international black list of notorious smugglers and dope peddlers. We convicted Joe on the evidence of a thumb print on a box of heroin seized in the traffic. The court gave him nine years. Joe insisted it was a bum rap. "Sure, I pushed a lot of it in my life," he said, "but this time I didn't!"

I looked into his case. Fingerprint experts had testified that it was Joe's thumbprint. "Are you absolutely certain?" I demanded.

The two men who had testified insisted that there could be no mistake. "Why should we be wrong now?" one of the men asked. "We've been doing this for years."

Some inner doubt still clung in his tone. I said, "Maybe so. But take another look anyway."

They came back with a whole new outlook. They showed me blowups of the prints. "There's one whorl in there we can't be sure of."

"Then your testimony may have been in error?"

Silence. Then, "We'll have to make a whole new appraisal."

They went at it again, as a result of that single suspicious whorl. Experts inside the Bureau and outside experts as well were brought in. They finally agreed that this was not Joe's fingerprint. We got Joe a full pardon.

There is always the danger, in narcotic cases, of planted evidence. In the Bureau we are constantly on guard against that technique, as a way of destroying an innocent man. Once a Southern politician was arrested after the postman delivered to him a package containing heroin. He was indicted on this charge. He came to see me, terribly disturbed, insisting it was a frameup. The package had been mailed from New Orleans. "I've no idea who sent it," he said. "Or why."

I had our people in New Orleans get on that one and within a short time we arrested the peddler who had mailed this package. The peddler did not know the man he was mailing the stuff to—he said he had done it on the orders of someone else. It became apparent that it was a calculated frameup, designed to wreck this man's political career.

He would have been ruined had we not intervened. The rival faction which had tried to destroy him by this smear were furious over my intervention. The man's chief political rival—chairman of a powerful committee in Congress—called me to his office. The moment I walked in, he began to put me on the grill. "You're intimidating witnesses in a narcotics case," he shouted. "You're supposed to enforce the laws and put violators in jail, not set them free."

I let him go on. When he paused for air, I said, "This case was framed all the way, Mr. Congressman. If you, the district attorney down there and the others concerned don't forget that indictment there will be other indictments in New Orleans, naming all of you." The man's face sagged. Then I added the finishing words: "The peddler who mailed the package has double-crossed you and will testify. We have his full signed statement."

The case against the political leader was dropped.

I do not imply that this Congressman is typical, of course; I have respect for the great majority of these men and the work they do. I think of men like Congressman Gordon Canfield of New Jersey who has fought many legislative battles to make sure we had the tools we needed to do our job, and Hale Boggs from New Orleans, who spearheaded the drive for stiff penalties for narcotic traffickers.

His success had a marked deterrent effect in Maryland, Delaware, throughout the South and the Northwest, and in the Hawaiian Islands. It will, I believe, eventually cut the narcotics traffic and addiction in this country to the irreducible minimum.

The question of whom we fight for depends usually not on any individual whim but on the evidence presented, either to one of our agents or to me directly. In Las Vegas, a high school professor was arrested when he claimed his baggage; authorities had learned that one suit case contained marijuana. A jury found him guilty and he was given two years. His academic career was finished.

This was a state case but the professor's family appealed to me for help. Our irrepressible West Coast supervisor, George White, did some remarkable detective work on this case. He discovered that the baggage had been transferred from one plane to another, en route to Las Vegas, that the professor had not touched the baggage at any time and that the baggage when weighed the second time was far heavier than when originally weighed before being put on the first plane.

The evidence was not conclusive but the doubts did seem to favor the professor. I asked White, "Why does a high school professor take trips to Vegas?"

He said he knew the answer. Vegas was the man's escape from all the humdrum of teaching high school kids, faculty meetings, class papers and all the rest. He gambled, had a few drinks, took in the shows—and went home restored in his own peculiar way. "But he isn't a user and wasn't out there selling dope," George insisted. And he was right.

Our critics often overlook the key fact that cases are not mass-produced tableaux that fall into precise, predestined patterns. Certain patterns recur constantly. But the case, the individuals, the complex of causes is as unique in any given crime as the single fingerprint whorl that kept a man out of prison.

Two young members of an organization fighting for civil liberties called on me at my office. They were sincere, decent, intelligent human beings, and they expressed some doubts about the things their organization was doing, not on the national but on the local level. I reminded them that their organization had just made charges against the Bureau for giving a hoodlum a black eye. "That is the gimmick a lot of criminal lawyers use," I pointed out. "If your man is guilty, you put on an act about the brutality of the cops. Sometimes it works."

"But couldn't you have been more humane in this arrest?" the women demanded.

"What about the other side?" I asked. "Do you know what he did to our people?"

"I never heard that he did anything to you."

"He shot one of our agents in the back. For five days our agent lay between life and death." It took five men to put that criminal in a prison cell. In my opinion, if he got off with a black eye he was very lucky.

What response could they make? They went away—I hope —with opened eyes.

Innocence and guilt crop up in unexpected corners. There is room for compassion, for pity, for help and for common sense in carrying out our responsibilities. But before all else is the safeguarding of the government and its laws and its people.

27. Final Report

In the position I have held since 1930, I have striven constantly to uphold the laws of our country and to protect its people. I have waged and will continue to wage unremitting war against professional hoodlums and their associates. My experience over more than thirty years in this post reaffirms my certainty that only stringent legislation, rigidly enforced, can safeguard us from this enemy.

The professional narcotic mobsters are the most ruthless criminals in the world. But like other rats they run for the holes when the power is turned on.

I warn the American public—and urge them—not to let irresponsible statements by misinformed people weaken our position in narcotic controls. Because of America's leading role in building these controls, any weakening of our stand would open the doors to world disaster. Only the organized underworld—and the Communists—would cheer.

I warn and urge Americans to be on guard against schemes that are untried and untested in this country, including plans to set up government or private clinics for dispensing dope.

I warn America to stand firm against the encroaching power of the syndicate. Much of the campaign for relaxing narcotic controls and setting up clinics emanates, in fact, from organized syndicate sources. Reefers and propaganda, too, go hand in hand.

I believe that the organized syndicate in America, with its strong Mafia influence, presents an immediate and present danger to our society. When we curtail their people-to-people dope pushing operation, they turn to other outlets for criminal cash—gambling, call girls, strong-arm protection rackets, blackmail, political corruption.

I believe especially that we must be on guard against the use of drugs as a political weapon by the Communist forces in China and elsewhere in the Orient, Europe and Africa. There is every possibility that some of the Commies and fellow travelers may join hands with the world-wide syndicate —for profits and subversive politics combined. There is every possibility that they may try to make narcotics a new "sixth" column to weaken and destroy selected targets in the drive for world domination.

I point out these dangers as a warning—not a prophecy of despair. I believe we can ward them off with alertness and firm action. A firm hand, a compassionate heart—and wisdom in the application of both—is the answer. By this approach we have already achieved substantial victories:

We have reduced addiction by more than ninety percent. We have built hospitals for addicts, we have established international law in narcotics and carried our agreements and treaties to a point beyond most other achievements in international fields. We have educated the world about drugs, we have awakened the conscience of nations to their responsibility within and beyond their own borders. We have developed techniques for getting the evidence to convict these gangsters and we have been able to teach these techniques to other nations. We have fought the underworld, we have fought the misuse of drugs, through treatment programs and research, while at the same time permitting the full use of these drugs for medical and scientific programs.

A cop is many things. He is the front-line fighter, the abuse-taker, the defender of public safety. He is the implementation of the laws of free men, the personification of society's courage, and need, in the face of wrong-doers. He is the protector of the weak, helpless, aged, crippled, injured; he is the defender of homes, families, principles, morals, ideals.

He is all of these things if he is the right kind of policeman, whether on the local scene, under the corner streetlight, or on the world stage.

We need a cop at the crossroads of the world, we need the fellow with the nightstick to root out the rats, to blow the whistle on evil. Perhaps it would be a better world if we did not need him. But we do. In this sense the honest, hard-working cop plays and must continue to play an indispensable role in narcotics and other matters of deep concern to us all—in the safe-keeping of our country and our world.

Appendices

MAJOR STEPS IN DEVELOPMENT
OF INTERNATIONAL CONTROLS

1909—Palace Hotel, Shanghai: First meeting of International Opium Conference. Called on the appeal of President Roosevelt acting on the suggestion of Philippine bishop Charles H. Brent. Thirteen nations participating. Passed nine resolutions, urging governments of world to begin restriction on opium smoking and use of morphine for non-medical purposes.

1912—The Hague, Holland: Meeting of essentially same nations to put resolutions of Shanghai meeting into formal written convention: The Hague Convention of 1912. First formal control agreement set up for distribution, manufacture and shipment of smoking opium, morphine and other narcotic drugs including Indian hemp. In addition to original nations, 24 additional countries were asked to ratify the convention agreed upon by original thirteen. Hague Convention also required signatory nations to enact strict narcotic control legislation within their own borders.

1919—Paris, France: All nations signing peace treaties ending World War I, who had not already ratified the Hague Convention, agreed in the peace treaties to accept and be bound by all commitments of Hague Convention.

1920—Geneva, Switzerland: Advisory Committee established by League of Nations on Traffic in Opium and Other Dangerous Drugs.

297

League Covenant authorized general supervision over narcotic traffic. The League Advisory Committee set policies and drew up treaties for improving controls.

1924—Far East conference on suppression of smoking opium by nations most immediately concerned. Adapted mild agreement aimed at suppression of trafficking in opium smoking in the Orient, by means of individual government monopolies and controls.

1925—Geneva, Switzerland: "Geneva Convention" reached, with 41 nations participating. Building on Hague Convention of 1912, Geneva Convention established system of permits and records for all transactions concerned with import and export of narcotic drugs, plus periodic reports of statistics to central international authorities from each signatory nation. Geneva Convention also established independent Permanent Central Opium Board, to examine the statistics furnished by the governments on the cultivation, manufacture, import, export, stockpiling and seizures of illegal narcotics within their borders.

1931—Geneva, Switzerland: Limitation Convention agreed to by 57 nations, to become effective in 1933. Required each government to furnish estimates of its annual narcotic needs for medical and scientific purposes. Established Drug Supervisory Body to examine these estimates and issue annual statement on world narcotic requirements. Also required participating nations to furnish additional detailed information—"an annual report" on narcotic administration and situation within their borders and with regard to other nations.

1931—Bangkok: Another conference on control of smoking opium. Participants: France, India, Japan, The Netherlands, Portugal, Siam and the United Kingdom. Little progress achieved.

1946—Lake Success, N. Y.: General Assembly of the United Nations approves Protocol transferring narcotics control functions of the League to corresponding agencies within the United Nations. The Economic and Social Council of UN sets up the United Nations Commission on Narcotic Drugs.

1948—United Nations, N. Y.: United Nations General Assembly, on recommendation of UN Commission on Narcotic Drugs, adopted a Protocol authorizing its agency, the World Health Organization, to place under full international control, with binding effect on all signatory powers to the narcotic conventions, over all synthetic and other new narcotic drugs, synthetic or not, not under control by earlier agreements. The Commission on Narcotic Drugs is also authorized to place under provisional control any new drug under "consideration" for permanent control by the World Health Organization.

1949—United Nations: A Commission on Inquiry to Bolivia and Peru, created on recommendation of the UN Commission on Narcotic Drugs, commended program for gradual outlawing and abolition of the chewing of the coca leaf, and the production of coca leaves for that purpose. (This recommendation and its implementation was supported by the full membership of the Economic and Social Council in 1954.)

1953—United Nations Opium Protocol adopted by plenipotentiary conference called under auspices of United Nations. This was the first control of production—cultivation—of opium. The Protocol agreed to by 34 nations by 1960—although not yet in force by that date—set up national opium monopolies in opium-growing countries, limitation of production and maximum stockpiles, with only a few nations named specifically in the treaty permitted to produce for export.

1954—United Nations: The Commission on Narcotic Drugs and the Economic and Social Council recommended that governments in countries where cannabis was still used for medical purposes explore possibility of discontinuing such use. (By 1958, the Permanent Opium Control Board reported that only 26 countries and territories continued to allow medical use of cannabis.)

1956—United Nations: The Commission on Narcotic Drugs recommended to all governments establishment of appropriate controls to prevent abuses of amphetamines and barbiturates. (A second such warning passed in 1957.)

1959—United Nations: Program of outlawing opium smoking, with strong United States support, results in accords eliminating such smoking in nation after nation over years following end of World War II. Culminates with outlawing of smoking opium in Thailand, making the practice illegal throughout the world with exception of incurables, put on slow withdrawal plan to be carried out over a period of years.

1961—Single convention of 1961 combined previous conventions into single protocol. Gravely weakened previous controls by replacing "requirements" with "recommendations" and "universally acceptable principles," as a result of compromise forced by Soviet bloc on Western nations, as price of Soviet acceptance of any international controls in this 1961 agreement.

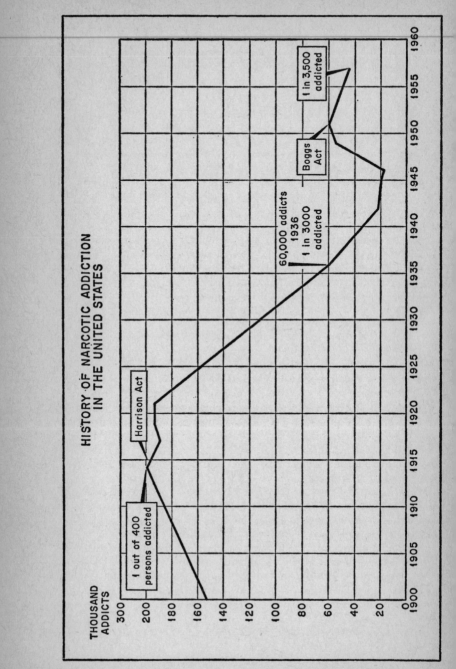

HISTORY OF NARCOTIC ADDICTION
IN THE UNITED STATES

APPENDIX 3

HARRISON ACT AND RELATED LEGISLATION

The Harrison Narcotic Act is a revenue measure; its enforcement is under the Treasury Department. Producers, manufacturers, handlers, druggists and physicians are all required to register under this tax act, to keep full records of purchases and sales and dispensing of these drugs.

Sale or possession without proper registration, or obtaining drugs without proper prescription or other authorization, is a criminal offense. Records kept by doctors, veterinary surgeons, dentists who dispense or sell narcotics to patients, must include date of sale, name and address of patient to whom drugs were sold or distributed. This is not required, however, if the drug is administered by the physician himself while personally attending the patient.

Under the act persons engaged in the import, production, manufacture or compounding of narcotic drugs are required to pay a tax of $24 a year; wholesaler dealers pay $12 and retailers $3 a year; doctors, veterinarians, researchers, chemists and those in kindred fields pay $1 each a year.

In addition, a commodity tax of one cent per ounce is imposed by the Act—with a few minor exceptions involving virtually infinitesimal amounts—on all narcotic drugs produced, manufactured or imported into the United States for sale or use. This is apart from and in addition to any customs duties that may be imposed on narcotics imported into the country.

The Narcotic Drug Import and Export Act of 1922 authorized controlled import and export of opium, coca leaves, their derivatives and other drugs for medical and scientific needs or uses. Import or export of smoking opium is specifically prohibited by this act.

Act of January 18, 1929, established two United States Public Health Service hospitals for treatment of drug addicts.

Act of June 14, 1930 established Federal Bureau of Narcotics.

The Marijuana Tax Act of 1937 put marijuana under the same type of control established for other narcotic drugs under the Harrison Act.

The Opium Poppy Control Act of 1942 authorized production—i.e., cultivation—of opium to supply medical needs in the event prolonged war should cut off foreign supplies.

The Narcotic Control Act of 1956 provided severe penalties for the unlawful sale of narcotics. First offenders are sentenced to a minimum of five years, without probation or parole; second offenders to ten years and third offenders to twenty years.

The Narcotics Manufacturing Act of 1961 provided manufacturing control by limiting the quantity of each basic drug which may be produced by a licensee.

MAIN NARCOTIC DRUGS AND DERIVATIVES

OPIUM

A white milky substance obtained from the unripened capsules of the opium poppy, known scientifically as *Papaver somniferum,* "the flower of sleep." Grown chiefly in China, India, Turkey and the Near Eastern nations, Bulgaria, Iran and in some parts of Mexico. Produces euphoric sense of well-being, restfulness, eases pain. Smoked or otherwise used for non-medical purposes, it induces fantasy dreams and eventually deep narcotic sleep. Highly addictive. With full-fledged addiction, deprivation produces agonizing pain, nausea and other withdrawal symptoms. Principal derivatives include:

morphine: a white crystalline alkaloid made from opium. It is effective medically but it is more addictive than opium itself.

codeine: not as dangerously addictive as morphine but dangerous enough to be on the controlled list. Used medically as pain reliever.

heroin: A derivative of morphine. Known scientifically as diacetylmorphine, it is five times as addictive as morphine. Used in France, Italy and to some extent in England medicinally but is banned for all uses in the United States and fifty other nations. Because of its potency it is the most "popular" drug on the illicit markets. A crystalline substance, it varies from almost pure white to greyish or brownish color. It induces intense reactions, fantasies, sense of exhilaration, power, well-being, lassitude and sleep. It dulls sexual desires. Withdrawal symptoms are violent: the addict lives in terrible agony without the drug, will lie, steal, commit acts of violence to get relief. Can be sniffed or injected; sniffing a grain or two can be enough to cause addiction.

Dilaudid: This opiate derivative, known scientifically as dihydromorphinone hydrochloride, is used as a substitute for morphine. A strong analgesic or pain killer, it has a shorter time of effectiveness.

dionin: Known scientifically as ethylmorphine hydrochloride, it has approximately the same strength and uses as codeine.

paregoric: An opium-based compound also used as an analgesic. Can lead to addiction if over-used or abused. Widely used medicinally, particularly in treating diarrhea in children.

laudanum: Another compound which was more widely used in the past medicinally, before wide use of morphine and various synthetic drugs.

thebaine: Highly toxic opium derivative with tetanus-like effects similar to that of strychnine.

papaverine: Opiate derivative and heart stimulant.

COCAINE

An alkaloid obtained from the coca leaves which grow on varieties of a South American shrub known scientifically as *Erythroxylon coca*, found primarily in Bolivia and Peru. This is a white crystalline drug which stimulates and excites the nervous system and sexual desires. It has been and still is used medically but is regarded as dangerously addictive. Used to excess or over any prolonged period, it causes sleeplessness and emaciation and leads to physical deterioration of the brain. Addicts sometimes blend heroin and cocaine in a mixture called dynamite. Cocaine, like heroin, can be sniffed, eaten, or injected either in the muscle, in a subcutaneous injection, or in the artery—known as main lining. The coca leaf has been chewed for centuries by South American natives, but the practice is now being outlawed and eliminated.

CANNABIS

Hashish, marijuana, dragga (South Africa), ahira, bhang, charas, gampa, and some three hundred other names in various parts of the world are applied to a narcotic weed known scientifically as *cannabis sativa*. This is the hemp weed, from the sap, seeds and stalks of which the drug is produced. Hashish is a product of Indian hemp—technically called *cannabis indica;* Marijuana—American hemp—is called Cannabis Americana. The products of the weed are smoked, although extracts have been made and used in varieties of liquid form. Effects vary with the individual and the strength of the drug. All varieties may lead to acts of violence, extremes, madness, homicide. Cannabis was used in a few parts of the world for medical purposes as late as 1960 but was virtually never so used in the United States. It is too unpredictable to be a good servant of medicine.

SYNTHETICS

By 1960, entirely synthetic analgesic drugs were under international control. Developed by pharmaceutical companies, the drugs are used medicinally with varying effects. They are sold under a number of trade names—often the same or essentially the same synthetic product being sold under several names. All are addictive in some degree. New synthetics are constantly being developed in the scientific quest for non-addictive pain-killers.

Methadone—used as a substitute withdrawal drug in treatment at Lexington. This drug is as effective an analgesic as morphine but while addictive is not as dangerously so as morphine.

Dolophine—similar to methadone.

Amidone—similar to methadone.

Demerol—somewhat like morphine in addictive qualities, equally effective as analgesic.

Propoxyphene—somewhat similar to codeine.

Normethadone—Federal Republic of Germany is main producer.

Trimeperidine—Manufactured in Soviet Union under trade name of "Promedol."

Ketobemidone—Highly dangerous. United Nations Economic and Social Council in 1954 recommended that producing countries cease manufacture and export, but Denmark and Switzerland, only producers, continued production.

Dextromoramide—manufactured in Belgium and Holland. Import figures indicate increasing popularity in many countries.

Over sixty new synthetic narcotic drugs have been discovered to date.

APPENDIX 5

ORGANIZATION: BUREAU OF NARCOTICS

Treasury Department

OFFICE OF THE COMMISSIONER

1. Enforces and administers generally the several federal narcotic and marijuana laws;
2. Cooperates with State Department in discharge of obligations under international narcotics conventions and treaties;
3. Cooperates with Customs, Internal Revenue, Armed Services and other federal agencies in matters relating to control of the use and suppression of the abuse of narcotics;
4. Cooperates with the several states in suppressing the abuse of narcotics and marijuana in their respective jurisdictions.

OFFICE OF THE DEPUTY COMMISSIONER

1. The Deputy acts as Commissioner in the absence of the Commissioner;
2. Exercises general supervision over the Bureau, including the field force, with particular emphasis on administrative functions;
3. Assists the Commissioner generally in all matters of narcotic and marijuana law enforcement and administration.

FIELD OFFICE SUPERVISOR
(under Deputy Commissioner)

Inspects field offices, making complete internal audits of operations; installs uniform procedures and organization; and reports on the effectiveness of operations and general conditions of narcotic law enforcement within the several districts.

DRUGS DISPOSAL COMMITTEE
(under Deputy Commissioner)

Examines and disposes of drugs seized or purchased as evidence, surrendered as excess stocks by registrants, or otherwise coming into custody of the Bureau of Narcotics.

THE DIVISIONS OF THE BUREAU

ADMINISTRATIVE DIVISION

1. Handles all details of matters of general administration, including:

(a) Budget and Fiscal
(b) Personnel
(c) Supplies and Equipment
(d) Messengers

LEGAL DIVISION

1. Interprets statutes, regulations and decisions;
2. Reviews narcotics and marijuana cases and the action thereon;
3. Recommends actions on pardons and paroles;
4. Assists in legal review of proposed international conventions and protocols and national legislation.

ENFORCEMENT DIVISION

1. Directs investigations of violations of narcotics and marijuana laws;
2. Gives general supervision to field force;
3. Maintains criminal identification files;
4. Directs activities of Bureau of Narcotics Training School.

RETURNS DIVISION

1. Directs matters pertaining to imports, exports, storage, manufacture and distribution of narcotics through legitimate channels for medical and scientific purposes;
2. Accounts for drugs coming into custody of narcotics and customs officers as evidence or by surrender;
3. Compiles miscellaneous statistics for administrative and reporting purposes.

STATISTICS AND RECORDS DIVISION

1. Receives correlates, distributes and dispatches all Bureau mail and other communications, including criminal investigation reports, related documents and classified material;
2. Compiles and prepares for study, research or dissemination, statistical reports concerning addiction, narcotic and marijuana traffic.

FOURTEEN DISTRICT OFFICES

1. Conduct investigations of violations of narcotic and marijuana laws;
2. Examine narcotic orders of pharmacists and practitioners for excessive purchases;
3. Maintain liaison with U.S. courts, state and municipal officials at local levels.

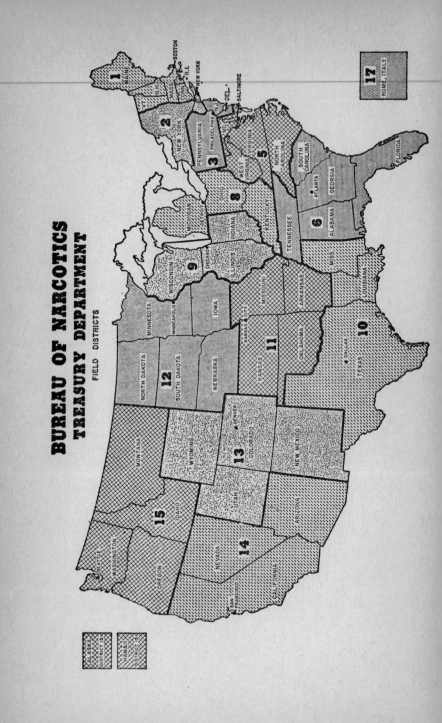

BUREAU OF NARCOTICS
TREASURY DEPARTMENT
FIELD DISTRICTS